AMERICAN WAR LITERATURE
1914 TO VIETNAM

AMERICAN WAR LITERATURE 1914 TO VIETNAM

Jeffrey Walsh

First Edition 1982
Reprinted 1983

Published by
THE MACMILLAN PRESS LTD
London and Basingstoke
Companies and representatives
throughout the world

ISBN 0 333 26149 6

Printed in Hong Kong

To my wife Natalie
and children
Andrew, Howard and Elizabeth

Contents

Preface

War is a literary theme on the grand scale, its relevance
confirmed by modern history; writers accordingly have envisioned the soldier as an image of man in society. In
particular, American novelists and poets, over the last sixty
years or so, have often come to understand their own country,
its social character, institutions and relations with the world,
through metaphors of battle. This book, in attempting to
offer a concise introduction to modern American war fiction
and poetry, examines some of the traditions and conventions
of twentieth-century war writing in the United States; it does
not aim to be either a synthesising or inclusive study. Clearly
there are enormous problems of an organisational kind in
writing about a topic as wide ranging as the literary treatment
of war from 1914 to Vietnam, and I have been conscious of
these in excluding much potentially interesting material. It
has seemed more important to establish parameters than to
furnish minute details.

Although there have been perceptive studies of some of the
areas of fiction and poetry discussed in this volume, it is fair to
say that there is no critical consensus about what constitutes a
distinctive body of knowledge or canon of modern American
war fiction and poetry. Because of this, it is particularly
difficult to decide upon a formula which will enable individual
works to be analysed while evaluating the notion of a tradition
of war writing, one which implies reworking and reconstitu-
tion into a living order. Other problems relate to the matter of
historical perspective, since it seems that certain writers and
works, viewed in broadly cultural terms, are more central and
representative than others.

In general I have been guided by the need both to suggest
historical development and to analyse through formal procedures of exegesis the internal complexities of the literary text.
Inevitably, in the last resort, I have had to rely upon my own

judgement about what is important. I have, therefore, set out
to write a series of arguments and analyses rather than a
comprehensive survey.

In making selections I have kept in mind the overall design
in two ways: first, through employing chronological methods
of study, and, secondly, by treating what I judge to be
representative issues and themes. The arrangement of the
volume is intended to show these priorities; it moves historically from the First World War to the present time and focuses
upon artefacts, writers and verbal modes that, I believe,
demonstrate authentic literary and socio-cultural significance
in the American imagination of war. I have tried to structure
individual chapters in such a way that they are both autonomous and complementary. A number of artistic and formal
questions are thus historically scrutinised. For example, the
problematic of representation occupies a major part of the
discussion. Another continuing concern is the manner in
which the poet or novelist faces the linguistic challenge of
countering the rhetoric that articulates official 'versions' of
war. A third consideration has been an attempt to recognise
and assess the oppositional literary politics of pacifism and
radicalism: in the latter case such crucial engagements are
overtly ideological in nature, and certain chapters are specifically designed to examine this constant political dimension
of war literature, its call to social action and commitment.

It will be clear from the above paragraphs that I have tried
to scale down the topic in order to make it manageable. The
value of such a methodology is, I believe, that it enables one to
address and theorise about a sub-genre of literature that
would otherwise be inaccessible, as a homogeneous entity,
because of its sheer bulk and complexity. It is helpful, for
example, to understand Vietnam not solely as a unique
literary event, but also as both an aesthetic re-enactment and a
radically new structuring of experience. War, then, is perceived as a flow of contending energies or as historical process.
From such a premise this study begins, that modern American
war literature shares the nature of debate, discourse and
consciousness rather than static form.

June 1979   T. J. W.

Acknowledgements

The author and publishers wish to thank the following who have kindly given permission for the use of copyright material:

Jonathan Cape Ltd, on behalf of the executors of the Ernest Hemingway Estate, and Charles Scribner's Sons, for the extract from *Across the River and into the Trees*.
Constable & Co. Ltd and Charles Scribner's Sons, for the extracts from *Poems* by Alan Seeger, ©1916, 1944.
Malcolm Cowley, for the extract from 'Château de Soupir, 1917' in *Blue Juniata: Collected Poems*, ©1929, 1957.
Doubleday & Co. Inc., for the extracts from 'The Peacemaker' in *Joyce Kilmer: Poems, Essays and Letters*, vol. I: *Memoir and Poems*, © 1914, 1917, 1918.
Faber & Faber Ltd and Farrar, Straus & Giroux Inc., for the extracts from 'Death of the Ball Turret Gunner' and 'A Camp in the Prussian Forest' from *The Complete Poems* by Randall Jarrell, © 1945, 1946, 1972, 1973.
Faber & Faber Ltd and New Directions Publishing Corp., for the extract from 'Hugh Selwyn Mauberley' in *Collected Shorter Poems* by Ezra Pound.
Granada Publishing Ltd, for the extracts from the poems by E. E. Cummings in *The Complete Poems, 1913–1968*, first published by MacGibbon & Kee Ltd, © Granada Publishing Ltd.
Houghton Mifflin Co., for the extract from 'Memorial Rain' in *New and Collected Poems, 1917–1976* by Archibald MacLeish, © 1976.
Liveright Publishing Corp., for the extracts from *Is 5* by E. E. Cummings, © 1926, 1953, and for the extracts from *Tulips and Chimneys* by E. E. Cummings, © 1923, 1925, 1951, 1953.
Penguin Books Ltd and Humanities Press Inc., for the extracts from 'The Language of Modernist Fiction: Metaphor and Metonymy' by David Lodge, and 'Imagism and Vorticism'

by Natan Zach, in *Modernism, 1890–1930*, edited by Malcolm
Bradbury and James McFarlane, © 1976.
Charles Scribner's Sons, for the extracts from 'February 1917'
and 'In the Dordogne' in *Collected Poems of John Peale Bishop*,
edited by Alan Tate, © 1913, 1941, 1948.
Martin Secker & Warburg Ltd, for the extract by Louis
Simpson from *The Poetry of War, 1939–1945*, edited by Iain
Hamilton (1965).

Every effort has been made to trace all the copyright-holders,
but if any have been inadvertently overlooked the publishers
will be pleased to make the necessary arrangement at the first
opportunity.

1 Introduction

There is a notion of separateness implicit in the term 'war literature' which sounds too prescriptive, as though war literature exists in a vacuum as a genre hived-off from other forms of writing. Such a schematic interpretation of war literature clearly needs to be resisted and full recognition accorded to the interactions and dynamics of literary production, and yet the conception of a corpus of imaginative work centrally concerned with the presentation and problematic of war is a valuable one. It is useful to refer to 'war writing' as a category in twentieth-century literature because the apprehension of war constitutes a distinctive and central element in the modern American literary consciousness. Military terrain and situations have become familiar, often assuming mythic connotations; the mass media, of course, have contributed pre-eminently to this process of dissemination, although the media do not truthfully render the actualities of war but tend normally to generate instead a new breed of inauthentic and obfuscating myths. As John Felstiner has recently argued, in discussing the poetic response to Vietnam, there is a current danger that the media, in over-exposing war, 'suffer' for us through their flow of surrogate war-visions.[1] Michael Herr, in his coverage of Vietnam, *Dispatches*, has coined the phrase 'jargon-stream' to name the attendant generative linguistic flux;[2] an obvious example is the term 'waste' which has now passed into idiomatic usage as a synonym for 'murder' or 'dispose of'. Through the conduit of the media, their textures, codes and conventions, versions of war infiltrate our homes; we consequently exploit the imagery and phraseology of battle to talk of mundane domestic situations. Paul Fussell, in his seminal study of the First War, *The Great War and Modern Memory*, has shown how the impact of 1914–18 became so widely communicated that its landscapes, forms and technologies acted as a staple of language

1

and conversation, as synecdoche or metonymy for a variety of different kinds of human experience. At present we frequently indulge in similar conceptualisations, talking for example of 'heading off another Vietnam' or of the dangers of 'triggering off World War Three'; such language usage enables us in this instance to structure in accessible clichés certain political options and contending theories that we believe to be part of public debate.

In an intellectual sense also the idea of a 'discourse' of war literature is valid because war has supplied writers with tropes and imaginative fictions of enormous vitality and symbolic energy. Vietnam, or more precisely American military participation in the Vietnam War (here the process of ellipsis is demonstrated at work), is an evident example. At the time of writing it seems that the American military experience in Vietnam and the former civil disturbances it caused are being redefined, given new kinds of public articulation: in movies and pulp fiction the once-forgotten war is being rescued from history in a particular way, its realities distorted, softened, mythologised in a subdued strain of jingoism. To an onlooker who is not an American it looks as though the national wounds and factions that were exposed by the war are still active, and that popular scriptwriters and motion film makers believe it is their role to manufacture and promote artefacts which seemingly heal the divisions or attempt to conceal them. (Such an opinion is, of course, difficult to substantiate and infers a level of market sophistication and conspiracy that it is virtually impossible to corroborate.) When the war was in progress in Vietnam the situation was very different; it was bitterly fought over in literature which functioned as a forum or social theatre for the debate of political issues (the term social theatre is here meant to describe in particular the role of war drama and popular protest ballads etc.). Literary works published during the immediate Vietnam war years could basically be divided into two kinds, the gung-ho or hawkish stereotypes which upheld the public, official and hegemonic version of what the war was being fought for and, in opposition, a vigorous, equally propagandistic body of dissentient writing. This protest fiction, drama and poetry often sought to instigate social action, to argue polemically against the conduct of politicians and ultimately to stop the war: it often proclaimed itself in favour of subversive acts to gain its objectives. In such contexts war literature revealed its true political nature as ideological battleground as well as offering its readers a formal representation of warfare. Using the example of Vietnam further, the critic can observe closely the way in which war as literary subject matter retains enormous symbolic potential. War as a theme acts out the great tragic vision of our time, the prime historical peripeteia and narrative. The soldier's traumatic first encounter initiates him psychologically into new realms of experience and marks him off from his civilian counterparts who have not served an apprenticeship under fire. In many cases writers who have attended college or been nurtured in leisured families en-counter in warfare their first and perhaps their only direct immersion into the industrialised realities that are collectively the daily routines of millions of their fellow citizens. The writer may, in the forces, become acquainted with new technologies, and therefore his military training, drill or combat duty will encapsulate for him the vast factory system of modern capitalist production and organisation. On the vast fields of battle, too, it is likely that a young American writer will marvel at the massive resources of his country expended in the pursuit of a seemingly mistaken idealism. The army or air force thus is transformed for him into an image of the American century, and the soldier who is also an artist takes on the role of what Frank Ross has called the 'assailant–victim': he becomes an agent of war and also its martyr.[3]

Since war is demonstrably the most pointless and destruc-tive of all human activities it frequently inculcates in the front-line writer a feeling of existential loss and disorienta-tion, a dawning awareness that the exemplary sacrifice of troops is meaningless and utterly futile: this may result in the participant experiencing a vision of *nada*. Such a bleak and nihilistic recognition, often profoundly expressed in war books, confirms the deep sense harboured by the intellectual of his own alienation, that war is truly what Philip Caputo called the Vietnam conflict, an 'ethical wilderness'.[4] The hunting of 'Gooks' in Vietnam in order to comply with the strategy of Search and Destroy results in Caputo's marines becoming so confused, in *A Rumor of War*, that they eventually forget the moral lessons learned in school and at church: conse-

quently their own identities become blurred and tenuous and
they sink into regressive barbarism. War in other ways may
demonstrate the worst fears Americans have of their own
culture; it may dramatise deep-rooted racial tensions or
re-enact in fable a brutish violence inherited from the
persecution of Indians in the old frontier days. Because of the
class oppression of enlisted men by officers that is so common
a theme in American war books, war may also serve as a
metaphor for the novelist or poet of prevalent social injustice
expressive of the dominance of hierarchies, through what
Norman Mailer in *The Naked and the Dead* termed the 'fear
ladder'. Taken together, then, such portrayals, images and
inventive fabrications that I have outlined in this paragraph
compose a picture of deep *angst*, and indeed much war
literature has, as its *raison d'être*, a trajectory of protest. It
protests against certain features of modern reality and life,
and can be a disguised lament for the disappearance of the
open plains and wilderness meadows, for vanished American
innocence, for the lost Edenic frontier spirit where once
flourished the pioneer virtues of self-reliance and a sturdily
wholesome independence.

And yet out of such holocaustal visions come stirrings of
redemption; if war can destroy a man it can also remake him
in a better mould; he may for example discover a more
permanent group identity in the army, and arrive at a lasting
solidarity with his fellow men. In the recurrent artistic vision
of honest infantry soldiers, whose love for each other transcends death in an unfailing bond, are reincarnated images of
community, of the frontier comradeship where a man helped
his neighbour, of hard times when the native American held
out a helping hand to the immigrant. This portrayal of
communion among brotherly officers or heroic dog soldiers
infers a literary theme which enables a writer to transcend
mythically both his own lonely and sedentary trade and to
escape also a spiritual alienation that he may feel deeply: in the
imaginative environment of war he may articulate myths
which break the deadlock of capitalist modes of production,
dismember the competitive ethic and postulate a social order
predicated upon collective interchange of property and
possessions. There is, in my speculations here, a great danger
of suggesting that writers live out their fantasies through their

books, and I do not wish to suggest this. I do want to indicate, though, the manner in which the heroes of war fiction and the symbolic renderings of poetic language frequently illustrate certain recurrent imagistic enactments.

There are, of course, uniquely American visions of self-renewal and discovery through the exigencies of warfare, and most of them draw upon the literary reworking of the writer's own experience. One such example will have to suffice here, that of the Whitman-like hero who volunteers for war and learns of its bestiality at first hand. The most famous illustration of this type is the First World War figure of the ambulance volunteer (like the real life Dos Passos or Cummings) who freely chooses to enter the war, propelled by idealism, and, scarred irrevocably by what he sees, becomes a disaffiliated anarchist or radical afterwards. Much of American war literature incorporates similar melioristic social overtones; a common pattern of the hero's progress involves some degree of reconstruction which may be roughly summarised thus: the hero, a good and young American, volunteers or is drafted to war, he enters the combat zone and mixes with men from different social classes from himself and of contrasting ethnic backgrounds. In uniform he learns what it is like to be born to drill and die; thus his experience parallels that of the hero of a *Bildungsroman*: caught in crossfire he learns to combat his loneliness and to submerge himself in the resistance subculture of his fellow soldiers. He is likely to cultivate a rebellious kind of behaviour, conducting himself less frequently in a solipsistic manner and sharing in social practices, argot and rituals of style which are creatively counteractive to the rigidities of militarism. As well as this flexing of a counter-cultural awareness, the soldier-hero may also participate in a collective generational consciousness. The myth of a lost generation of soldiers is one of the most potent imaginative impulses and orientations in the traditions of American war writing; it communicates an aura of betrayal, of intergenerational conflict, of a youthful and distinctively alternative value system contending with one expressive of a paternalistic dominant culture: the older culture is rejected as it is deemed responsible for the amoral conduct of the war. I am suggesting here that such a composite 'plot' or narrative-form is indicative of a central kind of American literary response to war, although the variations upon it and the totally different reworkings possible are, of course, numerous and too fre-quent to classify.

The discussion so far has, I hope, inferred the positions taken up in this study as a whole, that literature is both shaped by historical contingency and is also a relatively autonomous form. I want to argue that novels and poems interact in socially complex and dynamic ways, and that the most fruitful way to examine the relations of literature to social institutions, mechanisms and forces is to draw upon the discipline of literary criticism to explore formal and generic problems. The present work concentrates upon prose fiction, war journals and the qualitatively different genre of poetry where particu-lar attention is paid to the evolution, shaping, and traditions of poetic language. In order to try to avoid the pitfalls of a survey approach, which would be an inappropriate critical enter-prise, I have spent a good deal of time on the close textual analysis of language; such a methodology is intended to show in a structural way how a writer's socio-cultural tones, evalua-tions and nuances are meshed in with his particular verbal patterning, his public and private utilisation of myths, his constructions of symbolic language and his resources of imagery. As an example, I have tried to demonstrate in a chapter on Second World War fiction how the ideological dimensions of war novels (in this case shown by the contrasts portrayed between the hero's alienation and his transcen-dence of individual loss of identity through emergent group belonging) are aesthetically communicated by fictional strategies, locutions and analogies.

The chapters of this book are intended to be free-standing studies but not totally separate essays: they are written to be cross-referential, to comment upon each other, to provide comparisons and, hopefully, to create a dialectical sense of continuing debate and discussion. Although the links between chapters may not always be apparent from their headings, the chronological organisation of the study as a whole, and the classification of chapters into those which deal with fiction and those with poetry, should facilitate a unified historical perspective. All previous studies of modern American war literature have concentrated upon small segments of the subject; they have always selectively considered as topics the poetry or prose written in response to a particular war or wars. This does not seem entirely satisfactory, although obviously the critic who undertakes to investigate a more limited area has a good chance of probing deeply into particular circumstances. For better or worse this book attempts a wider investigation; it necessarily sets out, as a consequence of its wide range and scope, to isolate and explore representative themes, configurations and visionary nodes.

War writers are in essence literary warriors, and their embattled visions fought in words; yet battle portraits are shaped by actual histories. The critic needs, for example, to take account of the fluctuations of intellectual taste, the genesis and formation of sensibilities in both writer and audience. I have tried to meet such criteria by addressing larger more speculative issues and theories; for example, during the opening two chapters 'modernism' is examined as an emergent artist focus for reconstituting the war in new and complex paradigms; such a problematic mode is placed against the more traditional parabolic genre of war writing whose origins lie in the nineteenth century. In the case of Vietnam I argue the opposite, that the process is reversed when an oblique post-modernist mode gives way to one where military experience is expressed in more accessible public form. In both instances the social character of war literature is evidenced; its treatment of the epiphanies of battle structures in a symbolic way wider relationships and processes.

2 Poetic Language: First World War

If we set some of the symbolic fictions that were current at the time to dramatise the meaning of 1914–18 for Americans against the way Ezra Pound responded to the war, indirectly in the *Cathay* sequence and more overtly in two brief sections of *Hugh Selwyn Mauberley*, we can identify the problematic relationship of modernism to the war. In such *Cathay* poems as 'Song of the Bowmen of Shu' or 'Lament of the Frontier Guard' we encounter the modernist sensibility astringently at work in the hard-edged free verse, the absence of didacticism, the concealment of the poet behind his personae. Pound's oblique treatment of the experience of 1914–15 rests upon the modernist doctrine of impersonality. Hugh Kenner has drawn attention to the poet's 'structure of discourse' and the 'system of parallels' used in *Cathay*: 'Its exiled bowmen, deserted women, levelled dynasties, departures for far places, lonely frontier guardsmen and glories remembered from afar . . . were selected from the diverse wealth in the [Fenollosa] notebooks by a sensibility responsive to torn Belgium and disrupted London . . . .'[1] The method employs a non-representational way of talking about war, one in which holocaustal events are inferred by a series of elaborately disguised correlations. Pound's technique searches for that luminous stasis which haunted Stephen Dedalus in Joyce's *A Portrait of the Artist*, and his formalism led him to experiment radically with Chinese poetic devices. Donald Davie in *Ezra Pound, Poet as Sculptor* has explained how importantly syntax functions in Pound's scheme, and has noted 'the frequency with which a line of verse comprises one full sentence' or has an antiphonal effect when two sentences are incorporated into a single line.[2] Pound's way of writing about war, then, is to 'remake' it aesthetically, and his remaking may be related to

8

his definition of an image: 'that which presents an intellectual and emotional complex in an instant of time'. The war is imagistically fused with other wars in history, incorporated into a seemingly endless process and encapsulated non-referentially through different myths.

In the sections of *Hugh Selwyn Mauberley* where the persona speaks of the war Pound responds in a radically different way from *Cathay*: in place of the autotelic structures of the earlier verse there is a harsh analytical voice which objectifies the formerly received ideological assumptions. Here there is a displacement of earlier attitudes, a detached historical evaluation that has found them wanting. Pound's ironic use of Latin phrases such as *pro domo* or *pro patria* points to his modernist sense of collapse, his metaphor of the war as decreation:

> Died some, pro patria,
>   non 'dulce' non 'et decor' . . .
> walked eye-deep in hell
> believing in old men's lies, then unbelieving
> came home, home to a lie,
> home to many deceits . . .
>
> Daring as never before, wastage as never before.
> Young blood and high blood,
> fair cheeks, and fine bodies; . . .
>
> There died a myriad,
> And of the best, among them,
> For an old bitch gone in the teeth,
> For a botched civilisation.
>
> Charm, smiling at the good mouth,
> Quick eyes gone under earth's lid,
>
> For two gross of broken statues,
> For a few thousand battered books.[3]

If we contrast such acerbic lines with the patriotic verse of contemporary civilian poets such as Amy Lowell or Edgar Lee Masters we are likely to regret that the First World War did not figure more prominently as a theme in American moder-

nist art. The distillation of a factitious and 'botched' civilisation that we find in Pound's image of 'broken statues' and
'battered books' indicates metaphorically how he eschewed
earlier drum-beating war art. When a modernist such as
Pound seized upon the war as a theme it was likely to be
treated as one more example of cultural disintegration, if this
time of apocalyptic dimensions, a vision totally antithetical to
the treatment accorded by the more traditional American war
poets discussed in this chapter, such as Seeger and Kilmer,
who, in the main, articulated in their work self-regarding
public attitudes to heroism. In Edith Wharton's *The Marne* for
instance there occurs an image of the United States giving her
blood to revitalise Europe, and in the same work American
recruits are metamorphosed into crusaders willing to die for
their principles. The poetry of Alan Seeger evokes a similar
archetype in the figurative volunteer who links up with the
poilu in a chain entrusted with the defence of Renaissance
culture. Another poet, Joyce Kilmer, envisions the sufferings
of the soldier as an enactment of the Crucifixion, and
allegorises the warrior as a type of Christ. The imagery in all
four cases centres upon concepts of redemption and sacrifice.

It is an historical truism that the new cultural dispositions in
American life produced a reaction after 1918 against the
earlier myths of sacrifice. Those writers with first-hand
experience of military life either as conscripts or
volunteers – among them E. E. Cummings, John Peale Bishop
and Malcolm Cowley – re-experienced the war in their poetry
and perceived in it a paradigm of insanity and violation. For
the full impact of this later literary response to be evaluated it
is a valuable exercise to examine some of the symptomatic
poetry written during the war years. By first considering the
diction, the tropes and formal conventions employed by such
earlier poets as Alan Seeger or Joyce Kilmer we obtain an
added perspective when looking at later responses. Although,
as suggested earlier, there was little American modernist
poetry written in response to the war, one avant-garde poet,
E. E. Cummings, treated it in his work. It is helpful to consider
Cummings's profound modernism of spirit, his experiments
in grammar and syntax, his deployment of free verse forms
and his typographical innovations, as an attempt like Pound's
to remake the war artistically and dismantle the earlier

culture. Probably the most effective way to trace the emergence of such a modernist version of 1914–18 as Cummings offers is to begin by investigating the historical circumstances and then to concentrate upon a detailed examination of the changes and developments in the poetic language used to treat war from 1914 until about 1935; this analysis forms the substance of this chapter.

Often the reasons for American participation in the First World War are neatly divided into economic causes related to the benefits accruing from trade with the Allies, and the associated ideological justification that trade demanded. In this genre of historical account much importance is attributed to the rôle played by the emerging pseudo-science of propaganda in manipulating public opinion. Certain historical events, the sinking of the *Lusitania*, for example, or the German submarine blockade of 1917, are frequently cited as showing the interplay between economic and ideological forces. In his study of First World War fiction Stanley Cooperman analysed the popular civilian support for the war in America which continued until after the Armistice and which was manifested in the work of writers such as Edith Wharton and Willa Cather.[4] Cooperman argued that Entente propagandists, directed by Cecil Parker in Britain, were instrumental in assisting George Creel in the United States to persuade the American people into whole-hearted support for the war. According to this thesis the increased sophistication of propaganda techniques was employed to give the war an ideological basis peculiarly slanted towards the American consciousness. Leading figures in America's artistic, business and religious communities, Cooperman suggested, collectively reinforced the myth of a politically free, Christian and sexually pure America cleansing Europe of the degenerate Hun and reviving tired Allied spirits through the virility of her young manhood. In this version of reality, advertising, radio, films and the pulp press combined to support American capitalism in exploiting atrocity stories and anti-Teutonic racism; and the media are said to have portrayed the war as a crusade fought in defence of liberalism and democracy.

The theory of an orchestrated propaganda onslaught goes some way towards mitigating the inadequacy of the initial literary response to the war. If, with the benefit of hindsight, we can partially exonerate the American intelligentsia writing at the time of the war from charges of moral turpitude, it is hard to believe that they were naïve enough to be duped all of the time. The literature of the early stages of the war, written from the American continent, is imbued with the mystique of violence which vicariously exalts death in battle into a self-evident virtue. It is true that the war was fought a long way from America, that there was an element of culture shock in the increasingly technological conditions of battle, and that the public had little previous direct historical experience of the realities of warfare, but the majority of writers nevertheless seem perversely to have chosen to ignore the real and often accessible horrors of battle. Even those who had visited the front or those who were combatants, such as Alan Seeger, preferred to stress the heroism and sacrifice of the troops rather than show their deprivations. Consequently most American literature written during the war years induces in the reader a sense of historical disjunction. The code of high-minded rhetoric usually employed by writers serves principally to estrange the reader from the realities of the trenches. Exalted metaphor, which later writers operating from a base of existential uncertainty utterly rejected, appears to originate in wilful historical distortion.

Close cultural ties with the Allies and fat business profits do not prove fully adequate in accounting for the collective psychological responses of the American public in the years 1914–18. The degree and depth of concern, together with vast practical support for the Allies, suggests the working of more profound historical forces. Perhaps a clue is provided if we move beyond the purely American context. Bernard Bergonzi and R. M. Stromberg have located a fervent pro-war movement in progress well before 1914.[5] Stromberg's hypothesis documents the large numbers of European intellectuals who welcomed the advent of war in 1914, and explores the place of pro-war feeling in such modernist intellectual movements as Futurism, Vorticism and Expressionism. If such as Mann, Rilke, Apollinaire, Maeterlinck and Gaudier-Brzeska seemed to find in war the chance to regenerate the ailing cultures of their respective nations perhaps it is not so surprising to witness the enthusiastic approval similarly accorded to war by their American counterparts. Leading

British writers such as Masefield and Barrie visited the United States in the early years of the war expressly to influence public opinion, enlist support and contribute to the intellectual debate. By and large American intellectuals in the early stages of the war experienced a sense of euphoria at the prospects of a cause which seemed to enable them to transcend their own cultural isolation. This partly explains the willingness of those who rushed to join foreign armies, such as Alan Seeger, or who entered relief organisations like the Norton-Harjes ambulance volunteers, such as John Dos Passos. To an onlooker the generosity of the response is striking and parallels the national desire for some kind of moral renewal that was embodied earlier in Progressivism and later found articulation in Woodrow Wilson's abortive vision of a League of Nations functioning under America's spiritual leadership. The American historical experience for the fifty years leading up to 1914 had combined to limit the opportunities for gestures of valour and grand moral heroism, and the horizons of national life seemed more constricted both to intellectuals and to the masses alike because of the closing of the frontier in the 1880s and the slowing down of major rural settlement. The historical energy substituted for westward expansion, the massive growth of cities, led to a change of consciousness, a feeling akin to claustrophobia. A later illustration of this experience is dramatised in Arthur Miller's *Death of a Salesman* where the wilderness meadows have been replaced by skyscrapers and tenement blocks. Anomie, rootlessness and the social divisions consequent upon the rapid spread of urbanisation also contributed to the mass public acceptance of the Spanish American War. Large numbers of Americans, it appears, were a decade later, in 1914, disillusioned with materialist values and social Darwinism, and discovered in the far-off war a focus for collective identity; the rallying call of 'the Marne' linked disaffected intellectuals and proletarians alike in a fraternal cause which satisfied a longing for comradeship and dignity of purpose. Like most historical generalisations this account of American response inevitably misses the fact that millions of American citizens were too poor and hungry or too occupied with their own lives to give much attention to what was going on 'over there' in France. It was perhaps true though that current popular feelings of anglophilism and francophilism stimulated the widespread belief that 'civilisation' was in danger of collapse, and from this it was not far to the fashionable apocalypticism which can be detected in the work of early war writers such as John Curtis Underwood or the youthful Dos Passos. America, after a decade or so of isolation, seemed to move instead towards a worthy international commitment. Despite the reservations of Wilson, whose instincts were to remain neutral, the majority of the people supported the Allies, and in this patriotic feeling American intellectuals participated also, especially in the early years of the war. Edith Wharton symbolised the national response as analogous to a drawn arrow waiting to be released.

America possesses a popular tradition of gunpowder and glory war literature which must inevitably have entered into the consciousness of her First World War poets, and may have been a contributory factor in inhibiting them from writing of the war in a restrained, factually orientated way. A comprehensive anthology of war poetry confirms the potency of this tradition. In prose also in the nineteenth century the Civil War was often articulated romantically; two popular novelists, Sidney Lanier and John Esten Cooke, serve as exemplars, for they fed the public with chivalric images of the soldier and of the genteel conduct of the war. Cooke was particularly fascinated by the courtly figure of the cavalier embodied for him in such Southern generals as Robert E. Lee and Stonewall Jackson. There is one extraordinary example of the continuance of this myth that war is ennobling and tests the human spirit in the attitude of the novelist John De Forest in *Miss Ravenel's Conversion from Secession to Loyalty*; De Forest refrained from exhibiting the full horror of the Civil War because he felt the public was not ready for such realism in 1867. Towards the end of the nineteenth century popular plays written about the Civil War similarly ignored its adverse features: Bronson Howard, for example, in *Shenandoah* (1888) or William Gillette in *Secret Service* (1895) wrote sentimentally about the gentlemanly conduct of the war, the respect shown for civilians and of the essential humanity of the high commands on both sides. A reading of the popular poetry later composed in response to the Spanish-American War proves that the jingoistic strain was still active at the turn of the century. Poems written about Theodore Roosevelt and the Rough Riders, the Civil War veteran Wheeler's deeds of valour at Santiago and the gallantry of individual soldiers, typified by the heroic Lieutenant Miles at Santa Ana, all stressed the stirring deeds of combatants and their heroic transformation in battle. The victory over Spain is mythically interpreted in this genre of popular ballad as a direct result of individual gallantry. Even Crane's ironic war novel, *The Red Badge of Courage*, emphasises the subtle mystery of battle and its pageantry. It seems probable, therefore, that poets such as Seeger and Kilmer inherited a Dionysian view of war as a purifying experience from popular literature. An interesting collection of First World War poetry housed in the public library of Birmingham, England, confirms the comprehensiveness of this cultural inheritance for American popular versifiers. What is curious, though, in the case of poets such as Alan Seeger and Joyce Kilmer is that they continued to write broadly within this tradition and to uphold its values when their experience of battle must have dictated otherwise. There is an extraordinary disparity at times between the public rhetoric of Seeger's patriotic poems and the starkness of his private letters which portray the misery and death of his fellow soldiers. It is as if Seeger felt that in public he must act out the role of crusader.

No body of poems that may be corporately defined as American First World War poetry emerged from the war, and few individual war poems of merit have endured. America's late involvement in the conflict prevented most of her young poets from personally undergoing the rigours of warfare, and few of them proceeded in their work beyond the facile interpretation of the war as a crusade typified in English poetry by Brooke and Asquith. The most interesting American war poems are those that were written retrospectively when the poets had taken time to reflect, and consequently these poems are scattered in various collections. Only in the linguistic experiments and sophisticated ironies of modernist poets epitomised in Ezra Pound and E. E. Cummings do we find American poetry that comes near to enacting the historical realities of 1914–18. The most celebrated combatant poets of the war years, notably the charismatic figures Alan Seeger and Joyce Kilmer, were curiously genteel and conservative writers who were seemingly unaffected by the new energies at work in American poetry at this time. Nowhere in their poetry do we find the fertile and colloquial language practices found in Sandburg or Lindsay and neither is there any awareness of such innovatory artistic movements as Symbolism or Imagism. Seeger and Kilmer rely instead upon a mode of poetic discourse that derives from either the American Genteel Tradition, which Santayana referred to in 1911, or from literary sources, notably the English Romantics, Tennyson and the *Oxford Book of English Verse*. When they read modern poets, as Alan Seeger records in one of his letters, it was likely to be such as Rupert Brooke. Their poems, then, deploy an aesthetic that is pre-modernist and one which ultimately proved to be unworkable since the poets did little, unlike Wilfred Owen the English poet, to modify high literary language or to employ it for ironic purposes. Seeger and Kilmer were unable to express the contingencies of technological warfare because they were hampered by ineffective formal devices and a wholly unsuitable poetic language. This formal inadequacy is demonstrated in various ways, for example, in a dependence upon abstractions and personifications or in the patterning of essentially soporific metres and rhyme schemes; these close off complexity of response and induce instead acquiescence in the poet's own point of view through a spurious auditory and rhythmic harmony. John Felstiner, in an article written on the poetry of the Vietnam War, has argued that the poetry written in response to Vietnam illustrates a similar language breakdown but for different reasons.[6] In the case of Vietnam, he suggests, a number of factors combined to render the verbal felicities of traditional lyric poetry inappropriate. The cultural remoteness of the war, the alien language and climate, the euphemisms used by the American military establishment, and the inevitable public indifference induced by over-reporting in the media – all of these rendered the linguistic grace and private harmony of lyric forms polar and redundant. We find a similar malfunction and hiatus in the poetry of Seeger and Kilmer. Here the result of their basic reliance upon sonorous and declamatory vocabulary and rhythms contributes to an imprecise mediation of the war's realities, whereby the defunct aesthetic compounds the sense of historical fracture through the vagueness of an approving and over-confident diction. It is significant that when Cummings later presented a modernist version of 1914–18 he began by undermining these public modes of rhetoric and breaking down registers of established poetic language.

One of the clearest illustrations of the failure of American writers to grasp the reality of the war occurs in Edith Wharton's short novel *The Marne* (1918).[7] In this novel the reader is presented with an ideological assumption that the fabric of Western civilisation is threatened and the United States is morally obliged to come to its rescue. One of Mrs Wharton's recurrent images is the blood-transfusion metaphor where the American Republic 'poured forth from the reservoirs of the new world' her willing and courageous troops in order 'to replenish the wasted veins of the old'. *The Marne* envisages America's internal identity crisis being re-solved in the prophecy of her hero, Troy Belknap, who refers to American soldiers in Europe as 'the young crusaders'. Phrases such as the Horatian adage *dulce et decorum est*, chosen by the English war poet Wilfred Owen to indicate the obsolescence of classical rhetoric in a modern war, took on a new meaning for Troy and attained 'a beauty that filled his eyes with tears'. Here, unconsciously, Edith Wharton points to the battle for the control of literary language that was to be fought by the post-war generation of writers. Later artists made firm connections between this poetic language of 'beauty' and the ideological flaccidity of many of the pro-war novels and poems. In *The Marne* Troy comes to believe that America's 'inevitable mission' is to 'contribute the human element' to the war, which is the cannon-fodder argument against war used to legitimate it. Like the fictional Troy Belknap, several of America's soldier poets shared a belief in America's mission to revitalise Europe morally. Seeger, Kilmer, Peale Bishop, Van Doren and Edmund Wilson seem to have regarded them-selves romantically in terms not entirely unlike Mrs Wharton's symbolic crusader, purified by his quest and fit to represent a nation that is 'the world's fairest hope'; the crusader is a young man with 'a look of having got beyond the accident of living and accepted what lay over the edge, in the dim land of the final'. Behind much American poetry of this period there is often a sense, as here in this extract from *The Marne*, of an

encroaching public 'voice', as though the reader is attending a
church sermon or a rally.

Literature reflected and shaped other attitudes towards the
war that are vastly different from the didacticism and religio-
sity of Mrs Wharton's prose work. Very often and in some
unexpected places the reader is confronted with the strident
belief that war is the supreme test of manhood. The bohemian
poet Harry Crosby, who later became the *enfant terrible* of
expatriates in Paris, expresses this view in one of his letters
when he reflects upon the benefits he has derived from his
tour of duty in France: 'in the nine months that I've been over
here I can safely say that there's at least one vital important
lesson I've learned and that's to be a man. And I know that
those nine months have taught me more real good than all the
rest of the stuff I ever learned'.[8] Scott Fitzgerald in his short
story 'The Last of the Belles' also contributes to the cultural
glamorisation of the war. The officers in this story are
disappointed at not getting over to France and having the
kind of experience Crosby describes in his letters. In recalling
the fervour that the war generated in the American mind
Fitzgerald associates it with magnolia blossoms and nostalgic
tunes. In this fictional version of the soldier's life, a heavily
myth-dominated one, war has something of the illusory
nature of fairy tale, where the young man romantically enters
the field of battle in order to become a heroic 'young crusader'
such as the real life Alan Seeger, who volunteered for military
service with the French army.

Alan Seeger enlisted in the French foreign legion in 1914,
motivated by a firm devotion to French culture. Seeger
believed, as did many Americans, there was a special relationship with France, whose history had, since Lafayette, inter-
locked so critically with that of the United States; the sister
nation of France was commonly regarded rather grandly by
American intellectuals as the matrix of Western civilisation.
Seeger had a distinguished career as a soldier and fought both
at Craonne and at the battle of Champagne, where he was
killed in July 1916. In an edition of his work published in 1917
his letters reveal him to be an intelligent and accurate observer
of battle, perceptive enough to discount in private the myths
of military glory. Here, for example, he reports the miserable
living conditions of the front-line soldier:

The winter morning dawns with grey skies and the hoar frost on the fields. His feet are numb, his canteen frozen, but he is not allowed to make a fire. The winter night falls, with its prospect of sentry-duty, and the continual apprehension of the hurried call to arms: he is not even permitted to light a candle, but must fold himself in his blanket and lie down cramped in the dirty straw to sleep as best he may. How different from the popular notion of the evening campfire, the songs and good cheer.[9]

Paradoxically, the strain of realism evidenced here is subsumed in Seeger's poems and letters beneath a rhetoric communicative of fatalism, nature mysticism and often crude bigotry. Seeger wrote in one of his poems, 'The Hosts', that the soldier was privileged because he was enabled to transcend himself and to harmonise with 'the beauty of cosmic things', becoming in the process an 'instrument' of 'evolving nature'. His letters are full of this type of elevated language. Curiously Seeger, true to the crusader stereotype, minimises his own discomfort, preferring to stress the aims he is fighting for; 'the matter of being on the winning side has never weighed with me in comparison with that of being on the side where my sympathies lie'.[10] His attitude to the enemy often belies this moral intention and is far less idealistic; on one occasion characteristically he wrote, 'It was a satisfaction at least to get out of the trenches, to meet the enemy face to face, and to see German arrogance turned into suppliance.'

One of Seeger's early poems, 'The Aisne', echoes his letters in juxtaposing descriptions of hardship with exalted conceptions of war as sacred trust, spiritual trial and adventure. The River Aisne itself as other 'martial names' listed in the poem, Vic, Vailly, Soupir, Hurtelise, Craonne, is freighted with glamour. Here the place names are used for ostentatious effect unlike the bare dignity later apportioned to them in Hemingway's *A Farewell to Arms*. Written in sonorous and declamatory quatrains, 'The Aisne' is based upon an image of the war as sacred trust where dead soldiers hand on responsibility to those living in a never-ending chain:

> The charge her heroes left us, we assumed,
> What, dying, they reconquered, we preserved,

> In the chill trenches, harried, shelled, entombed,
> Winter came down on us, but no man swerved.[11]

By using the collective pronoun 'we' Seeger stresses the 'high fellowship' of the soldiers who achieved an augmented understanding and a collective identity in the trenches:

> For that high fellowship was ours then
> With those who, championing another's good,
> More than dull Peace or its poor votaries could,
> Taught us the dignity of being men.

Within 'The Aisne', as in many of his other poems, some of the reality of combat struggles out despite the counter strains of elevated diction:

> In rain, and fog that on the withered hill
> Froze before dawn, the lurking foe drew down;
> Or light snows fell that made forlorner still
> The ravaged country and the ruined town . . . .

Underlying Seeger's poem we may detect an implied disaffection with main street America. The mysticism of violence, expressed in phrases such as 'the majesty of strife' or the pseudo-pantheism which equates war with nature in enabling man to transcend his loneliness, are substituted by Seeger to rekindle lost American values. The initiation into the ritual of death thus acts for Seeger to alleviate materialism and the pointlessness of urban life. In the symbolic figure of the lone sentinel there is encapsulated a vision of the American thinking man become again plains cowboy and freely able to escape his previous alienation:

> And the lone sentinel would start and soar
> On wings of strong emotion as he knew
> That kinship with the stars that only War
> Is great enough to lift man's spirit to.

Scornful of non-combatants, many of whom he termed 'cowards, hypocrites, and fools', Seeger cultivated assiduously the business of living dangerously. Probably more than any of his contemporaries he stimulated the morbid glamorisation of death so prevalent in the early years of the war, and documented later in Edmund Wilson's and John Peale Bishop's prose work *The Undertaker's Garland*. The evocation of death as a lover in Seeger's work contributed to a cult that home-based intellectuals would have found more difficult to sustain if the war had been fought nearer the United States itself. This fascination with death is the central conceit of Seeger's most celebrated poem, 'Rendezvous':

> I have a rendezvous with Death
> At some disputed barricade,
> When Spring comes back with rustling shade
> And apple-blossoms fill the air –
> I have a rendezvous with Death
> When Spring brings back blue days and fair.
>
> It may be he shall take my hand
> And lead me into his dark land
> And close my eyes and quench my breath –
> It may be I shall pass him still.
> I have a rendezvous with Death
> On some scarred slope of battered hill,
> When Spring comes round again this year
> And the first meadow-flowers appear.
>
> God knows 'twere better to be deep
> Pillowed in silk and scented down,
> Where Love throbs out in blissful sleep,
> Pulse nigh to pulse, and breath to breath,
> Where hushed awakenings are dear . . .
> But I've a rendezvous with Death
> At midnight in some flaming town,
> When Spring trips north again this year,
> And I to my pledged word am true,
> I shall not fail that rendezvous.

What strikes one first about 'Rendezvous' is the dated use of poetic devices embodied in the archaic language and euphemisms unambivalently employed by the poet. The diction used is essentially nineteenth century in tone and lacks either particularity, irony or any modern linguistic precision; this is apparent not only through Seeger's reliance upon such upper case abstract nouns as Death and Love but also in the associated personifications, periphrasis and analogies. Death is rather ludicrously incorporated into the apparatus of traditional love poetry, the renewal of the seasons, spring's freshness and the clandestine meetings of couples. The language stems from an aesthetic that proclaims 'I am a poem'; the reality of death in battle consequently is transformed into a literary exercise with the result that Seeger's metaphors do not stand up to the human situation he tries to explore. Ultimately then this famous poem stands revealed as the narcissistic expression of a literary culture that is unable to respond to war other than in a stilted and unspecific way. 'Rendezvous' does not record or individualise the war, because we are not able to see beyond the ego of the poet himself.

Seeger's 'A Message to America', an influential polemical poem, declaims the poet's political convictions. In a crude verse argument constructed in couplets Seeger berates his countrymen for allowing themselves to be led by cowardly pacifists and for neglecting Roosevelt, the hero of the Spanish-American War. The moral imperatives structured in 'A Message to America' underlie 'Champagne 1914–15', in which Seeger appropriates the legitimate defence of 'Art' for the Allies, and pillories the Germans as the desecrators of cathedrals. In this scenario the Americans and French suffer a 'heroic martyrdom' for aesthetic reasons: they die in order to preserve the unchanging autonomous values of 'Art' and when they are dead they take their place symbolically in a fitting pastoral landscape:

> Here, by devoted comrades laid away,
> Along our lines they slumber where they fell,
> Beside the crater at the Ferme d'Alger
> And up the bloody slopes of La Pompelle,
>
> And round the city whose cathedral towers
> The enemies of Beauty dared profane,
> And in the mat of multicoloured flowers
> That clothe the sunny chalk-fields of Champagne.

Under the little crosses where they rise
The soldier rests. Now round him undismayed
The cannon thunders, and at night he lies
At peace beneath the eternal fusillade . . . .

The iambic pentameter and regular rhyme scheme comple-
ment the literary tonalities of the poem, and construct its
studied and rather grandiloquent manner. The unearned
resonances of heroic sacrifice intended by Seeger's traditional
formulation parallel the glorification of passive suffering that
also comprises the subject matter of Joyce Kilmer's work.

Joyce Kilmer, a convert to Catholicism, and formerly a
journalist with the *New York Times*, had published *Summer Love,
Trees* and *The Circus and Other Essays* before his war poems were
written and before his heroic death turned him into a cult
figure. His popular reputation as a war poet derives from his
two much-anthologised poems 'Rouge Bouquet' and 'The
White Ships and the Red', a parable on the sinking of the
Lusitania. Kilmer, although married with children, chose to be
drafted to France just three months after the United States
entered the war. Before his death on 30 July 1918, he was
promoted to sergeant, having also acted as editor of the AEF
newspaper. The most notable elements in Kilmer's poetry
relate to the underlying oxymoron of peace-loving warriors
killing only to preserve significant moral values. This ideology
is transmuted most often in his work in the analogy between
the soldier and Christ. As Paul Fussell has shown in his study of
British Great War literature, the paradigm of the crucified
Christ acts as a widespread motif in the work of many war
poets; Kilmer likewise envisions the soldier as a type of Christ
who welcomes death and whose militancy, being sanctioned
by a religious cause, is legitimate. In 'The Peacemaker' Christ
is conceived of in military terms as a Captain who smiles 'upon
a conquered world':

Upon his will he binds a radiant chain,
For Freedom's sake he is no longer free.
It is his task, the slave of Liberty,
With his own blood to wipe away a stain.
That pain may cease, he yields his flesh to pain.
To banish wars, he must a warrior be.

He dwells in Night, eternal Dawn to see,
And gladly dies, abundant life to gain.
What matters Death, if Freedom be not dead?
No flags are fair, if Freedom's flag be furled.
Who fights for Freedom, goes with joyous tread
To meet the fires of Hell against him hurled,
And has for Captain Him whose thorn-wreathed head
Smiles from the Cross upon a conquered world.[12]

This sonnet endorses the motives of the idealist who serves in a holy war where even 'the fires of Hell' can be faced by the spiritual warrior with equanimity. Kilmer noted in private, as did Seeger, the unheroic privations of the French *poilu* and yet he celebrates their pain as a religious necessity, a holy and terrible sacrifice enacting that of the crucified Christ. The difficulty for Kilmer's reader is compounded by the concluding image of Jesus smiling upon a war-ravaged battle scene. The Great War, allegorised by Kilmer, schematically symbolises the unending struggle between right and evil, an unhistorical projection. Kilmer's intentions of revealing the fighting man in a state of grace are invalidated because the poem's language conveys no close-up, no detailed intuition of the soldier as human being.

During the years of the war the dialectic of intellectual ideas and artistic theory that has since come to be formulated into Anglo-American modernism slowly infiltrated the United States. In 1915 the penetration of new currents of thought was instanced in the Disquisition address of E. E. Cummings at Harvard. The twenty-year old Cummings, in theorising about 'The New Art', ostentatiously fermented examples from beyond literature and showed a familiarity with the work (among others) of Brancusi, Schoenberg, Satie, Duchamp and Stravinsky. Cummings's models extended to the literary avant-garde also and he soon became familiar with the principles of Imagism and with the poetry and theory of Ezra Pound. For Cummings, as he began to make his reputation in the 1920s, the earlier literati, whose rhetoric was dependent upon a dramaturgy of sacrifice, were discredited as spokesmen for the generation that had profited financially from the war.

A helpful insight into E. E. Cummings's involvement in the

First World War is provided by the selection of his letters edited by F. W. Dupee and George Stade when complemented by the poet's own novel, *The Enormous Room,* a fictionalised account of his imprisonment in a French transit camp, La Ferté Macé, at Orne.[13] (*The Enormous Room* is discussed elsewhere in this book as a modernist artefact.) Cummings from the outset burlesqued the concept of war as holy cause, and he rejected both in his private life and in his poetry the rigorous moral code of the puritanical crusader figure as prescribed in the religious metaphors of such poets as Joyce Kilmer. Cummings's letters constantly ridicule solemnly held concepts of patriotism and heroism in combat (he frequently uses the term 'the front' in an ironic and disparaging manner, for example). For Cummings the war was not fought in defence of honour and sexual purity, but epitomised instead that wider conflict with authority which all too frequently annihilated the individual. Given this premise, it is the duty of the writer to rebel against the social conformity demanded by generals and presidents of warring countries: Cummings was duly engaged in a running feud with such authorities. At La Ferté Macé he refused to compromise himself by saying that he hated Germans, and later, when he was conscripted and sent to Camp Devens in the USA, he tried to gain his release by pointing to his own 'unsuitable' attitudes. In his poetry we encounter similar anarchic individuals; even the loving nephew who narrates 'my sweet old et cetera' harbours lecherous thoughts in the trenches!

Every war has two histories in literature: it has its own internal history in which literature may record a particularity of circumstance; and it has another history, its place in that wider history of events and nations that transcends the immediate and interprets situations more comprehensively in time. The most effective war writers are generally those who manage to live long enough after their military service to unite both kinds of history. Cummings is such a writer, a poet who had limited but first-hand knowledge of death in war as an ambulance driver and who suffered imprisonment through the vagaries of bureaucrats. His military training at Camp Devens sickened him by its crude uses of anti-German propaganda. Drawing upon these various personal experiences Cummings searched for an appropriate iconoclastic aesthetic in the new art forms that he admired. In the dozen or so poems that he wrote explicitly concerning the First World War and its effects upon individuals we encounter a modernist sensibility at work, demythologising, taking war out of the laudatory tradition of verse, and enacting a complete break with past war writing in the United States. Cummings managed, as did Pound, to integrate the treatment of war into the stream of American modernist poetry. This is, of course, most strikingly demonstrated in his use of free-verse forms so different from the regular rhymes and metres of Seeger and Kilmer, and in his typographical experiments. Other innovations included variations in syntax and grammar, word coinages, and what Pound termed logopoeia, language used out of its familiar contexts.

With the iconoclasm of a true modernist Cummings first made it new, and his amputation of the 'divine poesy' represented in orthodox war verse by Seeger and Kilmer forms an offensive strategy. The theory is set out poetically in 'Poem, or Beauty Hurts Mr Vinal' from *Is 5* (1926). Here his persona explicates a contempt for debased poetic language when he likens ennervated 'unspontaneous' verse to the verbal corruptions of slogan makers and advertisers:

> ... i do however protest, anent the un
> -spontaneous and otherwise scented merde which
> greets one (Everywhere Why) as divine poesy per
> that and this radically defunct periodical. i would
>
> suggest that certain ideas gestures
> rhymes, like Gillette Razor Blades
> having been used and reused
> to the mystical moment of dullness emphatically are
> Not To Be Resharpened ....[14]

Cummings's war poetry seems designed as a counterblast to the self-styled 'voices of liberty' the paid creators of verbal stereotypes such as public relations experts or politicians, who were, he believed, undermining the quality of American life by their 'pyrotechnic blurb'. The public statements of these bureaucrats and businessmen manifest a code of language used solely to defend the vested interests of institutional hierarchies, huge corporations and communications media. It is against these reductive practices of language which are self-reinforcing and which produce atrophy of thought that the *agents provocateurs* found throughout Cummings's war poems protest. The attack is managed by the poet in two ways: he draws upon the stylistic and linguistic innovations of modernism to satirise the language of military conformism, and he creates a cacophony of oppositional voices. The quirky personalities of his speakers in the portrait poems are affirmed through a variety of idiosyncratic linguistic effects or idiolects such as colloquialisms, mispronunciations, oratorical modes of speech, literary quotations or self-conscious archaisms. The critical intelligence surrealised in these wry collocations gives Cummings's personae an edge over the uninformed 'mostpeople'. His war poems also frequently capitalise upon the appeal to experience, and are peppered with knowing phrases such as 'I have seen' or 'take it from me kiddo'. The poet persuades the reader on the basis of his character having been there as one of the initiated; this air of authenticity is complemented by the verbal techniques of the satirist; parody is often used, for example, as when the speaking voice adopts the phlegmatic intonations and trite vocabulary of the British officer in

> it's jolly
> odd what pops into
> your jolly tête when the
> jolly shells begin dropping jolly fast you
> hear the rrmp and
> then . . .   (p. 269)

or of the bar-room soldier talking confidentially:

> lis
> -ten
> you know what i mean when
> the first guy drops you know
> everybody feels sick or
> when they throw in a few gas
> and the oh baby shrapnel
> or my feet getting dim freezing . . . .   (p. 272)

Cummings's old soldiers personalise the war, claiming inside knowledge and expertise, what Malcolm Cowley refers to as a part of the 'spectatorial attitude', as shown in the *vers libre* of

> the bigness of cannon
> is skilful,
>
> but i have seen
> death's clever enormous voice
> which hides in a fragility
> of poppies . . ..
>
> i say that sometimes
> on these long talkative animals
> are laid fists of huger silence.
>
> I have seen all the silence
> filled with vivid noiseless boys
>
> at Roupy
> i have seen
> between barrages,
>
> the night utter ripe unspeaking girls.   (p.45)

The converse of the speaker's claim that he *really* has been in action, seen events at first hand, turns into an impatient dismissal of those who have not had their verbal accounts of war authenticated by the epiphanies of battle; orators, for instance, who evoke 'these heroic happy dead/who rushed like lions to the roaring slaughter'. Other enemies of the war veteran are those who have chosen insensibility and who

> . . . don't and never
> never
> will know,
> they don't want
>
> to
> no   (p. 272)

'i sing of Olaf glad and big', originally published in the volume *Vi Va* (1931), employs Cummings's habitual mode of irony, and few poems more clearly specify his unquixotic, crusader in retreat attitudes. The pre-1918 ideals embodied in the work of such men as Seeger and Kilmer have been supplanted by a demonstrable assumption that the state entirely dehumanises the individual. 'i sing of Olaf' builds upon the iambic tetrameter and employs an eight syllable four stress line as its underlying metric pattern. The portrait of Olaf, the victim of the nation's all-American values, its 'blue-eyed pride', was drawn from someone Cummings knew at Camp Devens. The poetic meaning of his death in gaol is energised by Cummings into a satire of 'westpointers' who are 'succinctly bred' and who uphold the shibboleths of the Republic by religiously oppressing such rebels as Olaf whose only crime is to be a conscientious objector. The poet endorses by this presentation an alternative 'patriotism', that of rebellion. 'i sing of Olaf' is uncelebratory, antithetical in almost every way to the war poems discussed in the opening part of this chapter which rhetorically approve military glory. In place of Alan Seeger's sentry facing death from an enemy bullet in 'The Aisne' Cummings depicts a pacifist as hero, a man tortured and then executed by his own side. His murder, sanctioned by the president, is collectivised by 'all kinds of officers' and 'first class privates': Olaf's death is revealed as doubly ironic because he incarnates those 'brave' and 'blond' allegorical heroes found mythically in the poetry of such as Seeger. By directing precise attention to the brutal methods used to exterminate Olaf and by wittily underplaying his suffering Cummings concretises the ultimate effects of military disobedience. This humanised movement away from abstractions is paralleled in the shift towards a more particularised vocabulary which has been commented upon by Norman Friedman: 'The problem, as we have seen, is to counteract the abstract tendency of language, and the solution is to make nouns out of verbs, adverbs, adjectives and so on, thereby preserving motion in the midst of stasis, structure in the midst of function . . . .'[15] An elementary example of what Friedman postulates occurs in *Is 5* when Cummings demonstrates his 'inevitable preoccupation with The Verb' in the poem 'first Jock he' where the noun 'kilt' is instrumentalised as a verb:

> ... my youngest
> boy was kilt last with
> the big eyes i loved like you can't
> imagine Harry was o
> god kilt he was kilt everybody was kilt ....[16]

The effect is to intensify the impression the reader receives of first hand colloquial speech forming emotional experience of war. Such lines typify Cummings's instinct to discover a new poetic language expressive of war.

In order to redefine the war aesthetically, and follow the advice of such modernists as Pound to purge poetic language of its 'emotional slither', American poets ten years or so later occasionally returned in their work to 1914–18 to revalue the conflict poetically. Frequently this impulse towards recollection manifests itself in a single memorable poem such as Bishop's 'In the Dordogne' or MacLeish's 'Memorial Rain'. (A similar process may be detected in Second World War poetry when, for example, Louis Simpson as late as 1963 returns to 1939–45 in his fine poem 'A Story about Chicken Soup'.) In fiction and drama written in the thirties, too, novelists reassessed the First World War. *Paths of Glory* (1935), Humphrey Cobb's novel dramatising the French army mutiny, is concerned with military disobedience, a theme earlier treated very differently by E. E. Cummings in *The Enormous Room*; Dalton Trumbo's *Johnny Got His Gun* (1939) depicts in the figure of his womb-like vegetable, Johnny, the ultimate post-war communication crisis, a huge bandage attempting to send messages. Dramatists, towards the middle and late thirties, also reaffirming their pacifist commitment, looked back to Belleau Wood and Château-Thierry for inspiration and warned against the growth of militarism: Robert Sherwood, who had been gassed at Vimy Ridge with the Canadians and wounded at Amiens, wrote retrospectively in *Waterloo Bridge* (1930) a conventional lost-generation play about a wounded soldier and his sweetheart; Paul Green in *Johnny Johnson* (1937) recalls Wilson's promise to end all wars, and Green utilises the First World War milieu as a dramatic setting; Irwin Shaw in *Bury the Dead* (1936) stages a surrealistic mutiny of soldiers' corpses who are ironically 'ruining' the war for the brasshats.

In poetry the reassessment and historical mediation of the First World War involved a kind of metalanguage whereby the poem often self-consciously tests out internally the earlier rhetoric, confirms that such posturing did in fact convey historical distortion, and finally moves beyond analysis towards new vision. This complex second ordering, whereby attitudes to language itself become the subject matter of the poem, characterises Bishop's 'In the Dordogne'. MacLeish, Cowley and Bishop did not experiment in such extreme modernist fashion as Pound, Cummings or T. S. Eliot, but, in recollecting the war, the former group's attitude, subject matter, and linguistic resources exhibit profound differences from, say, Seeger's in 1917. (Bishop, who had in a 1917 volume espoused the imagery of redemptive sacrifice, in rewriting the war also revalues his own youthful poetry.)

The critic attempting to evaluate comparatively the occasional and retrospective First World War poem, written a decade or so after the war had ended, needs to retain a sharp impression of the nature of the popular poetic response in 1917–18 lest the initial shock value of the war be forgotten. The popular poems of war time, written by such prolific poets as Clinton Scollard, convey by their titles the attitude of their creators to the war: such works include Witter Bynner's 'Republic to Republic', Daniel Henderson's 'The Road to France', Amelia Burr's 'Pershing at the Tomb of Lafayette' and the famous Mary Raymond Shipman Andrews's 'A Call to Arms'. Mrs Andrews recalls in this poem the torpedoing of the *Tuscania* in February 1918, with two thousand American soldiers on board, and she ends her rallying call

> It is I, America, calling
> Hoarse with the roar of that ocean falling,
> Tuscania! Tuscania!
> Arm arm, Americans! And remember, remember,
>   the Tuscania![17]

Mrs Andrews frequently exploited anti-Teutonic feelings in her poetry, a preoccupation paralleled in the work of John Curtis Underwood. (Underwood's work, taken slightly out of chronology, forms the subject of later analysis at the end of this chapter.) *War Flames* (1917) demonstrates how Underwood, too, followed the curve of jingoistic myth-making demonstrated in American popular and magazine verse during the years 1914–18. He displays pre-eminently an antipathy towards what the poet believes to be the spirit of Prussianism, unhappily phrased in one poem as 'Teuton truculence'; another poem equally alliteratively describes a German regiment marching as possessed by 'the massive machinery of murder that Essen evolves'. It is difficult to admire Underwood's aesthetic obsession with analogies derived from prehistory and fairy tale: he tends to be excessively fond of referring to zeppelins and war dragons. In such a vision, war in 1917 becomes equated with the prehistoric battles of the cave-men of Mercia against the flying sea-lizards, wars waged with flints and arrows. Underwood attempted to convey the historical energy of the war by deploying meteorological symbolism and images from metallurgy: the conflict is said to move like 'a cyclone of ruin' expressive of the clash between two wills of steel. (Joyce Kilmer, Underwood's contemporary, likewise envisioned the First World War as an awesome collision whose vortex demanded symbolic fictions communicative of saints and angels engaged in cosmic moral warfare.) Later American poets, in order to reinterpret soberly the First World War, had to dismantle the vestiges of a grandiose myth-framework, still extant in the popular imagination of Doughboys in Picardy typified by the red-haired Alvin C. York of Tennessee. The metaphors current in the war years had been underpinned by an imagery of sacrifice that remained obdurate until well after the Armistice. An inquiry into the imaginative response of later writers to 'Armageddon' therefore demands from the critic an exegesis of the working of poetic language in action: particular poems need to be examined to demonstrate how the retrospection is formally structured. Such an enterprise will be attempted in the remaining part of the chapter which analyses several poems in great detail as case studies or foci where linguistic configurations may be located as an index of meaning.

  Cummings's linguistic experimentation, heavily dependent upon lexical and typographical effects, exemplifies a unique resolution of the aesthetic problem of treating the First World War as a theme in American poetry. The war, though, continued to occupy other poets such as Archibald MacLeish and Malcolm Cowley who, partly as a result of serving overseas, had become expatriates. Cowley recapitulates in *Blue Juniata* the feelings of disaffiliation engendered by the war: 'Having lost our illusions proudly at an early age, we felt the need of replacing them with others, and we had made a kind of religion out of the sordid.'[18] Although writers including Cowley, MacLeish and Peale Bishop were profoundly affected as poets by the historical demarcation that the war represented, they did not make as sharp a break as Cummings with established pre-war modes of poetic diction. The originality of their response to war often resides more in a measured and reflective attitude to tradition, language and history and a constant re-examination of the war's meaning in both public and private imagery. This is true of the work of Archibald MacLeish who had published *Tower of Ivory* (1917) before his finest war poem 'Memorial Rain' appeared in *Streets in the Moon* (1926). He continued to refer to the war in his writings, and wrote verse plays, for example, *Air Raid* (1938), at the time of the Second World War.

'Memorial Rain', written to memorialise the death of Kenneth MacLeish, Archibald's brother, who died in 1918, aged twenty-four, infers through its impersonal tone, the poet's exclusion of earlier poetic postures commending death in battle. In order to debar panegyric, MacLeish detachedly measures the fact of his brother's death against the rhetoric of Ambassador Puser who,

Reminds himself in French, felicitous tongue,
What these (young men no longer) lie here for
In rows that once, and somewhere else, were young . . . .[19]

The speaker of the poem has lain awake , aware only of the indifference of natural forces and remembering such things as 'lake winds in Illinois'. Ambassador Puser's bombastic words cease to have validity as the poet-narrator listens to them so that they become 'blurred', 'confused', 'thickened'; he remembers also the movement and energy of wind and rain together with 'the thin grating of ants under the grass'. Throughout the poem the narrator refuses to be drawn into hyperbole about the death of his brother whose only memorial is the impartial rain:

The living scatter, they run into houses, the wind
Is trampled under the rain, shakes free, is again
Trampled. The rain gathers, running in thinned
Spurts of water that ravel in the dry sand
Seeping in the sand under the grass roots, seeping
Between cracked boards to the bones of a clenched hand:
The earth relaxes, loosens; he is sleeping,
He rests, he is quiet, he sleeps in a strange land.

MacLeish exploits syntactical repetition to emphasise intrinsi-
cally important words such as 'trampled' or 'seeping'. Other
devices are ordered to connote the ambience of death, muted
full rhymes, present participles, intransitive verbs and au-
xiliaries, all controlled by a plangently restrained rhythm
which objectifies. In order to imply that war is a determinant
of modern life stark adjectival phrases such as 'clenched hand'
or powerful verbs like 'trample' are chosen by MacLeish to
generate an awareness of the agony suffered by any soldier
shortly before his death. Landscape, as an objective correla-
tive, poetically acts to 'denature' the human beings buried
there; the rain will not cease to seep into the decomposing
coffin, itself transformed into elemental process by the
nuances of 'shakes free' or 'gathered' and the poem's syntag-
matic structures mimetically break up the elegy into its parts.
Although MacLeish cannot resist the euphemisms 'sleeping' or
'strange land' the poem, in general, communicates a nihilistic
tone in its cold listing of data concerning the ageing dead, the
activity of ants, and the disintegrating coffin. The language
conveys a wariness of verbal flourishes appropriate to the
reticence of a war veteran. Against the 'felicitous' ambassado-
rial speech-making the tentative syntax and diction infer an
empirical attitude to experience.

Malcolm Cowley's poems often express a similar mood of
resigned melancholy to MacLeish's and the sense of restless
despair that one would expect from a man who had self-
confessedly reflected about war in 'a dry, reckless, defeated
and perverse way'. His verse chronicles the after-war years
when the lost generation toured Europe following the best
exchange rate for the dollar. Probably Cowley's most effective
war poem remains the much-revised 'Château de Soupir,
1917' which addresses itself to the impact of war upon a

French château. (This motif of the château despoiled by war recurs widely in American war literature and supplies a prominent theme in the work of other poets such as Anthony Hecht and John Peale Bishop.) 'Château de Soupir, 1917' is partly concerned with the issue that motivates Alan Seeger in 'Champagne 1914–15', the destruction of high cultural artefacts. In this context the château has resonant metaphorical associations, later explored by William Eastlake in his novel *Castle Keep* (1966). Cowley in 'Château de Soupir, 1917' identifies and affirms the splendour of the castle which houses 'genuine Flemish tapestries', 'gilded doors' and other associated irreplaceable works of art. The narrator of the poem, slightly bewildered by what he sees, responds ambivalently to the mixture of fact and legend which forms the accessible history of the château: this opaqueness is shown in the way constant reference is made for reassurance to the conduit of 'Jean's' opinions.

> Jean tells me that the Senator
> came here to see his mistresses.
> With a commotion at the door
> the servants ushered him, Jean says,
> through velvets and mahoganies
> to where the odalisque was set
> the queen pro tempore, Yvette.[20]

The past history of the château and its legendary role as transmitter of civilised values mean little to the Germans who attend to their battle positions; by discounting art they seem to live up to their attributes in Alan Seeger's earlier stereotype, 'the enemies of Beauty' and

> ... grown sardonical
> had used a bust of Cicero
> as shield for a machine-gun nest
> at one end of the banquet hall.

Jagged wire and trenches, assimilated into the history of the château, take on the attributes of surreal creatures so that war seems 'phantasmagorical' and the soldiers disorientated 'like drowned creatures of a dream'. The ambivalence of Cowley's

simile here typifies an intellectual uncertainty engendered by
the poem. The vocabulary, lacking the radical dissonance
occasionally employed in similar circumstances by such modernists as Eliot (say in *The Waste Land*), is somehow inappropriate to denote wider cultural fragmentation. Without a
vocabulary to dramatise his sense of collapse and cultural
chaos, Cowley's narrator undergoes only mild culture shock.
His gentle bewilderment is expressed in commensurately
conventional language, as he witnesses such comically inappropriate forms of destruction as

> Silenus, patron of these lawns,
> lies riddled like a pepper box.

Cowley's speaker, unsure of himself, stands wryly apart from
what he observes, able only to prophecy future devastation:

> The lake is desolate of swans
> In tortured immobility
> the deities of stone or bronze
> abide each new catastrophe.

Diction and imagery in 'Château de Soupir, 1917' cash in
upon the reflected glory of the château and borrow an ironic
elegance from such phrases as 'deities of stone or bronze'.
Poets such as Cowley co-inherited an awareness of war as a
force indifferent to the cultural monuments of European
civilisation, a viewpoint tested in John Peale Bishop's 'In the
Dordogne'. Both poets make literal the crumbling edifices of
old ways and values that the war destroyed: the château,
inviolable or violated, is a literally concrete form of old
life-styles that the war threatened.

John Peale Bishop's poetry demonstrates in microcosm
some of the difficulties experienced by American poets, such
as Cowley, in not being able to draw upon a poetic language
adequately decreative to symbolise the historical decimation
of the First World War. His early inoperative war poems
pictorialise his aimless leisure as a young recruit waiting to be
shipped to Europe; Bishop romanticises his slightly erotic
visions in a strained *fin-de-siècle* mode, as in these lines from
'February 1917':

... all my nights are filled with a violet-blue dusk of dreams,
And through the dusk,
The ripple of silk over white flesh
And the wistful eyes of immortal women.[21]

As this extract suggests, Peale Bishop apprehended the war conventionally in his poems of 1917, and his stylised and prescriptive metaphors grandly verbalise the challenge that he believed his country was facing. A young poet's reliance upon synecdoche cannot disguise the paucity of his ideology:

... if the call should come
I should go down with the rest,
And take my turn with the festered limbs of men,
The broken brains and the bruised eyes
And the dead that have no more dreams.

Military training appropriated days of languid beauty and excitement and Peale Bishop deplored their monotony. Such poems as 'Nassau Street' or 'Camp Zachary Taylor', which unambivalently scorns the 'cantonment in all its vast hideousness', testify to the poet's aesthetic distaste and his oscillating emotions before the onset of war.

During the early thirties Peale Bishop's responses to war had followed the anti-climactic pattern most common to those who lived beyond the immediate war years, and he wrote at this period one of the most perceptive American poems about the First World War, 'In the Dordogne', originally published in *Now With His Love* (1933). Bishop's earlier aestheticism and fondness for elevated language, such as 'if the call should come', or for synecdoche, as in 'the festered limbs of men', has been replaced by a controlled used of reflective public language and an intellectual curiosity about the real history of the war. The splendour of the château situated in the magnificent terrain of the Dordogne region, its adornments, such as the Virgin and Child and 'the aged magees scattering gifts of gold', are judiciously weighed against the fate of young men who died by the thousand and returned 'wounded or gassed'. Bishop's pacifism recalls Pound's section in *Hugh Selwyn Mauberley* where Pound similarly balances the war deaths against the broken statues of 'botched civilisation'.

Peale Bishop's poem likewise re-examines the ideals codified
in abstract words such as 'courage'. The poem interestingly
combines the first and third person methods of narration. Its
grave concluding stanzas contrast the voice of the anti-war
generation, 'We', the soldiers who lived after the war, with the
impersonal and omniscient voice which narrates the outcome of
history:

> And because we had courage;
> because there was courage and youth
> ready to be wasted; because we endured
> and were prepared for all endurance;
> we thought something must come of it;
> that the Virgin would raise her child and smile;
> the trees gather up their gold and go;
> that courage would avail something
> and something we had never lost
> be regained through wastage, by dying,
> by burying the others under the English tower.
>
> The colonel slept on in the bed of Sully
> under the ravelling curtains: the leaves fell
> and were blown away: the young men rotted
> under the shadow of the tower
> in a land of small clear silent streams
> where the coming on of evening is
> the letting down of blue and azure veils
> over the clear and silent streams
> delicately bordered by poplars.[22]

The cultural references in the poem, such as Périgord, 'the
tower of the troubadours', 'the English tower' and the 'bed of
Sully', do not minimise or attenuate the slaughter, and, the
dialectical tenor of the poem syllogises, the civilisation which
produced the château is indifferent to the soldiers who died to
defend it. The significant idea at the core of 'In the Dordogne', that wastage of lives was wrongly construed as
potentially beneficial, inheres in Bishop's usage of abstract
nouns. Inappropriately 'courage' and 'youth' have been
wasted in the pursuit of the mystical 'something'. Here the
ephemerality of abstractions becomes poetically effective

because only the cultural objects and the landscape remain; human 'endurance' counts for less than 'the tower of the troubadors' or the phonic glamour of Pound's Provençal 'Périgord'. The wheel has come full circle from Seeger's vision of aesthetically motivated soldiers dying in order to preserve a cultural ideal. Abstractions such as 'courage' now characterise an ironic poetic discourse about the validity of death in war.

Although MacLeish, Cowley and Peale Bishop were not innovatory poets, they absorbed into their work elements of the modernist sensibility. Their intuition that the war was the signifier of the passing of an untenable cultural order and a major historical determinant, was shared by John Curtis Underwood, a civilian poet who was in his early forties when he wrote *War Flames* in 1917. Underwood appears to have assimilated some of the scientism of American and European naturalism, a concern to register impulsive forms of behaviour and related social and biological compulsions. He envisions the war apocalyptically in drawn-out lines whose incantatory rhythms enact spatially the conflicting energies released by the catastrophe:

> London lies still and dumb under the night that crouches
>   over her,
> High in the sky through mist that hides the stars
>   comes a drumming of motors madly whirring in limbo,
> Death and the fear that fills the void of night, are
>   coming in new monsters made by man to smite the
>   monster city.[23]

Underwood's war poetry suggests a futurist obsession with the technological implications of modern warfare, 'the organic growth of steel'. Like the European Futurists he ambivalently exploits in his work the savage capability of machinery which he ostensibly conceived of as a regression to barbarism. The destructive potential of aeroplanes and zeppelins, the 'monsters' of the new primitivism, is denoted in Underwood's war poetry as a regimentation of spirit. Sophisticated military devices are ascribed to psychological darkness and act as metaphors for the atrocities that have become embedded in our consciousness of war. More than most of his contemporaries Underwood implicates civilians in the Darwinian struggle, the 'truceless wars of fang and talon', and he explores the deep structure of war as a process of 'vivisection'; the dehumanised image suggests the vision of later writers such as Dos Passos and Mailer who were interested in the psychological conditioning of soldiers. The large-scale projections of Underwood's language as evidenced in 'The mind and soul of a nation in its day of wrath and judgement' indicate a poet striving to articulate a historical reality in heightened artistic terms. The conceptual language Underwood uses does not fulfil this intention because it is historically inappropriate in formulating the nature of war as social process.

Perhaps the comparative weakness of Underwood's language, if we consider it in relation to Pound's in *Cathay*, stems from its over-explicitness:

They have mangled and distorted the mind and the soul of a
    nation in its day of wrath and judgement.
For the bottom of a sea of obscene consciousness has been
    heaved into sight.
And things inhuman and hidden have been hurled from the
    night into the knowledge of men that made them.

The image of a sea-bed vomiting its obscenities to the surface does not work independently because of the addition of the redundant epithet 'obscene' and the noun 'consciousness'. Because of the poet's pedantic explication of the metaphor its power of revelation is curtailed. In 1917 the oblique poetic method exemplified by Pound, and discussed at the beginning of this chapter, proved to be a more viable one.

3 Two Modernist War Novels

F. J. Hoffman in *The Twenties* interestingly links Cummings with Hemingway as major influences shaping the post-war period:

> Hemingway described the psychological results of the battlefield; Cummings portrayed the terrors and pointed to the survivors of the concentration camp. In each case, there was a suspension of time and a modification of customary space; in each case, conditions governing life were reduced to the borderline of consciousness; in each case, fundamental changes took place in the formation of the post-war attitude toward those who continued to live and believe 'conventionally'. The two more than any others, gave the 1920's the most complete rationalization of its postwar attitudes.[1]

Although Hoffman suggests the avant-gardism of Hemingway and Cummings, his comparison does not here indicate the bifurcation of modernism that their respective work represents. Hemingway, as this chapter will argue, may be related to imagist poetry in his concern to evoke objective reality; distrusting the validity of abstract ideas, he matches this conviction by mainly employing a denotative, non-figurative language which concentrates as far as possible upon the specific. Cummings subverts realism in a different way; like Joyce he is an elaborate and innovatory word-spinner whose formal configurations work through the deployment of abundant vocabulary and prodigal characterisations. Whereas Hemingway appears to handle words sceptically, having more faith in landscape, places and useful things, Cummings, like Mallarmé, is more interested in 'evoking an object little by little in order to show forth a state of the soul'. Cummings's modernism is characterised by a propensity to recreate inner landscapes and to explore verbally colours, textures and shapes rather in the manner of a graphic artist (he was, of course; a talented painter) and in this quality his work has affinities with that of the French Symbolistes. Cummings's celebratory attitude to the unbeautiful and his desire to penetrate beyond surface reality also led him to a non-representational presentation of character and to restless linguistic experimentation. His figures in *The Enormous Room*, Lily, Le Directeur, Judas, Celina, Black Holster, the Young Pole, Bill the Hollander, Lena, the Three Wise Men, are portrayed in spiritual movement. Hemingway's novel *A Farewell to Arms*, austere in its formalism, sparing in its verbal constructions, focuses more upon physical action, whereas Cummings, taking *The Pilgrim's Progress* for counterpoint, investigates what his early reviewer Dos Passos called 'the spark of God' in individuals. The chapter begins by considering how E. E. Cummings, operating through innovatory fictional techniques, such as the departure from a chronological time scale, managed to achieve a revaluation of the lives of individual men and women. Ernest Hemingway's *A Farewell to Arms* is reviewed after the discussion of *The Enormous Room*, and, like Cummings, Hemingway is examined as a modernist artist formulating an aesthetic adequate to enact (in Hoffman's term) 'the borderline of consciousness'.

Norman Friedman has described E. E. Cummings's early enthusiasm for new developments in the arts, in music admiring Satie and Stravinsky, in literature Eliot and Gertrude Stein, and in art praising the experiments of Gaston Lachaise and arguing for the aesthetic relevance of Futurism and Cubism (which may have influenced the formal shaping of *The Enormous Room* in 1922).[2] Cummings's rejection of Bostonian academicism and his crossing over to Europe augmented his modernist credentials. Partly in order to escape the confines of his New England cultural environment, Cummings volunteered in 1917 to join the ranks of gentlemen volunteers at war. On board ship, while making the ritual journey to France, the recognised theatre of action, he met a Columbia student, William Slater Brown, who was to become his companion in La Ferté Macé internment camp. *The*

Enormous Room, written at the instigation of Cummings's father who persuaded his son of the affirmative value of such a book, grew out of Cummings's experiences in the detention camp of La Ferté Macé where the author was sent, seemingly accused only of untidiness and of generally setting a bad example. Cummings's friend Brown had written a letter which seemed to be hostile to the spirit of the French war effort, and both he and Cummings offended their superiors by their casual attitude to dress and to military discipline. Under interrogation Cummings refused to say exactly what was expected of him, and this further proof of his non-co-operation resulted in imprisonment.

The patterning of *The Enormous Room* reflects the modernist preoccupation, common in Joyce, Eliot and Pound, with literary borrowing to create analogical structures. The narrator–hero of Cummings's novel revalues past experience to arrive at a more profound mode of visionary insight, and in order to achieve this evaluation he draws freely and often ironically upon the symbolism of *The Pilgrim's Progress* for structural underpinning. His experiential journey in its broad outline resembles Pilgrim's: on his path to awareness he encounters criminals, vagrants and outcasts as well as divine, ineffable, and kingly beings; such latter figures whom he likens to Bunyan's Delectable Mountains possess the transformatory quality of allegory. Like Christian, Cummings's narrator confronts, in his Ambulance section, a version of the Slough of Despond and is tested by hardship and by filth, which proves edifying and completes his moral break with well-scrubbed America. The narrator undertakes two journeys in a dual perspective: one is a mundane, geographical movement from the ambulance barracks to La Ferté, and a secondary voyage, involving the novel in its totality, conducts the reader to the prison cell, which takes on the aura of pristine holiness despite the obscene language of its inhabitants and their insanitary living conditions. Finally, the persona, through contact with his fellow men and women, attains social beatitude and aesthetic grace.

Through such a symbolic structuring of experience, *The Enormous Room*, which derives its title from the church-like hall where the prisoners are incarcerated, functions as an extended metaphor for life outside its perimeters and offers a poetic model of the social dynamism. Police and prison authorities, individualised energies, relate to their prisoners in a kind of symbiosis. The novel thus enacts a concentration camp view of the world superseded triumphantly by a vision of aesthetic and moral liberation. The gaolers and military bureaucrats represent insensitive authority, and implement the attitudes of their political masters by bullying the imprisoned soldiers and civilians. Such a theme, of caged man defying his captors, is complemented by the motifs of pilgrimage and progress, for each man who, like Jean, resists subjugation advances spiritually. The enormous room where the inmates live implies a central reality of the modern world, as only in conditions of such squalor can true freedom clearly develop unhindered by extraneous factors. The gentle nonconformists most easily singled out by the security agents of the state and victimised accordingly paradoxically incarnate insights and collective wisdom denied to their oppressors.

The Enormous Room incorporates an artist-fable, through the high modernist credo of its narrator. Only art, the hero hypothesises, has the potentiality to explode false social myths and discredit mechanistic ways of thinking. Authentic art demands a quality of human response denied to 'The Great American Public' at large, which feeds on 'defunct ideals and ideas'. The true artist–seer has no option but to submit himself prophetically to creative self-amputation; a 'vast and painful process of Unthinking' amputates his past in order that he may begin anew.[3] The aesthetic impetus in *The Enormous Room* also incorporates a social trajectory through Cummings's satiric animus. In practice the narrator demonstrates the affirmative value of art in his fictional treatment of character, his response to individual men and women, who are apotheosised.

Characterisation in *The Enormous Room* is multiform, because Cummings's persona delights in rampant and avant-garde subjectivism. The patchwork effect generated by his mosaics of imagery and verbal texturing shows affinity with the style of Cubist painting. Characters, fluidly conceived in shaped movement, are mythologised through the hero's attempt to suggest their inner spiritual rhythms. Celina Tek exemplifies the complicated optics of Cummings's prose, its bold lyricism and excess, its commitment to creative pandemonium, its regenerative thrust towards social vision:

> Celina Tek was an extraordinarily beautiful animal. Her firm girl's body emanated a supreme vitality. It was neither tall nor short, its movements nor graceful nor awkward. It came and went with a certain sexual velocity, a velocity whose health and vigour made everyone in La Ferté seem puny and old. Her deep sensual voice had a coarse richness. Her face, dark and young, annihilated easily the ancient and greyish walls. Her wonderful hair was shockingly black. Her perfect teeth, when she smiled, reminded you of an animal. The cult of Isis never worshipped a more deep luxurious smile. This face, framed in the night of its hair, seemed (as it moved at the window overlooking the *cour des femmes*) inexorably and colossally young. The body was absolutely and fearlessly alive. In the impeccable and altogether admirable desolation of La Ferté and the Normandy autumn, Celina, easily and fiercely moving, was a kinesis.
>
> (The French Government must have already recognised this; it called her *incorrigible*.)   (p. 175)

The force of Celina countervails the depredation of war and resists the dehumanisation that assails her. The artist–narrator suggests her inviolable identity by emphasising her incorrigible animal vitality encapsulated in the concept of 'kinesis'. Another example of Cummings's epiphanising probes into the mystery of human personality energises the portrait of Zoo-Loo, who is transformed into a part of speech, literally verbalised, so that he borrows the energy of 'a verb' and becomes 'an Is'. Cummings is fond of this kind of projection, and on another occasion notes that a planton's face has the properties of an 'ellipse'. These insights into the identity of men and women are utopian and transcendental, stepping stones on his progress towards the final chapter, when he sees New York as a transfigured city.

Like Joseph Heller and Kurt Vonnegut later, E. E. Cummings envisioned war as manic incoherence whose illogic demanded a formal enactment commensurate to its madness: language and form must be shaped in new and seemingly disruptive ways. The counter-language of protest in Cummings is sumptuous, comprising constellations of metaphor, adjectival and adverbial barrages, superlatives and frequent slang. It is common for Cummings's narrator to pile up qualifying clauses and phrases, to include variable parentheses and lists and to modify statements in extreme fashion. One of *The Enormous Room's* most effective achievements from such concatenations of ultra-individualistic language is the Chaplin-like scene of comedy. This is demonstrated in the chapter, 'En Route', when Cummings's narrator evidences his cartoonist's eye for the ludicrous. After describing his painful attempt to relieve himself on Ça Pue, whose 'incense' mounted 'gingerly upon the taking air of twilight', he insists upon having his cane, which is finally given to him. The gendarmes, as usual, are described with belittling humour. Cummings rarely tries to understand their problems; they exist, as the v-f-g, targets for him to perform his mental gymnastics against. One translates into a 'rube movie-cop' personage; another has 'pork-like orbs'. Zestfully the hero pillories them. He may use high falutin' language, 'the prestigitatorial vanishment of the v-f-g' or depict instead the comic gestures and movements of these subhuman 'brigands'. He derives consistent pleasure from delivering his laconic insults – 'I looked several blocks through him' – or in narrating the occasions when the mouse outwits the cat. In one instance the v-f-g believed his captive was penniless, but the 'criminal' had hidden money in his clothes:

> The gendarme offered a suggestion, in these words: 'Have you any change about you?' He knew of course that the sanitary official's first act had been to deprive me of every last cent. The gendarme's eyes were fine. They reminded me of . . . never mind. 'If you have change', said he, 'you might hire this kid to carry some of your baggage.' Then he lit a pipe which was made in his own image, and smiled fattily.
> But herein the v-f-g had bust his milk-jug. There is a slit of a pocket made in the uniform of his criminal on the right side, and completely covered by the belt which his criminal always wears. His criminal had thus outwitted the gumshoe fraternity.   (p. 52)

This type of humour, dependent upon slang for its effects, stems from the pleasure felt in any situation when authority is outsmarted. It is the triumph of the little man over the magnitude of comic–evil forces arrayed against him. In the details of his captors, the gallery stretching from the Fencer to the plantons, Cummings's humour works sometimes through irony or periphrasis, but more often by hyperbole and exaggeration. Thus the Fencer takes on a 'renovated look' with a 'rooster-like body', and is compared with Napoleon 'reviewing the armies of France'. The Gestionnaire strikes one as 'a contented animal, a bulbous animal; the only living hippopotamus in captivity, fresh from the Nile'. The plantons are said, with comic irony, to have 'three plantonic virtues', which are '(1) beauty, as regards face and person and bearing, (2) chivalry, as regards women, (3) heroism, as regards males'. The levity is necessary, and the plantons have to be treated flippantly because they are a foil for the galaxy of splendid people we meet, the 'Delectable Mountains'. Thus it is a vital part of the pattern when Cummings's narrator queerly describes their mannerisms. For example, when one of them conducts the hero to be interrogated by the Gestionnaire, the planton grows impatient for his prisoner to enter: 'The planton threw the door open, stood stiffly on the threshold, and gave me the look which plantons give to eggs when plantons are a little hungry.' The predatory nature of the relationship is not entirely masked by comedy!

Another variety of Cummings's idiom is a public mode when his persona acts out the role of witty agitator. This means of address deploys raw irony or mock urbanity, as in his analysis of treason:

> By treason I refer to any little annoying habits of independent thought or action which *en temps de guerre* are put in a hole and covered over, with the somewhat naive idea that from their cadavers violets will grow whereof the perfume will delight all good men and true and make such worthy citizens forget their sorrows. Fort Leavenworth, for instance, emanates even now a perfume which is utterly delightful to certain Americans.   (p. 132)

The ironic method often yields to a more directly threatening tone as when the hero considers the treatment accorded to his companion, the Machine Fixer. He remains coolly in control, and thus his bitterness and anger are intensified:

> O *gouvernement français*, I think it was not very clever of You to put this terrible doll in La Ferté; I should have left him in Belgium with his little doll-wife if I had been You; for when Governments are found dead there is always a little doll on top of them, pulling and tweaking with his little hands to get back the microscopic knife which sticks firmly in the quiet meat of their hearts.   (p. 157)

Characteristically the passage exploits metaphor to reinforce its polemical urgency.

What linguisticians call code-making, the creation and manipulation of new linguistic relationships and contexts, together with Cummings's other innovatory language uses, are appropriate for him to render his novel impressions. The narrator also responds to the problematic of narrating the story-less tale by jettisoning conventional formulations of time. His insights necessitate a digressive time viewpoint, one unschematic and elaborate, unstructured and radically free. At the beginning of the chapter 'A Group of Portraits' a decision is taken to escape from 'temporal dimension'. The captivity, with the benefit of hindsight, crystallised in the mind 'helter skelter' into periods or spheres: this effect further produces a convergence into halted flow, imaginative stasis. What the narrator perceives retrospectively is 'the actual present', the unsegmented, seamless forms of the imagination expressed through the colours, shapes and textures that cohere when the artist has passed through a creative amputation of the world. In such an interface between time and art the conventional memoir lacks the capacity to articulate inner harmony and aesthetic order:

> each happening is self-sufficient, irrespective of minutes, months, and other treasures of freedom ... It is for this reason that I do not purpose to inflict upon the reader a diary of my alternative aliveness and non-existence at La Ferté – not because such a diary would unutterably bore

him, but because the diary or time method is a technique which cannot do justice to timelessness.   (p. 131)

The theory at work here, of the aesthetic pause, the suspension of dead chronology, recalls part of the doctrine of Aquinas explored by the young Stephen Dedalus in *A Portrait of the Artist*. People within *The Enormous Room* like Stephen have been enslaved by routine, and it is to demolish this false social regulation that the young artist–hero must rebel. After the first four chapters *The Enormous Room* substitutes for chronology an internal and rhythmic principle of organisation which is more appropriate than the diary method to dramatise the actual suspension made explicit in lives diverted from their normal course by imprisonment. The narrator rejects the chronological in favour of the symbolic, wishing to evade the constrictions of 'temporal dimension' because his power of imaginative recall contrariwise is associative and teleological. The effect of Cummings's abandonment of chronological time is that his narrator creates the illusion of a suspension of time in which he is better able to profile the evolving structure of his consciousness and his parallel disenchantment with tradition. 'Fixed' change, implied by what one critic of Cumming's work has referred to as 'novelistic' time,[4] embodies the idea that man is the incarnation of time, a product of the formal standardisation imposed by the state's institutions. Cummings's transfigured men and women, the heroes and heroines of his novel, are liberated by their imprisonment from this systematisation. The barely perceptible plot of *The Enormous Room* and its unorthodox break from the sequential both contribute to our understanding of this process of liberation, the form of the novel thereby felicitously embodying its meaning.

The 'personages' the artist–narrator celebrates in his image-laden slangy prose he conceives of as affirming the victory of human spontaneity over the rigidities of militarism. The occasional and oblique references to war (as in the account of how French soldiers fired on their Belgian allies from behind) provide a reminder of other externally threatening and discordant situations. Given the reality outside the *porte de triage* (or receiving station) of what Cummings often calls ironically the Great War for Humanity, the individual must attempt to transcend events and situations destructive of the true, pre-social self. This propositon puts into gear the loose unity of the novel, its metaphors of quest and change, which reinforce and augment the rapidity and often breathless movement of the prose as it jousts against the dehumanising world of the Three Wise Men who interrogate the hero. By aestheticising the world, Cummings's hero opposes the morally unbeautiful and, with jesting intelligence, he celebrates individuals whose diversity is truly regenerative. The narrator's farewell to Surplice, the camp's scapegoat, who cheerfully empties lavatory buckets in order to be noticed, supplies a suitable illustrative passage. The risks, intended to produce through synesthesia a pluralist perception, bring a high degree of success; Surplice

> has the territory of harmonicas, the acres of flutes, the meadows of clarinets, the domains of violins. And God says: Why did they put you in prison? What did you do to the people? 'I made them dance and they put me in prison. The soot-people hopped; and to twinkle like sparks on a chimney-back and I made eighty francs every *dimanche*, and beer, and wine, and to eat well. *Maintenant... c'est fini. . . . Et tout de suite?* (gesture of cutting himself in two) '*la tête*'. And He says: O you who put the jerk into joys, come up hither. There's a man up here called Christ who likes the violin.   (p. 273)

The growth towards understanding, instanced in this revelatory portrait of Surplice as perceived through hindsight, is conveyed in the contours of Cummings's narrative as it moves from chronology to stasis, from personal to seemingly beatific vision. The reader accompanies the hero through a voyage from atrophied tradition to the experimental functions of art, from abstractions such as La Patrie to the actuality of human beings such as Lena or the Wanderer. Cummings's exploitation of the dynamics of artistic form places him firmly in the mainstream of modernism.

The narrative of *A Farewell to Arms* articulates a modernist vision of collapse; as did Gide, Kafka, Musil, Lawrence, Yeats and Eliot, Hemingway structured his work upon a dislocation of sensibility. Frederick Henry, his most celebrated hero, embodies the manner in which settled ways of living are overturned to be replaced by disaffiliation and rootlessness. Henry has the pattern of his life severely disrupted; he experiences initial comradeship with his Italian war-brothers as an ambulance driver and finds love with Catherine Barkley, but other forces act centrifugally: after having received serious wounds, he re-enters battle, is confronted by treachery and betrayal at Caporetto, deserts to make a separate peace, and finally loses both his surrogate wife and his child. Events compel him to rely upon his primal instincts, to live empirically and to be suspicious of abstract formulations of all kinds. The arena of war teaches him that fatherhood, marriage and the potentialities of family life are, like his son, strangled at birth. In such a world of loss and *Angst*, where war, alienation and death move deterministically at the core of behaviour, no institutions either public or private can provide shelter against the larger social and cultural upheavals. The artist faced with evidence of disintegration mimes through his art responses to disorder. T. S. Eliot in *The Waste Land*, sharing a similar vision of crisis, explored the break-down through various poetic strategies, by the imagery of neurasthenia, by the deployment of broken syntax and parataxis, and by the use of disconnected voices. Hemingway, claiming modernist credentials, needed to devise a fictive method to transmit his awareness of war being at the epicentre of contemporary life. If man is envisioned as a hunted and shackled animal then the artist searches for an aesthetic that enacts such restrictions. The problem suggested here underlies this part of the chapter which seeks to prove that *A Farewell to Arms* displays kinship with such modernist artefacts as *The Waste Land* principally through its presentation of Frederick Henry's consciousness, which is communicated through a series of restricted language codes. The chapter will argue that, unlike E. E. Cummings in *The Enormous Room*, which explodes language in copious verbal innovations, Hemingway's aesthetic functions antithetically; it implodes language and restrains both lexicon and dialogue.

The realist strain in *A Farewell to Arms* inheres chiefly in its authentic accounts of war on the Austrian front. Hemingway's study of war, which took him imaginatively to Crane, Tolstoy and Stendhal, and to military text-books, ensured that his combat descriptions were precise and expert. The novelist also constructed his fable with a view to its accessibility; the narration evolves sequentially without time shifts or complex stream of consciousness devices. Clearly, any claim that *A Farewell to Arms* is shaped by modernist influences needs to be justified on different terms from a novel, say, by Joyce or Virginia Woolf. David Lodge has drawn attention to modernist and realist fusions in Hemingway's fiction when discussing the novelist's language resources as evidenced in his short story 'In Another Country'. Lodge attributes Hemingway's search for a language properly faithful to the instantaneousness of experience partly to the influence of Gertrude Stein:

> This was largely the basis of her influence on subsequent writers, like Hemingway, who saw that the artful use of repetition, with slight variation, both lexical and grammatical, combined happily with an imitation of casual vernacular speech; it was thus possible to be a realist *and* a Modernist. The opening paragraph of his story, 'In Another Country', is a representative example of how he applied to the American vernacular an elaborate and hidden verbal craft, so that the magical incantatory quality of Symbolist poetry is given without losing the effect of sincerity, of authentically observed experience.[5]

Another major influence upon Hemingway derived from the artistic impulse underlying Imagism. Natan Zach has noted the suitability of Imagism as an aesthetic creed in the First World War situation:

> the outbreak of the First World War seemed to vindicate Imagism as a philosophy of style. The hardness which the movement required for its modern medium suddenly became the common experience of a generation on both sides of the trenches. The 'softness' of late nineteenth-century Aestheticism, itself a reaction from a hardened world, was now being superseded by a state of mind in tune with an even harsher reality.[6]

Given the premises of Imagism, Gertrude Stein's interest in sentence structures, and his own experience, Hemingway presumably experimented until he felt equipped with adequate formal procedures. Such a neat proposition does not take account of Hemingway's sensibility, which suggests a predisposition towards 'toughness' of language. The movement of *A Farewell to Arms*, both linguistically and structurally, is reductive, and its hero, Frederick Henry, conducts himself in an increasingly solipsistic manner. Upon this persona the novelist imposes formal and lexical restraints, including the first-person narrative method, the coded language of love and war-brotherhood, a concern with action rather than speculative thought, Henry's preference for the tactile and sensory instead of the intellectual: all of these trajectories point to a masculine consciousness taking refuge against the encroachment of war. The larger fragmentation of consciousness outside the hero is internally countered by a defensive segmentation of experience, a containment displayed within the novel pre-eminently through its distinctive discourses or language registers. The remainder of this discussion of *A Farewell to Arms* will concentrate upon selected passages which demonstrate both the interplay between and the autonomous nature of these discourses.

Perhaps the most apparent mode of discourse in the novel is that analysed by David Lodge in the passage quoted earlier. For a convenient example of this synthesising method the much-quoted opening paragraph is chosen:

> In the late summer of that year we lived in a house in a village that looked across the river and the plain to the mountains. In the bed of the river there were pebbles and boulders, dry and white in the sun, and the water was clear and swiftly moving and blue in the channels. Troops went by the house and down the road and the dust they raised powdered the leaves of the trees. The trunks of the trees too were dusty and the leaves fell early that year and we saw the troops marching along the road and the dust rising and leaves, stirred by the breeze, falling and the soldiers marching and afterwards the road bare and white except for the leaves.[7]

The prose-rhythms of this description depend upon skilful syntactical suppression and repetition together with plain

vocabulary. The absence of complex sentences works to
signify the flow of a story, as does the drawn-out last sentence,
which creates an illusion of spontaneity, the action related
exactly as it happened. A notable feature is the infrequency of
latinate or 'feminine' words; Hemingway's diction adopts
a 'masculine', largely Anglo-Saxon word stock to generate
the ethos of the soldier as hero. In the juxtaposition of the
beauties of the fall with the marching of the soldiers, the
antipodes of Hemingway's experience, the Michigan Lakes
and Caporetto, are adumbrated.

The impersonality of the opening passage, where the stress
is an 'objective' one upon the firm contours of nature,
characterises a large part of the novel. Certain values, of clean
swift action, for example, or of the emotional stability to be
drawn from natural objects underlie the prose. A very
different kind of language from this detached observation
and enactment is that used to register movements of ideological crisis or insight when decisions are made or intuitions
distilled. Such a moment occurs when Frederick Henry,
travelling upon the freight train after having deserted,
decides that he must escape permanently from the war. In this
passage figurative language connotes emotional tension:

> You did not love the floor of a flat-car nor guns with
> canvas jackets and the smell of vaselined metal or a canvas
> that rain leaked through, although it is very fine under a
> canvas and pleasant with guns; but you loved someone else
> whom now you knew was not even to be pretended there;
> you seeing now very clearly and coldly – not so coldly as
> clearly and emptily. You saw emptily, lying on your
> stomach, having been present when one army moved back
> and another came forward. You had lost your cars and your
> men as a floorwalker loses the stock of his department in a
> fire. There was, however, no insurance. You were out of it
> now. You had no more obligation. If they shot floorwalkers
> after a fire in the department store because they spoke with
> an accent they had always had, then certainly the floorwal-
> kers would not be expected to return when the store opened
> again for business. They might seek other employment: if
> there was any other employment and the police did not get
> them.   (pp. 204–5)

Lacking the apparently uncomplicated shape of the earlier unemotional passage, this moment of heightened experience deploys convoluted syntax in order to evoke the internal conflict of the protagonist. Verb tenses, crudely mixed, enact the problems of conceptualisation, a usage which frequently brings forth oddities as in 'was not even to be pretended'. The switching of tenses and the employment of conditional verb forms, producing the effect of thought-processes, both imply Frederick Henry's inner struggle when he feels compelled to leave the battle arena, the testing ground where nothingness can be verified. In addition to the colloquial anti-art devices, though, the reader is presented with a powerful modernist metaphor of rejection, the war conceived of as a fire in a shop where a floorwalker dutifully protects his goods. Having been betrayed by his own side, Henry, like the threatened floor-walker, has no option but to relinquish his earlier responsibilities. The image is suggestive of reluctant exile, an analogy and a condition of mind that indicates Hemingway's attune-ment to the modernist sensibility.

For a man such as Henry who was not born to think, such moments of psychological tension represent a painful close-up of that other abyss, the one located within the psyche. In general, though, Henry is presented through his conversa-tions with others and according to his own estimate of himself. This unmediated presentation projects Henry's life-style very often through dialogues with Rinaldi and Catherine, the two people with whom he feels most secure. The dialogues with Catherine are different from those with Rinaldi, as they are 'edited' and communicated through a 'love-register' of lan-guage. Characterised by apparent banality these conversa-tions edit the most intimate side of Frederick Henry's person-ality, his most private aspirations and values. The stylised and reductive language, which seems to withhold information from us, is based upon a startling register-change if we compare it with the two passages already mentioned. It purports to reveal by its limited linguistic resources the narrow conventions of lovers. Essentially the omissions ob-served in these dialogues and the repetitions of syntax and vocabulary depend upon a restricted language code. The theoretical underpinning for this usage, which draws upon synonyms and such terms of approval as 'fine' or 'splendid', relates to a principle of Imagist art: art should be controlled, hard and precise, cutting out non-contributory matter.

Before Catherine enters hospital she discusses with Frederick Henry the proprieties of marriage:

> '. . . if I marry you I'll be an American, and any time we're married under American law the child is legitimate.'
> 'Where did you find that out?'
> 'In the New York *World Almanac* in the library.'
> 'You're a grand girl.'
> 'I'll be very glad to be an American and we'll go to America won't we, darling? I want to see Niagara Falls.'
> 'You're a fine girl.'   (p. 258)

In this exchange important issues such as citizenship, marriage and illegitimacy are broached, but they are hedged in and curtailed by the bland adjectives and endearments. The effect is to infer that such large and important matters are less significant than being a 'grand' girl or a 'brave' soldier. The value-system, one which dismisses large abstract notions as dishonest, is carried through into the lovers' talk and thereby normalised.

In Hemingway's fiction the ethos of the camp-fire never seems far away either, providing another counter to the consuming energy of war that breaks all the brave ones. This brotherhood of war, its fraternalism and esoteric camaraderie, expresses itself through another kind of discourse where Henry communes with Rinaldi, his Italian war-brother. In these exchanges Henry emerges as the dominant figure through his relative taciturnity; he contrasts in both vocabulary and manner with the voluble, more effeminate surgeon, who kisses him and calls him 'baby'. When he visits Frederick in Chapter 10, Rinaldi's garrulousness and ornate speech are notable:

> 'How are you, baby? How do you feel? I bring you this – '
> It was a bottle of cognac. The orderly brought a chair and he sat down, 'and good news. You will be decorated. They want to get you the medaglia d'argento but perhaps they can get only the bronze.'
> 'What for?'

'Because you are gravely wounded. They say if you can prove you did any heroic act you can get the silver. Otherwise it will be the bronze. Tell me exactly what happened. Did you do any heroic act?'

'No,' I said. 'I was blown up while we were eating cheese.'

'Be serious. You must have done something heroic either before or after. Remember carefully.'

'I did not.'

'Didn't you carry anybody on your back? Gordini says you carried several people on your back but the medical major at the first post declares it is impossible. He has to sign the proposition for the citation.'

'I didn't carry anybody. I couldn't move.'   (p. 63)

Henry's inner thoughts about his wounding are carefully shielded from the reader, and his ironic articulation of the event disguises his pained sorrow. The specificity and familiarity of the dialogues between Rinaldi and Frederick Henry, based upon mannered and coded verbal exchanges, signify the human face of war, its only redeeming feature. Interestingly, although Henry loses touch with Rinaldi, their friendship lasts, one of the few things that remain spiritually unaltered by the war. The laconic understatement, so recognisable in Hemingway's style, may also conversely undermine the intended credibility of his narrative.

In the exchange with Rinaldi the litotes and ironic withholding of details are acceptable, but on other occasions, as when an Italian deserter is shot, such understatement suggests an evasion of authorial responsibility. The deserter, one of two Italian sergeants who have left their regiment, is shot on Henry's instructions for refusing to help remove the ambulances from mud (pp. 180–1). The reader is left wondering whether Frederick Henry was saddened by the event, whether he had made a mistake or whether the sergeant had indicated by his conduct some more traitorous potential than merely running away. The irony here derives from the fact that Henry shoots frightened men on his own side who are deserting and he himself later almost suffers the same fate. Perhaps this structural irony is complexly intended, but there is no evidence to assume this. Such concealments and the use of codes, of both language and conduct, confirm Hemingway's modernist credentials. His model of the artist was a Flaubertian one, excising from his manuscript redundant words, and searching for a unity of structure and language. The method of constructing coded language was later put to effective use also in *For Whom the Bell Tolls* in those passages purporting to render colloquial Spanish with grace and formal beauty.

In conclusion, we may identify the formal differences between Hemingway and Cummings by noting Hemingway's central method of articulation as constituting a series of distinctive linguistic discourses, separated off in contained fashion, whereas Cummings, contrastingly, explodes language in sustained metaphorical utterance. The tensions and dynamics of Hemingway's pared down language differ from Cummings's in being more dependent upon the use of staccato syntax to produce checks and repetitions, so that meaning may be intensified in finite linguistic segments; Cummings's prose works antithetically in its attempts to engage the infinite dimensions of human personality and social relationship; it seeks to rival a field of force in physics, as waves and particles of language interact kinetically. Both novelists exhibit the modernist instinct for breaking down in order to rebuild; in both instances stultified and conventional language, taken to symbolise defunct ideas and values, is rejected in favour of a regenerative and innovatory language practice which is counteractive to war's decimation. Both modernist artists display an idealist attitude to form; their artistic focus seeks to celebrate the mystery and integrity of human individuality. In war, their work seems to imply, historical energies bear down upon individual men and women curtailing potentialities for communal relationship and productive social interchange; given such premises prose fiction should concern itself with the notion of individual liberty as an index of social morality.

4 Radicalism: *Plumes* and *Three Soldiers*

Richard Plume, the protagonist of Laurence Stallings's novel *Plumes*, desperately needs his war wounds to be validated by the outcome of history. To this end he examines the war settlement at Versailles and scrutinises the political actions of Wilson and the Senate League. His reasoning that the amputation he suffered must have ideological value is founded upon the premise that America entered the war borne upon a tide of humanitarianism so overwhelming that its momentum must inevitably produce a rearranged social order, one sympathetic to any deprivation or suffering of its member individuals. His experience, of course, teaches him otherwise, and what he comes to understand of politics and authority is emblematic of the fictional war veteran's 'disillusionment'. After the national economic advantages of being a supplier of armaments have passed, the former pro-war hysteria and the patriotic fervour of 1918 which greeted victory are also dissipated. The United States had 'sized up its flurry into European affairs' and returned to 'normality', the pursuit of self-interest.[1] In place of the altruistic culture he anticipated as an outgrowth of war, Richard Plume registers his disgust at finding instead a ruling class motivated by nepotism and comprised of political cabals whose ingratitude to disabled soldiers is symbolised by the latter's inadequate pensions.

Richard Plume, before the conflict began, identified with the myths expressed in the poetry of Alan Seeger through such archetypes as crusaders, Christian soldiers, hands linked across the sea, all expressive of an American people willingly shedding blood to defend its European heritage. After having made the 'sacrifice' in exemplary fashion by losing his leg, he feels entitled to expect fulfilment of the ideals he previously

59

cherished. Ironically the most apparent justification for Richard's wound derives from its surgical significance: by operating upon his leg, surgeons at the Walter Reed hospital have developed techniques for plastic work upon gunshot wounds. Socially his wound is productive, too, for the cultural freedoms the war engendered; now 'the conventions of Montparnasse' have been imported to America. There is even a philosophical benefit accruing from mass warfare, as one may fairly deduce from its carnage the non-existence of a loving deity. Faced with Belleau Wood, Richard also theorises about the war's historical implications; what lesson does it offer concerning the origins and nationhood of the United States? His conclusions are tentative: it seems to him that America's greatest men have been deflected from worthier aims by their preoccupations with the ritual shedding of blood, and he wonders additionally whether 1914–18 would ever have happened if the American colonies had not won their independence (p. 205).

Ultimately Richard Plume adopts the viewpoint so common to lost generation fictional heroes, that intellectual empiricism is the only course left open. It must be acknowledged that the war demonstrates above all the pointlessness of industrialised slaughter; the fundamental illogic of history inheres in the decimation at Verdun and the Somme. A sentence deployed by the omniscient narrator of *Plumes* towards the end of the novel signifies the new fictional historiography of war, that any notion of war service for one's country which is based upon the concept of crusading is a delusion. The narrator draws upon ironic conjunctures in futurising a war vision: 'Even the tall towers of Arlington, snapping their steel fingers at battleships in the roadways of Manilla and Pearl Harbor, seemed dancing in the brisk afternoon wind, unmindful of their skeleton significance above the bodies of illusioned patriots.' Novelists such as Dos Passos and Stallings, who form the subject of this chapter, were constantly mindful of what had happened to those 'illusioned patriots'. A discussion of *Plumes* is followed by an analysis of one of the most influential of all American war novels, *Three Soldiers*.

Laurence Stallings, born in Georgia in 1894, married the daughter of a college professor and volunteered for the First World War. His distinguished war service at Belleau Wood culminated in Stallings having his leg amputated, elements of his life which broadly authenticate *Plumes* (1924), his war novel. Like the fictional Richard Plume, Stallings rushed into the war, discovered its horror, and bore by his disfigurement the permanent results of his service. Stallings developed his analysis of 1914–18 in a sequence of war books; *What Price Glory* (1924) was closely followed by *Plumes*, and nine years later Stallings wrote captions for *The First World War* (1933), a photographic record of the war. *The Doughboys* (1962), a history of the American Expeditionary Force, reworks the themes of heroism and disillusion found in Stallings's occasional writing, such as his film script *The Big Parade*, and his dramatisation (in 1930) of *A Farewell to Arms*, which emphasises Hemingway's pacifism. Like Hemingway, Stallings compulsively observed war; he accompanied Ethiopian troops in 1935 as a correspondent, served during the Second World War on General Arnold's staff, and 'saw the backwash of the Korean War a generation later'.[2]

Despite the commercial success of *Plumes* Stallings will probably remain a minor literary figure whose contribution to war literature retains interest because the war shaped him as a writer and his work, in turn, contributed to the formation of popular anti-war attitudes in the twenties. His play *What Price Glory* (1924), like its author's other works, remains primarily interesting in this symptomatic or documentary sense. Written in collaboration with Maxwell Anderson, *What Price Glory* principally depends for its effects upon the reproduction of previously taboo soldiers' language. *Plumes*, the novel paralleling Stallings's own war experience, is the author's best known work of fiction. Although in considerable vogue when first published, *Plumes* has inevitably shed its topicality and has since been generally neglected by literary historians and critics.

The novel traces the volunteer, hero, disillusioned patriot pattern of Stallings's own traumatic experiences. Its hero, Richard Plume, commits an act of folly by enlisting for the forces, not knowing his wife, Esme, is pregnant. He suffers grave wounds, and like his ancestors, the martial Plumes, who predictably rush into war and are invalided out, he becomes a returned warrior, a potential focus of attention. Now that he is faced with the difficulty of adjusting to society, his alternatives are clarified for the reader: he may capitalise on his disability and assume the role of the professionally wounded veteran or use his life to protest against the glorification of war, and solve his financial problems by taking a job no matter how difficult this may be. Richard Plume chooses not to yield to his disablement, and prefers to work in a laboratory and accept the consequential low wages and housing difficulties for his wife and son, to slinking home to the easy life awaiting him at his former college where he may romanticise his wounds.

Ultimately the stresses of living as a cripple overwhelm Richard: he drives his wife and son away, and enters hospital where his leg is amputated. The limb serves as a metaphor for his angry spirit, and when the poison has left his system his humour improves. His former colleague at the government laboratory, Gary, a cynical invalid who erodes Richard's remaining illusions about war, tries to persuade him to return to his job, but Richard refuses and becomes a journalist, a piece of living propaganda, for a political magazine, *The Wounded Doughboy*. Towards the end of the novel, after being tempted by a relative who offers to find him a well-paid sinecure, Richard rejoins his wife and boy. Ironically, Richard's son, by his action of collecting used cartridges, suggests that the Plume tradition of rushing foolishly into battle will be perpetuated in the next war.

To erect a framework for his novel, Laurence Stallings uses chivalric terminology; the first and last books are entitled 'Battered Plumes'; the others 'The Shorn Helm', 'The Caitiff Knight' and 'Tourneys'. Richard's experience is to be ordered by a structure of knightly concepts, so that his actions and thoughts may be placed in ironic perspective and related to a martial tradition. A somewhat similar technique is employed by William Faulkner in *Sartoris*, which likewise links the First World War with past wars. The Plume who bears most responsibility is Noah, who 'founded the war-like tradition, persisted in unto this day among the Plumes, of going to war to save your neighbour's property'. Other descendants continue this practice, among them Noah's son, who illustrates what generally happens to the Plumes: they fight, are gravely wounded, and return home to foolish retirement. Stallings's narrator, reflecting on Noah's injuries, caustically particularises the uniformity of soldiers' wounds:

There is a superstition among the ignorant that the World War was more cruel than any other: yet Noah Plume, with a round hole in his groin, must have there experienced sensations and misgivings identical, in so far as physiology is concerned with those of the German assault regiments at Verdun.   (p. 11)

Refusing to learn from this, Noah, when asked by his son if he had been hurt by the war, said, 'Naw', thereby 'drenching his descendants in blood'.

Old Hickory Plume, who lost part of his arm at Buena Vista and then 'made the mistake of setting up house in the path of Sherman's troops', is another described half-humorously, half-ironically by Stallings's narrator, yet he lost two sons in the Civil War. Stallings's initial method is to refuse to take war seriously: if he had continued to do this when narrating the experience of his hero, Richard, the novel would have been aesthetically more consistent and satisfying. Richard's father, who suffered from 'frustrated valor', regretted his inability to get into a war and experience 'the drumming pulse and blanched cheek of the man who feels the hot blast of enemy fire'. He compensated for this by reading Froissart's *Chronicles*, naming his son Richard Coeur de Lion, and teaching him a Confederate interpretation of history. The reader is prepared by Stallings's emphasis upon the absurd deeds of Richard's ancestors for a novel somewhat like *Catch-22*, an anarchic, comic rejection of war. However, Stallings does not long continue in this surreal humorous vein, and the parody of chivalry that he apparently intends soon loses energy. Although not fully developed, the figures in the early Plume tradition are treated with considerable detachment; Stallings utilises both periphrasis and comic understatement to burlesque military glory-seeking. Such an instinct towards irony, displayed in these opening sections, suggests an aesthetic solution that, if pursued throughout the novel as a whole, would have led the novelist in the direction of greater objectivity.

Stallings prefers to concentrate upon the tragic qualities of his hero whose error was to enlist for the war and repeat the mistake of his predecessors. A look at the dust-cover of *The Doughboys* (1962), Stallings's popular, loosely-written account of the American Expeditionary Force, illuminates the fictive character of Richard Plume. Two pictures of Laurence Stallings are placed before the reader: one shows the author when he first joined the army, and the other him after he had been badly wounded. Stallings comments on the second picture: 'I could not walk at the time, and Genthe, a great artist, more or less reveals this.'[3] The contrast between two pictures such as these and the ideological attitudes revealed in their presentation are explored more fully in *Plumes*, where war acts out the great historical peripeteia underlying the photographs. Physical independence, the core of Richard's self-respect, is taken away by war. When described before his wound, the details of his physique are clearly emphasised. His body 'was a beautiful thing' and he possessed 'flat hips and shoulders of a Rodin mould' (p. 4). He also had a 'cavernous torso', 'glistening shoulders', 'sleek sides'. His virility is conveyed by his supple nakedness: the boy 'squeezed the pinpoint scratch under this left nipple – a boss on a bronze shield', and two French women remark, 'vous êtes plus grand'. The hero, who now easily disarms a powerful Sengalese trying to knife him, later becomes a helpless cripple involved in a crisis of identity.

After the war Richard's wound visually marks him off from his contemporaries and psychologically alienates him from the past. He feels emotionally separated from his ancestors and family whose attitudes he rejects, and from the society that produced his disability and now denies him both material reward and mental ease. In the conflict Richard has within himself and which is externalised in his social relationships inheres the tragi-comic potentiality of the story that Stallings fails to capitalise, a lost opportunity which is apparent in the novelists's presentation of character. Richard's use of language, for example, suggests an ambivalence on Stallings's part. The difficulty the hero has in adjusting to his wound is embodied in his self-descriptions, on one level terrifyingly apt, on another seeming to verify Scott Fitzgerald's comment that Stallings 'had not genius enough to whine appealingly'. Richard refers to himself on different occasions as 'mutilated', 'shattered', 'twisted', 'tortured', 'mis-shaped', 'crippled'. In portraying fictionally a situation so close to his own experience of having been wounded and undergone a process of social rehabilitation, Stallings needed considerable artistic detachment, especially if Richard were to be regarded as a heroic victim of society. Richard, as a fictional creation, conversely appears at times to be merely a mouthpiece for his creator, which originates from an apparent lack of technical sophistication on Stallings's part, an unawareness of some of the problematic issues involved in writing a war novel which apparently blends a strain of documentary realism with one of impersonal comic irony. Formal considerations do not always seem to be taken into account as when the reader is offered an unmediated narrator's description of Richard as 'a hopeless cripple' or of Gary, his friend, as 'bitter', 'acid', 'sardonic'. Given the predominance of a realistic mode of presentation dependent upon characters undergoing social readjustment, it is reasonable to expect that the novelist as narrator will not pre-empt in this way the reader's own evaluations too frequently.

Stallings writes of Richard, 'Not only had his system of locomotion been changed, but his emotions as well' (p. 84). The imagery of the hospital ward, restricted in Dos Passos and Hemingway to the precincts of the hospital, carries over into civilian life. The reader gains an intimate knowledge of Richard Plume's injury, of the monstrous 'engine' the hero has to wear and the varying stages of his fight to conquer his wound. Thus the novel communicates a medical case history and a concomitant frenetic concern with self, rather like the hero's self-dramatisation in Hemingway's *Across the River and into the Trees* (1950). Richard does, though, try hard to externalise his experience on occasions, envisioning the fate of Richard and Esme as historically typical: 'people are all over the world, weeping into one another's arms this minute, crippled, blinded, insane. Crippled Richards killing pitiful Esmes, and little children unconscious of it all.' Once he analogises his own situation with that of the crucified Christ, a motif found commonly in First World War fiction. He has grown atheistic and his anger spurts out, directionless, blasphemous:

I can walk into a church with its promises of peace hereafter and its scorn to consider this present room and your terrible little tin oven and my horrible brace, and laugh into a preacher's face. I have died. What does he know about death? He'll tell me how Christ died to save me. . . . I did the same thing, and voluntarily. . . . A foolish little Christ all over again. . . . And after all, the man of Nazareth had only three short hours upon a cross. I've had hundreds. How many expiations must there be before I can approach death with serenity?   (p. 199)

Outbursts such as this occur frequently in the novel, because like war itself they render disordered consciousness.

Henri Toxier, a character in William Eastlake's *Castle Keep* (1966) deplores heroism as 'stupid cavalier or silly', a course of action made inevitable only when thoughtful cowards have left no alternatives. Toxier also cynically theorises that Americans, like lemmings, commit such suicidal acts out of an uncontrollable national impulse; thus death in war for the doughboy attains a charismatic aura and manifests both the childish innocence and misplaced bravery of the New World. Richard Plume's lemming-like rush to war evokes afterwards a pathogenic flashback to the scene of his wounding, conveyed in language that expresses the terror of being hit: 'Funny that he had felt nothing from his foot and yet he had seen the feathers fly from it an hour ago when the man in the church tower had hit him again. The foot was turned exactly round, its heel and toe reversed and was swarming with gnats' (*Plumes*, pp. 240–1). The hero's completely twisted foot infers wider cosmic disorder; from Richard's unnatural injuries issues the true meaning of war; for he is transformed into 'centrifugal' energy, becoming for an instant 'the centre of all living things'. One of the strands of definition in Eastlake's *Castle Keep* draws upon the elusive nature of war, its processes of transmutation that can transmogrify at random. In 'trying to forget the killing and the hurt that happened', the soldier in *Castle Keep* is moulded by the shock of combat into a different selfhood: 'war is a Cinderella story where each man turns into a soldier'. War in Stallings's novel goes beyond oxymoron and fantasy into nightmare: Richard Plume not only changes from 'a man' into 'a soldier', but into an ambling creature with 'bear-like' steps. It is one thing, the narrator infers, to erect fantasies about death, another to wake up, outraged, and find one's leg amputated.

Stallings writes at the other end of the spectrum from later war novelists like Heller, Vonnegut and Eastlake who give formal perspective to war through the non-representational devices of post-modernism. The desire for authenticity in Stallings's case, his determination to show it as it really was, seems to have inhibited other fictional possibilities of comic vision and satire which are hinted at especially in the early stages of the text. The occult bandaged figure in Heller's *Catch-22* points to other fictional and comedic ways of treating the topic of wounding, for example.

In later life Stallings returned to the theme of wounding in an impressive story, 'Vale of Tears' (1931), and in the Prologue to *The Doughboys*, where he observes that the wounds of his 'buddies of the past' were more agonising than those of Korean war veterans, because in 1917–18 there existed 'no miracle drugs, no sulphur or antibiotics, to quieten the canvas air at Coulommiers'. *Plumes* illustrates a commensurately direct fictional treatment of wounding by centralising industrialised military violence within the person of Richard; his pain is often evoked through imagery of factory kilns, acting, for example, like 'hot coal' to make his torso 'furnace-like'. Stallings's narrator makes little attempt to understate Richard's mutilation in order obliquely to stress its horror in the manner, say, of Remarque's *All Quiet on the Western Front*, where the multifarious ways of being wounded are on one occasion coldly listed. Richard Plume by obsessively describing and talking of his own wounds reminds the reader more of the battered Colonel Cantwell in *Across the River and into the Trees*; in Richard's case wounding generates social anger, and contributes to the formulation of social analysis; his rage, being justified, enables him to attain insights denied to others.

Stallings later writes in the Prologue of *Doughboys* of President Wilson's curt dismissal of Sergeant York, his country's most celebrated hero, and implies that Theodore Roosevelt would surely have behaved with more understanding towards the old soldier. The many references to the mood of post-war society which gave *Plumes* its topicality, similarly picture the American people and their leaders as hostile to returned soldiers. The society, because it rejects its own veterans as expendable, deserves its shabby representatives at Versailles, sanctimoniously extracting war reprisals from innocent Germans who had been fed a similar diet of 'shining swords' to Richard himself. This strain of writing catches a radical tone of protest that is crystallised in the author's attacks on the post-war government for perpetuating a 'gigantic hypocrisy' by investigating chemical warfare and yet continuing to produce armaments. Thus it is implied that the government's illness is more serious than Richard's. Men such as Gary, the cerebral pacifist and the novel's most successful character, are isolated. Gary has the unique experience of being a 'hybridisation' of 'victim and profiteer', because he invested in war stocks after his injury. Thus he fights society on his terms, learning acquiescence to his disfigurement, and displaying a non-co-operative attitude to the political authorities who betrayed him. Gary explicates his basic viewpoint when he tells Richard that a war wound has exactly the same nobility and causes the same amount of suffering as one caused by a freight truck. Such an opinion, authenticated by combat experience, authoritatively articulates the intellectual justification for pacifism and revolt. Other philosophical or ideological positions, the attraction of religious rhetoric or political idealism, have little cogency for men who have been appallingly wounded like Richard.

As a whole, *Plumes* remains an interesting novel because of the serious social concern of its author evidenced fictionally through the conduct and debate of such characters as Richard and Gary. Their assumption that society would, after their hospitalisation, reform its governance, stays unfulfilled. Instead the novel dramatises the continuance of false rhetoric and slogan-making, outward manifestations of a debased social morality: clerics continue to talk of 'service to the Christian ideal', politicians still seem bent upon self-advancement; the ruination of Richard's family life and aspirations thus depicts the total failure of pre-war progressivist ideals. Only one solution presents itself to Richard, pacifism and more pacifism. The ending, when young Richard is told by his father that a general is a man who 'makes little boys sleep in graves', clarifies the novel's pacifist trajectory. Richard Plume will accept no more bluff, will no longer allow war to be prettified through the platitudes of politicians. He will do all he can to help his own son, against the drawing power of the war dead, to keep his kneecaps all through life.

He has become cognisant of the hypocrisy of men such as Wilson who pretend to hate war and yet still keep conscientious objectors in prison for their 'crimes'. Above all, Richard has learned what it is to fight and come back, 'broken fool', taught by kilowatt hours of pain not to sentimentalise war. Richard's concluding position, that of a liberal conscious of the betrayal of liberal principles by politicians who have never 'lacked for cheese' during the war, may be taken as a representative one in the twenties. Where *Plumes* is of exceptional interest is in its exploration of the domestic implications of such an ideological position. The novel exhibits powerful pacifist and meliorist energy.

Ernest Hemingway, writing of *Three Soldiers*, praised its seminal influence: 'the writing of it was as valuable a pioneering feat in American letters as some minor Lewis or Clark's expedition into the North West'.[4] David Sanders, discussing the same novel, refers to Hemingway as among novelists who learned a great deal from Dos Passos: '*Three Soldiers* was the original example, in subject and tone, of the American war novel as thereafter developed by Hemingway, William March, Hersey, Mailer and James Jones.'[5] Such formulations aptly suggest the impact of *Three Soldiers*, whose treatment of army totalitarianism shaped the dissenting attitudes found in a wide range of later American war fiction. Dos Passos became the first important novelist after Stephen Crane to treat war as a major fictional theme, and his tutelage of American war writers may be fairly likened to that of Barbusse upon Europeans. Significantly, Barbusse's total denunciation of war seemed to the young Dos Passos to correspond most closely to his own position, a debt acknowledged in Dos Passos's autobiography, *The Best Times*. Frequently *Le Feu* recalls the similarity of sensibility and attitude between the young Dos Passos and Barbusse. This seems most apparent in passages where the violent tone of protest is expressed in heightened metaphorical language, as in this reflection:

> Après tout, qu'est-ce qui fait la grandeur et l'horreur de la guerre? . . . C'est la grandeur des peuples . . . . Mais les peuples, c'est nous! Celui qui avait dit me regardait, m'interrogeait. Oui, lui dis-je, oui, mon vieux frère, c'est vrai! C'est avec nous seulement qu'on fait les batailles. C'est nous

la matière de la guerre. La guerre n'est composée que de la chair et des âmes des simples soldats. C'est nous qui formons les plaines de morts et les fleuves de sang, nous tous – dont chacun est invisible et silencieux à cause de l'immensité de notre nombre. Les villes vidées, les villages détruits, c'est le désert de nous. Oui, c'est nous tous et c'est nous tous entiers.[6]

In *The Best Times* Dos Passos records how his father tried to dissuade him from volunteering for Eliot Norton's ambulance drivers and packed him off to Spain instead. After his father's death, Dos Passos joined the Norton-Harjes Volunteer Ambulance Service on the Verdun front and transferred to northern Italy with the American Red Cross. During this period, drawing upon Barbusse and *The Masses* for ideological inspiration, he aspired to write a radical and pacifist war novel. Fuelled by his disappointment at Woodrow Wilson's declaration of war after being elected to office for a second time, Dos Passos remembers, 'I began listening seriously to the Socialists. Their song was that all that was needed to abolish war was to abolish capitalism. Turn the industrial plant over to the people who did the work and man's aggressive instincts would be channelled into constructive efforts.'[7] Such political theorising was seemingly validated by a change in the novelist's own circumstances when he escaped the privileges of his class to serve with a Medical Corps Casuals Company. His experience at Camp Crane helps to account for the vacillations Dos Passos himself experienced between the roles of 'gentleman volunteer' with its Elizabethan swashbuckling connotations and that of 'buck private'; a similar transformation may be noted in the metamorphosis of Martin Howe, the rather effete hero of *One Man's Initiation*, into John Andrews, the artist–rebel of *Three Soldiers*.

One of the revelations manifested to the cerebral John Andrews in *Three Soldiers* is the correlation between war and the dynamics of social change. Andrews comes to realise that war is not a historical digression, an accident unfortuitously interrupting the flow of civilisation, but the fullest expression of civilisation, its most perfect metaphor. The ideological framework of the novel rests upon this assumption, a truth that the composer Andrews, on behalf of the war artist, seeks the aesthetic means of articulating: 'If only he could express the thwarted lives, the miserable dullness of industrialised slaughter, it might have been almost worth while for him; for the others it would never be worth while' (p. 269). This prescriptive viewpoint, that society's workings and its counterpart, war, are equally products of an insignificant and humanly random spate of events dominated by the machine consciousness, totally informs *Three Soldiers*. Dos Passos consistently enacts in the novel the pre-eminence of the machine, the processing of the infantryman by inorganic systems, self-perpetuating and geared only to achieving 'industrialised slaughter'. The American army, a hierarchical model of the social infrastructure, and not the act of killing in combat, now becomes the object of the novelist's detestation. Talking about war is portrayed as being more obscene than actually fighting it. The organisation formed in order to instrumentalise war, the American army, Leviathan-like oppresses its victims, and the imagery appropriately seizes upon inhuman substances, metal, rust, copper, moulds, treadmills, grinding wheels, rolling stock, broken clockwork toys, automatons, superannuated machinery, steamrollers, bundles on the production line – all suggestive of steel juggernauts. One is reminded of how Marinetti and the Italian Futurists approved of machinery as part of the purifying hygiene of war. Dos Passos was similarly fascinated, although his motivation originates from aesthetic distaste of war.

Jonathan King, writing of *Le Feu*, has drawn attention to the aesthetic difficulties Barbusse faced in combining the documentary and prophetic modes of writing within a social realist form. The First World War, he notes, was 'this most plebeian and democratic of wars . . . also the most obviously apocalyptic'.[8] Barbusse's uncertainty of language, according to King, stems from this ironic conjunction; King writes,

the awkward lapses into the language of prophecy are not always wilful. They are symptomatic of a crisis within the history of realism itself, of a problem not easy to overcome. Realism had at some stage to bring within its orbit the masses as well as the individual, just as it had to take account of suggestions emanating from the world of science that some kind of blind, but not necessarily malevolent, force was at work in human history. Realism was forced to be increasingly close to documentary journalism at the same time as being forced in the direction of prophecy and vision, allegory and symbol. It acquired the subject matter associated with Naturalism together with the methods of Symbolism . . . .[9]

King's insights into the contradictory impulses at work in *Le Feu* have validity also if applied to the fiction of Dos Passos, Barbusse's admirer. The strain of documentary authenticity in *Three Soldiers* clearly inheres in the novel's fidelity to detail in depicting the multifariousness of barracks life. Fuselli, Chrisfield and Andrews are fully displayed at work: the reader encounters them in conversation with 'Y' men and talking to a range of other civilians, for example, hypocrites such as the Reverend Dr Skinner; the soldiers are observed in the company of French prostitutes or behaving deferentially to officers; military routine expressed in drill sessions or cookhouse duty is similarly treated. Transposed against this seemingly factually orientated account of military life is a pattern of symbolism of a more poetic kind. These configurations are intended to evoke the debilitating action of what Andrews calls the 'psychology of slavery', a yoke designed to break men and collapse ordered structures of thought. Such an aesthetic tension, which remains unresolved, between documentary realism and symbolic prophecy signifies one of many polarities running through the narrative of *Three Soldiers*. The pulling apart of the individual's freedom and aspirations by the tyranny of the army's treadmill is built into the novel at many levels. One such insight into the violation of individual rights is elaborated through John Andrews's great-man theory of history; Andrews envisions history as a process dominated by a series of extraordinary individuals: this sequence has broken down into the sterility of the present. Whereas in the past towering figures such as Socrates, Christ or Da Vinci were able to transcend their environment, in the industrialised present such greatness is impossible, because of the omnipresence of dehumanising forces which block human potentiality and induce in its place intellectual and emotional stagnation.[10]

The tripartite patterning of *Three Soldiers* is, paradoxically,

another instance of Dos Passos's dualistic imagination, his
tendency to work through contraries, since the structure
of the novel seeks both to provide a cross-sectional view of
American society and, at the same time, to offer a rendering of
three individuated lives. Clearly such an ambitious formal
patterning proved beyond Dos Passos's scope until the advent
of *USA*, where the camera eye and newsreel techniques acted as
more suitable enabling devices for a panoramic novel. Dos
Passos's basic narrative method in *Three Soldiers* is to dramatise
the separate military careers of three representative Americans, Fuselli, Andrews and Chrisfield. All three are shown to
hate the army, an institution jointly experienced as profoundly destructive because it seeks to deprave the individual
by stimulating in him the negative emotions of competitive-
ness, cruelty and self-disgust. Thus Fuselli, who tries to play
along with the system, and is an equivalent of one of James
Jones's 'jockstraps', in *From Here to Eternity*, is deterministically
frustrated in not gaining his desired promotion: he is merely
tricked into obedience, and appropriately in view of his
psychic experiences, he finally contracts venereal disease.
Chrisfield, a prototype of Norman Mailer's sadistic Croft, has
embryonic pathological tendencies fostered by his situation,
and these culminate in the murder of an officer; finally he is
thoroughly perverted and deserts. Like Chrisfield, John
Andrews also deserts, after his artistic sensibility has been
violated by the army's brutality. *Three Soldiers*, through its
wide-ranging panoramic narrative, attempts to convey a large
and tragic perspective of war. The historical pessimism of Dos
Passos falls short of tragedy, though, because his principal
characters invalidate his tragic objectives. He cannot reinforce
his central belief that organisation, whether from above or
below, annihilates personal development, which is the radical
standpoint of *Three Soldiers*, if he does not as a novelist create
individuals who are at least potentially capable of the 'organic
completeness' he desires men to have. *Three Soldiers* was the
work of a novelist finding his feet artistically, a state of affairs
demonstrated by the rather inchoate presentation of character. The reader is likely to experience difficulty in fully
differentiating between the individuals treated (instanced
most readily in the way the ill-educated Fuselli, the deprived
boy from California, sometimes aestheticises like the artist

Andrews). There is virtually no psychological change displayed throughout the narrative of *Three Soldiers*: Fuselli,
having lost his illusions of rising meritocratically, remains in
the same state of defeated bemusement. Chrisfield, the
stereotypical Indiana farm-hand, continues until the close of
the novel to experience erotic feelings of violence, and Dos
Passos does not assist the reader to explore the psychological
origins of his sadism. Fuselli seems to be the most plausible
fictively in the way he allows his confused notions of the
meaning of the war to impinge upon his personal situations;
he tries to personalise the army's activities and processes,
believing mistakenly that its processes are humanised and will
acknowledge his merit. Inevitably the officers neglect to
reward his co-operation, and he is utterly broken by the end of
the novel. Fuselli has always been duped by propaganda,
formerly believing in atrocity myths, and his low level of
articulateness and education combine to create the aura of a
genuine victim.

   Dos Passos's fictional techniques are represented fairly
by Chapter 1 of 'Under the Wheels' when John Andrews is
finally pressured into desertion. In the preceding chapter the
novelist has shown the army's sadistic cruelty when Andrews is
beaten up by military police for not having his papers, and the
hero becomes the first of a line of army prisoners (one recalls
Jones's stockade men in *From Here to Eternity*) working in a
symbolic environment of 'bloody bandages, ashes, and bits of
decaying food'. Dos Passos's narrator intends to reveal how
military tribalism, the army's pernicious herd instinct,
punishes its victims. Andrews befriends one of these misfits, a
boy of seventeen who has lied to get in the army, and they
work in appalling conditions symptomatic of army totalitarianism. Dos Passos devotes himself in chapters like these
to arguing a case against the army, and his novel risks the
overall accusation of bias since it rarely, unlike, say, Jones's
From Here to Eternity, shows the positive side of barracks life.
Andrews over-reacts to instances of military brutality perhaps
because his creator, as John Aldridge has said, is 'using him all
along to make a point'.[11]

   In *Three Soldiers* Dos Passos attempts to evaluate fictively the
suffering of men of different cultural backgrounds. Hoggen-
back, a companion in the labour squad, cannot understand

why the educated Andrews did not try to evade the army: 'I kinder thought an edicated guy like you'ld be able to keep out of a mess like this. I wasn't brought up without edication, but I guess I didn't have enough' (p. 368). Andrews, a suitable hero for a *roman à thèse*, replies that despite their different social origins their situations are essentially similar: 'A man suffers as much if he doesn't know how to read and write as if he had a college education.' After this speech, and for once throwing aside his cerebral flabbiness, Andrews acts swiftly, and deserts from the labour squad.

Dos Passos's poetic reinforcement of thematic material by an integrated strand of heightened imagistic prose merits some discussion also in an analysis of *Three Soldiers*. The novelist's aesthetic concern in such contexts is to convey both the inner and externalised rhythms of military life, its routine and monotony. One example taken from the paragraph that opens Chapter 3 of 'Machines' illustrates well how the novel succeeds mimetically in communicating the 'erect paralysis' that encompasses the infantry soldier and which takes away his identity as an individual. The symbolism, that elsewhere often seems rather inflated, in this passage energises the prose. The corporateness of collective enslavement is enacted through drawn-out syntax and imagery suggestive of metallic inertness:

Chrisfield's eyes were fixed on the leaves at the tops of the walnut trees, etched like metal against the bright colourless sky, edged with flicks and fringes of gold where the sunlight struck them. He stood stiff and motionless at attention, although there was a sharp pain in his left ankle that seemed swollen enough to burst the worn boot. He could feel the presence of men on both sides of him, and of men again beyond them. It seemed as if the stiff line of men in olive-drab, standing at attention, waiting endlessly for someone to release them from their erect paralysis, must stretch unbroken round the world . . . . (p. 151)

John Andrews, the cultivated hero of *Three Soldiers*, enters the war voluntarily. Like his creator, he enlists to uphold the values of the gentleman volunteer, acting out initially his own sense of adventure, grateful for the benefits of travel and motivated by an altruistic concern for his fellow men. Andrews, a Harvard man, composer and aesthete, wishes to transcend himself in the army's turmoil, to explore the lower half of the social pyramid and thus outgrow his previous self-centredness. Because he chooses to enlist and is not duped by propaganda, he believes that his decision will lead to spiritual growth. The structure of his romantic world has collapsed at the outset of war, and he wishes to face Armageddon in company with the huddled masses. Such grand gestures, out of fashion in Second World War fiction, are founded upon Andrews's unexamined 'philosophy of scorn' whereby slavery and negative experience germinate social understanding. Andrews's idealism, which stems from his liberal sensibility, is inevitably frustrated. Ultimately he discovers only a stark equation: the army represents the total enslavement of the individual. It crushes any impulse towards redemption or renewal.

Andrews initially believes that with his social and educational advantages he can contribute to the achievement of freedom for his fellow soldiers, but Dos Passos depicts him in what now seems to be an ambiguous way and makes it inevitable that this aim will remain unachieved. From the outset of *Three Soldiers* there are factors that detract from the post Second World War reader's sympathetic approval of Andrews. He appears in hindsight to be something of a mother's boy and a snob, who abandons a French girl, after he has seduced her, merely because she is working-class, in favour of a rich Parisienne, Genevive Rod. Andrews's flashes of social conscience are too intermittent to be either dialectically or morally productive, and his remark to Jeanne that deep down he 'must be a socialist' is never borne out by action. His political sympathies stay uncodified so that when French working people strike for better social conditions Andrews remains detached from their cause, although he is a deserter at the time and is himself in conflict with the social hierarchy. What Andrews learns, that to exist in the army means that one must be either a sheep or a deserter, calls for a revolutionary creed that the dilettante composer seems entirely incapable of formulating. Because of Andrews's limited political understanding, the radical impetus of *Three Soldiers* remains unrealised, latent only in the sub-text of the novel; thus the intellectual implications of the book, towards political activism, is unhelpfully divorced from its narrative action. As Stanley Cooperman has noted, Andrews's principal sacrifice is an aesthetic gesture when, at the end of the novel, facing arrest, he leaves behind his music.[12] The interest of John Andrews in the context of war fiction is that he embodies an artist fable, whereby the artist at war seeks to distill creatively his growing insights into the enlisted man's humiliation at the hands of a fascist-like supervisory class.

Three Soldiers adumbrates many of the controlling ideas found in later American war fiction. The iconoclasm of its ending where Andrews fulminates against the military system proved more ideologically appropriate to later novelists than the enigmatically uplifting ending of Stephen Crane's *The Red Badge of Courage*. It is possible also to detect in Dos Passos's work many of the motifs that later became standard in novels such as *The Naked and the Dead* and *From Here to Eternity*. The army, in these later novels, is similarly envisioned as an expression of American totalitarianism which induces the individual to conform to a pattern of values that combine to destroy his identity. In *Three Soldiers* the reader encounters for the first time in American fiction a radical note of protest against the army's bureaucratic and hierarchical organisation. John Andrews, like a succession of later heroes, feels that he is psychologically enslaved by the social structures that surround him, caught on a treadmill, his consciousness seared. Fuselli and Chrisfield also come to disavow the values of their own side, and what happens to them all suggests that war is an instrument of politics designed to subjugate both a proletarian class and the middle-class artist alike. One of the characters in Dos Passos's earlier novel *One Man's Initiation* remarks suspiciously that the dominant capitalist class is expert in disguising its real intentions which are to maintain its dominance: 'Think of this new particular vintage of lies that has been so industriously pumped out of the press and the pulpit. Doesn't it stagger you?'[13] In reaction against such dishonest propaganda the soldiers like Martin Howe or John Andrews feel alienated from the agents of the ruling class such as the 'Y' men and the military police. In consequence, as a soldier remarks in *One Man's Initiation*, enlisted men are 'nearer, in state of mind, in everything, to the Germans than to everyone else'. The determination to be just to the enemy, so much an integral part of *Three Soldiers*, was a counter-product of the earlier propaganda that confused Fuselli and made him think of figures with spiked helments dressed like Ku-Klux Klan men and spitting babies on their bayonets. Dos Passos's John Andrews and Martin Howe are purified not by heroism in battle but by the revolutionary stirrings of social conscience; above all they strive to preserve their identity in a social system where everything is rigged.

5   Lost Generation at War

The experiential connotations of 'lost generation' have often been appropriated by novelists and poets wishing to measure their own situation against the aura of the First World War. William Eastlake in *The Bamboo Bed* (1969) scrutinised the phrase in his disanalogy of a Vietnam 'lost generation' of GIs: 'This is not a lost generation. This is the ignored generation. The generation that is used by old people to kill young people. The generation that is kept fighting a war in nowhere so that there will not be a revolution somewhere.'[1] Other writers have similarly exploited the war-weary implications of 'lost generation' as a basis for generalisation. John Hersey, for example, in his Second World War novel *The War Lover* (1959), creates a narrator who denies that he belonged to a 'wised-up' generation: 'There's too much idiocy at large about how we were disenchanted young men who'd been wised-up by *A Farewell to Arms* and *Soldier's Pay* and *Three Soldiers*.'[2] Karl Shapiro, writing in 1968, is likewise haunted by the incubus of the earlier lost generation:

> our generation lived through more history than most or may be any. . . . We were reared as intellectuals and fought the Second World War before it happened and then again when it did happen. . . . None of my generation were war heroes that I remember. . . . Unlike the war poets of the First World War, who never recovered from the experience, our generation did . . . the tragedy of our generation — and I believe it is the tragedy — was that our army never melted away . . . .[3]

William Styron, in his novel about Korean reservists, *The Long March* (1952), enters the dialogue by portraying his characters as being 'trapped' because they are born into a generation of 'conformists' unlike the earlier rebel heroes.[4] Thus the phrase 'lost generation' dialectically interacts with later variations, and becomes traditional, like the first inscription of a palimpsest overlaid with later versions.

Hemingway, in *A Moveable Feast*, suggests that the phrase 'lost generation' had its genesis in an occasion when Gertrude Stein was having her car attended to. The garage proprietor, bemoaning lack of 'respect', referred to his Italian mechanic, an ex-serviceman, as one of 'une génération perdue'.[5] The catchword came to symbolise many of the younger novelists who began writing after the war, the constellation Arthur Mizener refers to as a coherent artistic grouping:

> These novelists constitute perhaps the first coherent group of novelists in the history of American literature. . . . None of these novelists of the Lost Generation was as gifted as the great and lonely giants of nineteenth-century American fiction. But, taken together, as the impulse common to their generation requires that we should take them, they constitute the finest group of novelists America has produced.[6]

Malcolm Cowley, a poet himself, supplies an authentic impression of these lost-generation novelists when he investigates the various phases of literary response to the war. American apprentice writers, he argues, tested their creative mettle in France, experienced the flavour of war and, as far as possible, minimised its dangers. Death in war had inevitably become, in the immediate war years, a common literary theme. (John Dos Passos encapsulated its glamour in the title of his early novel *One Man's Initiation: 1917*) Cowley noted, 'You went to the war, and it was like going to the theatre that advertised the greatest spectacle in history.'[7] Both Cowley and a fellow critic, Charles A Fenton, in the latter's conspectus of the American Ambulance Field Service,[8] confirm the humanitarianism that motivated First World War volunteers. Only when these American observers grew more involved in the conflict and became more than spiritual participants did they become soured by what they saw of latent mutiny, pointless mass butchery, false arrests and revolutionary discontent; these writers then began to capitalise upon their self-image of separateness, of being initiated, an élite different in their values from their elders, a process that culminated, as Cowley

theorises, after the war had ended in the mask of 'disillusionment'; Cowley's gloss on 'disillusioned', when used in relation
to American writers, introduces a salutary note of caution.[9]
Interestingly enough some of the older novelists, particularly
such women writers as Edith Wharton, Willa Cather and
Dorothy Canfield Fisher, often commented in their fiction
upon the conduct of their younger contemporaries in similar
ironic fashion. A side-glance at the novels of these women
writers is productive in order to challenge the self-evaluation
of the lost generation.

Troy Belknap in *The Marne* wishes to become an ambulance
driver because he believes that the volunteer is entitled to be
'ranked as a soldier of the great untried army of his country',
but in *A Son at the Front* Mrs Wharton has shifted her position;
like Mrs Belknap she 'began to take a calmer and more distant
view of the war'. With glacial disdain, and perhaps sensing the
way future literary historians would report the war, she
dismisses by implication the aura of the lost generation, as this
extract, which is spoken on behalf of the artist, Campton,
suggests: 'for whom was the country being saved? Was it for
the wasp-waisted youths in sham uniforms who haunted the
reawakening hotels and restaurants, in the frequent intervals
between their ambulance trips to safe distances from the
front?'[10] Dos Passos acknowledged the glamour and relative
comfort of driving an ambulance in *The Best Times*, as does
E. E. Cummings in letters home to his parents, and a similar
apologetic tone surfaces when Adrian Fort in Dorothy
Canfield Fisher's *The Deepening Stream* outlines the life-style of
the ambulance volunteer: 'You must not think I'm suffering
or a hero. The danger doesn't amount to much, and as for
hardship we live like princes compared to the infantry.'[11] (In
fact, one in seventeen American ambulance volunteers died in
action and many more were wounded.)

Through the conduit of the mass media the technology and
terrain of the First World War have become so familiar that
mortars, trench landscapes and field ambulances have acquired a popular mythic value wherein civilian readers of
literature feel themselves to be fully conversant with First
World War battlefields. The other side of war, that waged in
cities behind the lines, the relief work and the suffering of
bereft families, is not so readily taken account of by the lost

generation myth; what is omitted is the often inaccessible
perspective of the estranged and bereaved parents, who, no
less than their children, were disorientated by what was
happening in the front lines. John Campton of *A Son at the
Front* is a fictional creation who communicates this sense of
psychological and cultural confusion in the way his evasions
and machinations to keep his son out of the army give way to a
dawning realisation that the war means something. Edith
Wharton, with a sociological energy missing from her earlier
works, *Fighting France* (1915) and *The Marne* (1918), particularises in *A Son at the Front* the paradoxical conduct of
Allied civilians in Paris, the devotion of many expressed in
philanthropic work and the contradictory pull towards
hedonism and black-marketeering shown in 'this hideous
world that was dancing and flirting and money-making on the
great red mounds of dead'. *A Son at the Front* rarely trivialises
the ideological issues underlying the war, and offers some
thoughtful insights into its socially catalytic effects; an example is Mrs Wharton's analysis of the linguistic obsolescence
accelerated by war when a character, Paul Dastrey, speculates,
'I was considering how meaning had evaporated out of lots of
our old words, as if the general smash-up had broken their
stoppers. So many of them ... we'd taken good care not to
uncork for centuries. Since I've been on the edge of what's
going on fifty miles from here a good many of my own words
have lost their meaning....'[12] The strain of liberal idealism
concretised in such works as *A Son at the Front* reflects the
earlier stance taken by the American literary intelligentsia. In
a gesture of recognition Henry James had become a British
citizen in 1915, and in the same year contributed, together
with fellow Americans, W. D. Howells, George Santayana and
Paul Elmer More, to Edith Wharton's artistic symposium *The
Book of the Homeless* which raised funds for Franco–Belgian
relief. *A Son at the Front*, a later artistic product of this spirit, is
an interesting novel to set beside such accepted war classics of
its time as *A Farewell to Arms* and provides an illuminating
ideological source of comparison, as Peter Buitenhuis has
noted:

The botched civilisation to use Ezra Pound's words, that
France and her allies represented, was for many who fought

infinitely preferable to that model of efficiency and inhumanity that Kaiser Wilhelm and his Junkers apparently had in mind for the new German empire that was to be built on the ruins of a conquered Europe. Are we to say that the conviction of value and purpose in the Allied cause that Mrs Wharton represents in *A Son at the Front* was less valid than what, in art at least, had so far passed as *the* truth about the First World War.[13]

There is clear evidence in the work of Edith Wharton, Willa Cather and Dorothy Canfield Fisher that any vestiges of romantic egotism accruing from the self-dramatisation of a lost generation were critically placed. In Willa Cather's *One of Ours*, for example, Claude Wheeler, the inexperienced Nebraska farm boy, aspires to be a war hero, and the poised narrative tone evaluates satirically the implicit narcissism stemming from such a self-projection: 'This was one of the things about this war; it took a little fellow from a little town, gave him an air and a swagger, a life like a movie-film, and then a death like the rebel angel's.'[14] The category of novels, including *A Son at the Front* and *The Deepening Stream*, which treated the refugee problem, legitimately enlarged the vortex of the war to beyond the context of youth, and incorporated the civilian traumas of its hinterland. Dorothy Canfield Fisher's *The Deepening Stream*, published in 1930, with the benefit of hindsight recalls the exhaustion of the older people who attempted to order life behind the lines: 'The war had grimly hastened the process of ageing. People went into it middle-aged and came out of it decrepit' (beginning of part IV). Matey, the heroine of *The Deepening Stream*, has her experience broadened in France where she undertakes charity and relief work; she observes war profiteering and notes also profound intergenerational changes in sexual morality, an awareness confirmed by other characters, as when Mr Fort discloses to Adrian his reservations about the cult of war bravado and its attendant permissiveness: 'It's the fashion nowadays to maintain that a man can't be sure whether he's alive unless there are guns going off around him, and some weaker person to knock down once in a while, and a new woman every week or so' (p. 69). The novel ends, like Laurence Stallings's *Plumes*, commenting upon the defeat of

Wilsonism, and deploring 'the future [which] brought no spiritual rewards for the ignominy of the war'. Bereaved women are pictured 'guarding their dead from desecration', and the men round Wilson, who 'destroyed the future' and brought about the shameful peace settlement, are castigated. There is also, towards the end of *The Deepening Stream*, more than a hint of the recriminatory attitude of later war novels (such as *Slaughterhouse-Five*) when unambiguous reference is made to the Allies as 'butchers' and 'murderers', our 'gallant airmen' in reality being guilty of 'dropping tons of bombs on Cologne' (p. 359).

Claude Wheeler, the Prairie states hero of Willa Cather's *One of Ours*, dies before he has time to grow disaffected with the war. Magnetised by the connotations of the word 'Marne', he abandons the restrictions of the mid-West to leave behind for ever the provincialism of his background. Claude is 'predestined' to 'get over', and to implement his idealism (p. 229). Previously he 'used enviously to read about Alan Seeger and those fortunate American boys who had a right to fight for a civilisation they knew'. Claude dies heroically but unaware, 'believing his own country better than it is, and France better than any country can ever be'.[15] Few notable American writers, save for Alan Seeger and Joyce Kilmer, died in the First World War; many, after military training, were denied by the Armistice the opportunity for heroism accorded to the fictional Claude Wheeler. The ambience of war, though, continued to haunt several major lost-generation novelists who drew upon its aura in their fiction without having themselves experienced war directly. Two such novelists, Scott Fitzgerald and William Faulkner, will be considered in the remainder of this chapter.

Scott Fitzgerald's fiction interprets the First World War as a prelude to the Jazz Age, a far-off event whose repercussions mysteriously alter behaviour and invest young men and women with a meretricious beauty and *élan*. In *This Side of Paradise* (1920) 'one of the effects of the war' emerges through Rosalind's emancipated conduct; she is caricatured as 'average – smokes sometimes, drinks punch, frequently kissed'.[16] The novel apportions political blame for the war, which produced these social mores, to the greedy ancestors of Rosalind's generation, 'all the people who cheered for

Germany in 1870, all the materialists rampant'. *This Side of Paradise* articulated the protest of early 1920s youth, its feeling of betrayal and sense of unity when confronted by an older generation manifestly discredited by the war. Amory Blaine voices this feeling of collective identity:

> As an endless dream it went on; the spirit of the past brooding over a new generation, the chosen youth from the muddled unchastened world, still fed romantically on the mistakes and half-forgotten dreams of dead statesmen and poets. Here was a new generation, shouting the old cries, learning the old creeds, through a reverie of long days and nights; destined finally to go out into that dirty grey turmoil to follow love and pride; a new generation dedicated more than the last to the fear of poverty and the worship of success; grown up to find all Gods dead, all wars fought, all faiths in man shaken.   (p. 270)

The romantic tone of this meditation is followed in Fitzgerald's work whenever mention is made of the generation that his heroes represent. Again, in *This Side of Paradise*, the young Tom D'Invilliers, whose prototype is thought to be John Peale Bishop, reflects upon leaving college, 'we're breaking all the links that seemed to bind us here to top-booted and high-stocked generations.... "The torches are out", whispered Tom. "Ah, Messalina, the long shadows are building minarets on the stadium" ' (pp. 155–6).

Like Joseph in Saul Bellow's *Dangling Man*, Scott Fitzgerald was personally opposed to war and yet cognisant of its aesthetic value, conscious of war's potentiality to extend the range of his artistic vision. Such an ambiguity characterises the way war is treated in his fiction as a powerful but veiled force, motivating human behaviour, although seemingly of marginal importance only. Formally this is epitomised in the novels by the way war is explored, always as a subsidiary motif, a concealed social factor obliquely moulding action. Nick Carraway in *The Great Gatsby*, for example, suffers one of the most far-reaching effects of the 'delayed Teutonic migration known as the Great war'; this is a sense of 'restless disorientation', like Faulkner's young men in *Soldier's Pay*, a feeling of malaise and rootlessness, stemming from a conviction that things are mysteriously different, one's hopes are less certain to be fulfilled, and one's home is less central. Nick is driven by the war to travel, feeling that, 'Instead of being the warm centre of the world, the Middle West now seemed like the ragged edges of the universe.' Jay Gatsby lost money in the 'big panic' of the war, but gained in status as a distinguished soldier who was highly decorated for holding off three enemy divisions with the depleted troops under his command.

Fitzgerald's novels and stories embody an increasingly complicated response to the war, the fairly unsophisticated dislike of military training evidenced in *Beautiful and Damned* becoming subsumed in the more complex and ambivalent military references in *Tender is the Night*. The narrative seems to approve in this later work the Hemingway-like Tommy Barban, the ostentatious man of action who had 'worn the uniforms of eight nations' and needs constant war to stimulate him. Barban is the antithesis of Dick Diver who displays interest in the war, but did not fight, like Fitzgerald himself, and had only been 'around the edges of the war'.[17] His colleague the psychiatrist Franz Gregovorius, observing that shell-shock can be caused from a distance or merely through reading a newspaper, inquires if Dick had been 'changed . . . like all the rest' by the war. The question implies the existence of a disaffiliated younger generation. Dick has an interest in military matters: he visits the battlefield of Beaumont-Hamel and the 'tragic hill' of Thiepval, where land cost twenty lives a foot. Fitzgerald, later reviewing the Swiss setting of the novel, refers ironically to the 'contagious glory' of the war years, and his description of the Thiepval battlefield, probably the most exact passage that he wrote about war, and, according to Andrew Turnbull, based on Ludendorf's memoirs, implies a dualism of attitude (p. 129).[18] The war infers a line of historical and socio-cultural demarcation, and also confers upon its participants a mystique. Fitzgerald's narrator caustically closes the battlefield scene by observing that Dick 'had made a quick study of the whole affair, simplifying it always until it bore a faint resemblance to one of his own parties' (p. 132). This may not be far from Fitzgerald's own position, as he himself read cursorily in military science, and had a diffuse knowledge of war literature.

Retrospective interest in the psychological ramifications of army life shaped Fitzgerald's story 'I Didn't Get Over' (1936), which utilised the novelist's own involvement in a training accident when a raft overturned and some soldiers were drowned on the Tallapoosa River. This short story elaborates a conflict of will between two men, one a Captain Hibbing, the other the war veteran, Lieutenant Abe Danzer. Because of Danzer's superior combat experience and his consequent arrogance Hibbing is driven to act impetuously and make a wrong decision. He orders Danzer's men to cross the river on an insecure raft, which sinks resulting in the deaths of twenty-two men. This compact story is commented on by Arthur Mizener, in relation to Fitzgerald's own life:

> Fitzgerald could see that Hibbing's . . . feeling of inferiority at having missed something mysterious and important in 'not getting over' was absurd. But it was a feeling Fitzgerald had all his life; he kept a German helmet in his bedroom at Ellerslie and spent a good deal of time trying to learn from books what he believed he would have learned from experience had he got over.[19]

It is interesting to compare Fitzgerald's lack of direct war writing with the treatment of war in William Faulkner's early work. Faulkner projected himself into combat situations, which Fitzgerald never attempted in his fiction. Andrew Turnbull is probably correct in assuming that 'the sort of violence that concerned Fitzgerald required a social rather than a martial setting', and Fitzgerald's artistic discrimination probably censored any attempts at this kind of direct war writing.[20] Fitzgerald's intuition of the significance of the war and his treatment of it as a secondary theme in his fiction attests to his lost generation sensibility, for to write in post-war America as a younger novelist demanded an obligatory recognition of the war as a spiritual catalyst.

William Faulkner's treatment of war displays an aesthetic instinct towards the mythopoetic; the First World War is formalised as belonging to a flow of historical energies extending back to the American Civil War and earlier wars. (Faulkner's own family possessed a military tradition, the novelist's great-grandfather having fought the British at Cowpens Mountain.) In *Sartoris* this foredoom is suggested by the death of a generation symbolism surrounding John Sartoris, which reverses the realist impulse and implies the problematic relationship between history and folk memory. "All the Dead Pilots', a short story, explores this interaction through a process of enlargement whereby John Sartoris is amplified, his actual fate accorded a mythic charge. In this legendary apprehension of war, real events are less important than their 'grid' effect upon survivors; war is mediated by the poetic imagination, its heroes haloed through time. Faulkner seeks the unattainable recapitulation, the semiology of heroism. Significantly his principal archetype is the airman, flying to his doom, or, like Gray in 'Victory', a fallen angel. War is conceived of in grandly tragic terms, renown or rejection depending on the turn of a wheel.

Soldier's Pay (1926) lacks the esoteric awareness of military life found in First World War novels such as *Three Soldiers* or Barbusse's *Le Feu*. H. H. Waggoner has noted how its opening chapter seems to be an academic exercise, in contrast to the unliterary and more authentic fiction of Hemingway: 'The opening chapter of *Soldier's Pay* makes us think of Hemingway, to Faulkner's disadvantage. The disillusioned returning soldiers, drinking to deaden their awareness of the great nothingness behind and before them, are like classroom examples of lost generation attitudes.'[21] *Soldier's Pay* infers an element of vicariousness in its narrative development, American society being indicted for first cultivating a taste for war and later rejecting the outcome of its action. The rather maladroit structural irony of the novel is hinted at by its title, since the doomed aviator Mahon receives only a gratuitous interest in his illness. The axis of *Soldier's Pay* is formed by the reactions of the citizens of Charlestown, Georgia, to Donald Mahon's impending death:

> Curious, kindly neighbours came in – men who stood or sat jovially respectable, cheerful: solid business-men interested in the war only as a by-product of the rise and fall of Mr. Wilson and interested in that only as a matter of dollars and cents, while their wives chatted about clothes to each other across Mahon's scarred, oblivious brow . . . girls that he had known, had danced with or courted of summer nights, come now to look once upon his face and then quickly aside

in hushed nausea, not coming any more unless his face happened to be hidden on the first visit . . . .[22]

The explicit nature of this passage ('Mahon's scarred, oblivious brow', for instance) or its querulous antitheses ('dollars and cents' opposed to 'respectable') illustrates the tendentious tone of *Soldier's Pay*. Marred by such polemical formulations, the novel's satiric animus is directed principally at women who are portrayed as being totally unaware of how soldiers have been re-created spiritually by the war and how they are consequently marked off from society's materialist concerns. An interesting subsidiary theme in *Soldier's Pay* is Faulkner's fictional study of the young men, abandoned by former women friends, who have become outsiders. This destructive consequence of the war generates a change in manners, which alienates the 'poor kind dull boys', who have never known war or heroism. The young men have been nurtured in a war-oriented society like Claude Wheeler in *One of Ours*; now, when society changes from fashionable patriotism to flippancy, they feel stranded, without a clearly-defined social role, 'eternal country boys of one national mental state lost in the comparative metropolitan atmosphere of one diametrically opposed to it'. Society, which had once put a premium on heroism, now behaves in a latently hostile way towards these boys, who were too young to fight; they now seem obsolete, the detritus of war, lacking either the blunted heroism of veterans like Gilligan or Mahon or the necessary poise to adjust to new social conventions. Once used by girls in a 'detached, impersonal manner', now they seem 'the hang-over of warfare in a society tired of warfare. Puzzled and lost poor devils. Once Society drank war, brought them into manhood with a cultivated taste for war; but now Society seemed to have found something else for a beverage . . .' (p. 198). A. C. Bross has argued that the *fin-de-siècle* shimmer of *Soldier's Pay* owes something to the influence of Aubrey Beardsley and the English Decadents of the 1890s.[23] Faulkner's ornamentation, notably visible in the language patterns presenting the satyr-like Januarius Jones, does seem to express the flexing of a literary style. The motif of the returned soldier appears to be almost incidental and less important than a quasi-symbolic exploitation of pictorial language by an apprentice author.

The male Sartorises in *Sartoris*, like the Plumes in Laurence
Stallings's novel, are obsessed by war almost to the point of
masochism: the family's chronicles, adorned with heroism,
are symbiotically blighted by misplaced war bravado. The
family inhabit a fictional world where the Civil War frequently
exists in conversation, still spoken of as a warning that war
remains a cyclic pestilence. The women in *Sartoris* live with the
contingent reality that male Sartorises are prone to run
recklessly into battle: Miss Jenny's characterisation of the Civil
War as a 'gentleman's war' when a horse conducted itself in a
more dignified way than a flying machine, while implying
historical discrimination, leaves the history of war unaffected.[24] The novel concentrates more fully upon the martial
proclivities of obstinate male Sartorises and draws upon the
resonances of past wars. Faulkner characteristically
fictionalises war within the evolving relationships of a family.

The tragic potentiality of *Sartoris* should grow from
Bayard's retrospective visions which motivate his suicide.
Bayard, hardly more articulate than the mute Donald Mahon
of *Soldier's Pay*, feels impelled by his brother's death in combat
to seek escape routes from the past. He shares responsibility
for his brother's pointless death, and its ironic circumstance
intensifies Bayard's suffering. John's death prescriptively
seems intended to take on the significance of the death of a
generation implied by Bayard's emblematic vision of young
men 'like fallen angels, and of a meteoric violence like that of
fallen angels beyond heaven and hell and partaking of both:
doomed immortality and immortal doom'. Such an attempted
epiphany fails because the inoperative elevated language
observed here is imprecise, over-rhetorical and too explicit:
this makes it difficult for the reader to accept that John's death
acts as a symbolic index of wider loss. (H. H. Waggoner has
drawn attention to Bayard's sickness, in suggesting that war
nerves are no substitute for the interplay of tragic feeling.)[25]
The emphasis upon Bayard's pain centralises the social
violence incipient in war, and yet the reader cannot detect
spiritual development in Faulkner's hero.

A comparison between *Soldier's Pay* and Faulkner's later war
writing in *The Unvanquished* (1938) and the nucleus of his
study of war, 'Victory', 'Crevasse', 'Turnabout', 'All the Dead
Pilots' and 'Ad Astra', suggests how fiction may exploit a

dichotomy between fact and legend. Faulkner displays interest in the epic qualities of war, its mythic grandeur. Consequently, in his fiction legends are created, numinous figures such as Colonel Sartoris, Cousin Drusilla, and John Sartoris in 'All the Dead Pilots'. Olga W. Vickery has suggested an aesthetic logic informing this cyclic creation of folklore: the experience of war must be manipulated because

> the passing of time not only removes the confusion which accompanied the experience but permits and even encourages poetic licence until, at last, the experience is formalized and expressed by a series of significant gestures or words. The 'truth' of these legends is not in question since cold, unadorned facts, measurements, and statistics are no substitute for the vision of the enthralled imagination and the passionate heart making out of the brutality and confusion an enduring spectacle of human courage and faith and self-sacrifice. Each post-war generation must discover disillusionment which must, in turn, be replaced by a renewed faith in the legend. In other words, the legend which has its source in history finally replaces history . . . .[26]

The core of Faulkner's war writing resides in *These Thirteen* (1931), together with 'Turnabout' from *Dr Martino* (1934): these stories appear in his *Collected Stories* (1951) under the heading 'In the Wasteland'. They reflect Faulkner's interest in war as a proving ground for morality, testing human capacity for endurance and bestiality. 'Crevasse' takes a detached look at soldiers lost in a trench landscape of terrible portent, a wasteland recalling Melville's Encantadas. The terrain, conveyed poetically through impersonal symbolism, focuses the lack of individuality of the men. Animal imagery reinforces their degradation, as they fearfully carry out their patrol. Their names and their feelings are kept from the reader as 'they burrow furiously, with whimpering cries like dogs' in their Golgotha.[27] 'Crevasse' employs an imagistic method whereby men are anthropomorphised to communicate the dehumanisation of men in battle.

'Victory', 'All the Dead Pilots' and 'Turnabout' narrate contradictory aspects of heroism. 'Victory' reworks earlier themes; how war brutalises the individual, the lack of com-

munication between soldiers and civilians, and the exile
forced on the veteran after the war. Gray, its hero, revisits the
scenes of war, a France devastated like the wasteland in
'Crevasse'. The people he encounters, like the Chorus in a
Greek play, comment on the ravages of war, ironically turning
their anger against Gray, oblivious of their ingratitude.
Faulkner now switches the time-sequence to when Gray, a
young recruit, is corrupted until, in a scene of appalling
horror, he kills the sergeant who has victimised him, in a most
brutal way. Paradoxically, like other 'assailant–victim' heroes
in American literature, he shortly afterwards becomes a hero.
The story treats fictively a different and unmerited kind of
heroism from the legitimate kind in 'Turnabout' or the
legendary in 'All the Dead Pilots'. Alec Gray 'had long since
found out that no man has courage but that any man may
blunder into valour as one stumbles into an open manhole in
the street'. Like Krebs in Hemingway's 'Soldier's Home' or
Bayard in *Sartoris*, Gray has been nullified by war and
estranged from his family until all that is left is the cultivation
of a protective stoicism. He maintains a facade of elegance in
the way he replenishes his cards and waxes his moustaches
when reduced finally to street-hawking (one recalls the
stereotyped street-hawker ex-soldier in *Plumes* and in Paul
Green's play *Johnny Johnson*). Finally Gray, lost in despair, lives
with abandoned soldiers who huddle together for comfort,
and he scratches a living by begging: 'In his eyes now is not
that hopeful resignation of a beggar, but rather that bitterness, that echo as of bitter and unheard laughter of a
hunchback' (pp. 454–9).

Whereas 'Victory' addresses itself to the social implications
of war and is modelled upon the tragic laws of nemesis and
reversal, 'All the Dead Pilots' aspires to a metaphysical
dimension. It specifies the valour of John Sartoris, one of the
legendary fliers, mythical beings 'like that of some dim and
threatful apotheosis of the race seen for an instant in the glare
of a thunderclap and then forever gone'. The narrator, who
tries to focus the fortitude of such prophetic figures, can
record only aesthetic inadequacy; they appear only in 'a series
of brief glares in which, instantaneous and without depth or
perspective, there stood into sight the portent and the threat
of what the race could bear and become, in an instant between

dark and dark' (p. 512). The narrative action of 'All the Dead Pilots', based upon a comic vendetta, is less significant in itself than for the opportunity it provides for the narrator to elegise all the dead pilots memorialised in the title. The voice eulogises in awed tones as if the transitory lives of these past heroes offers a benediction for the living:

> And that's all. That's it. The courage, the recklessness, call it what you will, is the flash, the instant of sublimation; then flick! the old darkness again. That's why. It's too strong for steady diet. And if it were a steady diet, it would not be a flash, a glare. And so, being momentary, it can be preserved and prolonged only on paper: a picture, a few written words that any child can engender, can obliterate in an instant. A one-inch sliver of sulphur-tipped wood is longer than memory or grief; a flame no larger than a sixpence is fiercer than courage or despair. (p. 531)

Faulkner's treatment of war demonstrates copious formal variation. The novelist's range extends from the narrative derring-do of 'Turnabout' to more static and reflective modes of war writing. The pacifist debate in 'Ad Astra' instances this more theoretical assessment of war and links dialectically with other Faulknerian analyses – as when Gavin Stevens in 'Knight's Gambit' philosophises about the soldier's adjustment to society or when, in the opening of 'The Unvanquished', the two schoolboys play at fighting the battle of Vicksburg. It has been suggested that 'Ad Astra' may have been influenced by the last pages of Chapters 25 and 26 of *A Farewell to Arms* when Rinaldi, Henry and the priest discuss the spiritual benefits of defeat and the insubstantiality of human attainment in war.[28] The Indian Subadar in 'Ad Astra', similarly envisions the psychic death of a generation with as great sensitivity: 'Out of nothing we howled, unwitting the storm which we had escaped and the foreign strand which we could not escape; that in the interval between two surges of the swell we died who had been too young to have ever lived' (p. 408). The Subadar in 'Ad Astra', together with a defeated German POW, talks on Armistice night about 'the pitiableness of man'; through his belief in brotherhood he excuses the drunkenness, the wild laughter and the continual arguments of the war-weary soldiers. The German POW, another articulate spokesman, channels the 'accrued despair' of all soldiers into an apocalyptic vision of war as a calamity which transforms frontiers and breaks up continents. After the war the German has learned to reject the term 'fatherland', believing it to be 'the symbol of the hierarchy which has stained the history of man with injustice of arbitrary instead of moral; force instead of love'. The Subadar and the captured German have faith in humanity to transcend war which indicates a strain of affirmative didacticism found elsewhere in Faulkner, for example in his essay 'To the Youth of Japan', in his Nobel Prize speech, and as an ideological substructure in *A Fable* (1954). Such an impulse towards affirmation and renewal is wholly typical of the writing of lost-generation novelists.

6 Hemingway and Bessie: Education in Spain

Robert Jordan takes a practical view of progressive politics towards the beginning of *For Whom the Bell Tolls* (1940); he believes that he can be an instrument, and, through doing his duty, the bridge 'can be the point on which the future of the human race can turn'.[1] The bridge, therefore, attains schematic importance as a significant event in the history of the evolving Spanish Republic. When Pilar later teases Jordan about the religious seriousness of his politics, he expands upon his political convictions and disclaims Communist affiliations while asserting his credentials as an anti-fascist of ten years' standing (p. 71). In addition to this rejection of fascism, Jordan infers that he has inherited a Republican consciousness from both his father and grandfather, which transfers easily to the Spanish situation and allows him commensurate 'faith' (p. 95). Informed by an identical viewpoint to that found in the commentary to 'The Spanish Earth' and in Hemingway's anti-fascist speech to the American Writers' Congress, Jordan's political reflections are essentially anti-fascist and Republican rather than Communist. This discrimination is articulated frequently in the context of the prosecution of the war when discipline and military astuteness are associated with Communist strategy:

> He was under Communist discipline for the duration of the war. Here in Spain the Communists offered the best discipline and the soundest and sanest for the prosecution of the war. He accepted their discipline for the duration of the war because, in the conduct of the war, they were the only party whose programme and whose discipline he could respect.   (p. 167)

After having rationalised his acceptance of Communist discipline, Jordan acknowledges that he is basically apolitical: 'What were his politics then? He had none, he told himself' (p. 167). Jordan's apolitical stance offers a way of understanding his presentation as a character. Hemingway locates in his hero the central ideological valuation of the narrative, and Jordan's political scepticism acts as an essential counterforce to the excesses dramatised in the novel. Language provides Robert Jordan with a case in point when, on one occasion, he scrupulously analyses revolutionary and patriotic clichés and caustically satirises his own hardened political attitudes as 'hide-bound' (p. 167). In such thought-soliloquies Hemingway deploys a vital formal method, the inward meditation where moral judgements may be activated and communicated truly and privately. The omniscient narrator supplies the complementary enabling device of authorial commentary, as here when the pristine joyfulness of Jordan's revolutionary feelings are distilled: 'He was very happy with that sudden rare happiness that can come to anyone with a command in a revolutionary army' (p. 202). Another mechanism for the working through of political doctrine inheres in the debates, when frequently the American social and economic experience is utilised for the purpose of historical analogy. Such an occasion occurs when Augustin, Andrés and Primitivo discuss with Jordan American agricultural organisation. Homesteading, in this exchange, is interpreted by the Spaniards as agrarian reform, and Jordan's explanation of land taxes and inheritance duties recalls the genre of socialism whereby reform occurs in an evolutionary rather revolutionary manner (pp. 208–9). Jordan's crucial ideological significance in this exchange with the Spanish peasants is, though, his revelation of latent American fascism, which, he argues, must inevitably be confronted.

The presentation of dialectical politics is enacted principally in *For Whom the Bell Tolls* through the dialogues of the guerrilla band, but the chapters centred upon Gaylords supply an alternative source of debate. In conversation with Karkov, the Russian general who more than anyone else informs him of the political realities of command, Jordan discovers the darker side of the war, the shooting of spies and the internecine quarrels. His chief discovery at Gaylords is his recognition of the historical necessity of Russian intervention when he accepts that such peasant leaders as El Campesino, Enrique Lister and Juan Modesto have necessarily to be Russian-trained in the Lenin Institute by the Comintern. Jordan experiences rather confused feelings about Gaylords; initially deploring the luxury of life-style revealed there, he comes to condone it as a countervailing force acceptable in the conditions of wartime (pp. 278–47). He enjoys the esoteric excitement of military command and its attendant theoretical discourse, while accepting 'the necessity for all the deception'. Even when Karkov refers to the practice of political assassination as distinct from acts of 'individual terrorism', Jordan refrains from a moral critique. He does not himself 'like' the killings, although he does not 'mind' them and seems to prefer the corrupt pragmatism of Gaylords to the 'puritanical religious communism' of Velasquez 63, the HQ of the International Brigades.

As a contrast to the spy-disease and conspiracies that flourish in Gaylords, Jordan recalls the early days of the Civil War, which, to participants, felt like the feeling expected but not achieved at one's first communion. This feeling, articulated in conjunction with the highpoints of Spanish culture and art, stemmed from a conception of the Republican cause as a 'crusade', and involvement in it attained the feeling of 'consecration' (p. 234). Jordan, in this interior monologue, does not recoil from using the kind of abstract words that Frederick Henry, so fond of understatement, deplores in *A Farewell to Arms*. It is important to consider this passage, where Jordan reflects upon initial entry into the Republican cause, as one which communicates through hindsight; it represents a definition of past experience and should be read in context as such. Jordan has placed this pure revolutionary feeling which cannot survive in war against a more programmatic later one in which he endorses Karkov's doctrine of political development. The Spanish people must be instructed into an awareness of the movement in order to understand the need for discipline and to distinguish between the sound policies of the Popular Front and the undisciplined ones of the POUM and Anarchists, 'the crackpots and the romantic revolutionists'

(p. 246). Peasants such as Augustin, Pilar and Anselmo embody an unharnessed revolutionary impetus which needs shaping and the consolidation of discipline.

War has taken on for Hemingway an ideological dimension since the publication of *A Farewell to Arms* in 1929, and it demands of the soldier hero a concomitant political education so that he may fairly evaluate revolutionary creeds; the outcome of such an education in Robert Jordan's case is that he perceives, with a measure of inner objectivity, that the Spanish War cannot be subsumed within a single revelatory truth. Some hint of the perplexity found within Jordan's psyche may be implied from Hemingway's earlier play, *The Fifth Column* (1938), where esoteric doctrine is likewise bandied about, Philip initially regarding Dorothy Bridges as 'uneducated' and himself, the IB soldiers and Max as 'educated';[2] such an ambiguous juggling with various concepts of education also characterises *For Whom the Bell Tolls*.

Robert Jordan's instruction begins with his insights into Spanish national identity; he learns that loyalists behave with a barbarity equal to that of their fascist counterparts, although, when Pilar recounts the thrashing of the fascists, Jordan is clearly hurt by the knowledge (p. 139). Frequently Jordan corrects his tendency to formulate half-truths about Spanish culture, which eventually contributes to a more profound understanding. Such an intuition of genuine worth stems from his realisation of the territorial imperative underlying Spanish conduct, the manner in which Spaniards, in the last resort, demonstrate loyalty only to their own localised unit (the village, the band). This insight is dramatically verified at the end of the novel when Pablo kills Spaniards from another band in order to steal their horses. Jordan, as well as growing acquainted with peasant life, forms an opinion of the Republican hierarchy, noting that they have gained influence through behaving like a bunch of unprincipled 'horse thieves' (p. 167). Gaylords, the hub of the military establishment, offers lessons too; by radiating outwards from its corruption, Jordan, by contrast, appreciates the decency of such men as Anselmo or El Sordo, which authenticates his own maxim, 'the closer to the front, the better the people' (p. 247). Through being interested in the development of his own education, Jordan possesses a readily available education metaphor to apply to the Spanish situation. His political apprenticeship produces in him an assimilation of ideological awareness, which enables him to consider fascism in morally-structured terms as a system of social organisation. Fascist atrocities, such as Maria's rape, are judged as the product of a refined political code: 'I know that we did dreadful things to them too. But it was because we were uneducated . . . . But they did that on purpose and deliberately. Those who did that are the last flowering of what their education has produced' (p. 349). To balance this judgement, elsewhere in the novel Jordan acknowledges that few of the enemy are 'real fascists . . . very few'.

Besides the process of education connected with the development of Robert Jordan as an individual, one notes a wider process of collective education plotted in *For Whom the Bell Tolls*, perhaps most explicitly seen in the agency of the Russians as tutors of the Spanish revolutions. Pilar acts as an exemplar to Jordan through her atrocity story of loyalist brutality: she also, in her account of the tubercular Finito's deprived upbringing, carries a socialist trajectory in castigating the pampered Spanish bourgeoisie. Pilar instructs Jordan and other members of the band about the smell of death; she also teaches Maria how to please a man and prepare herself to be a worthy wife for Jordan. Anselmo seeks to deprive the fascists of their planes and weapons and to teach them dignity instead. Jordan's daydreams of his grandfather possess pedagogical inferences; he wishes his grandfather could pass on the lessons learned in the Indian wars and the American Civil War. Gomez and Andres, duped by previous propaganda, learn of the duplicity of André Marty and of his treachery towards his own loyalist troops when they encounter him personally.

Perhaps the major educative force that Robert Jordan experiences in Spain is the transcendent force of love, given its articulation in both the hero's solidarity with the gipsy band and through his relationship with Maria. He loves her, he says, as he loves also 'liberty and dignity and the rights of all men to work and not be hungry' (p. 343). The apprehension here evidenced of the social power of love seems intended by Hemingway to dignify Robert Jordan's military engagement in Spain. When he says to Maria, as he confronts death, 'I go

with thee', his statement should equate personal and individual sexual love with political duty and commitment. Such a
resolution, as critics have noted, is not fully communicated
either textually or imaginatively, and therefore results in a
measure of 'ideological' collapse. Jordan's education does
have a positive side, though. A complicated instance resides in
his attitude to killing. Although he demonstrates an awareness
of the military necessity for carrying this out, he appears to
hold in check his 'tainted' pleasure; he does not, either, seem
as eager to kill as some early Hemingway heroes, and one may
legitimately speculate that Frederick Henry, under similar
provocation from the dangerous Pablo, would have dis-
patched him without much thought. Admittedly Jordan's
restraint in refraining from killing Pablo is initially tactical,
but he does demonstrate a reverence for human life when
examining the papers of the young fascist soldier; the dead
man, he reflects, would probably have been a drinking
companion in the festival of the bulls. Jordan's experiential
education causes him also to revalue the role of democratic
institutions; he deduces, for example, from events in Spain
that there should be an attempt made to educate American
proto-fascists out of their social perverseness. The frequently
contradictory nature of Jordan illustrates his complex assessment of events and his confused interpretation of them. For
instance, his attempt to understand Marxist dialectics while
accepting Communist organisation reflects a meritorious
intellectual enterprise for a non-Communist and one likely to
result initially in a measure of conceptual difficulty. Jordan
clearly perceives his own limitations in matters such as
theoretical awareness when he confesses, 'I have the very
smallest beginnings of an education' (p. 375). The irony
accruing from this intimation relates to Hemingway's narrative plotting, as the sensitised university instructor soon finds
himself deprived of the opportunity to hand on his insights.
Jordan wonders, when he faces his inevitable death, if there is
a potential reservoir of education within man and whether an
overflow level is ever reached. Such a metaphysical query will
remain unanswered in Jordan's case, curtailed by events.
Ironically, Robert Jordan's aptitude for self-instruction becomes heightened shortly before his premature death. He
experiences in action intense feelings of comradeship and a

selfless love for the old man Anselmo, truly confirming that he possesses the small 'beginnings' of an education.

The principal affirmation of Jordan's life, perhaps the major product of his 'integration', is one related to the cultural status of *For Whom the Bell Tolls* as a fictional transposition of American values to the Iberian Peninsula. Jordan is invested by his creator with an unsynthesised but powerful value system, revealed through his interior monologues. He never wavers from a commitment to free elections, from a belief that a people should be enfranchised and should, if necessary, be prepared to fight and die to uphold their civil rights. *For Whom the Bell Tolls* fictionalises in this manner American moral energy, a social dramatisation clearly demonstrated in the opening chapters when the skilled bridge-blower arrives to energise the tired band of Pablo. He comes not in the guise of coloniser but in the role of revolutionary. Such an interpretation of the narrative would suggest that Jordan epitomises America's capacity for democratic leadership and that the historical experience of the United States in making a fresh start away from the tradition and reactionary conservatism of Europe is imported ideologically into the structure and tone of the novel. Citizen Jordan has much to offer the Spanish cause through his talents as a man of action, and his politics should consequently be assessed as a soldier's politics. The reader's abiding memories of Jordan's family background are likely to be of his buckskin grandfather, of war bonnets and the native Smith and Wesson. From such a tradition it is inevitable that Jordan should be more Fortinbras than Hamlet.

Throughout *For Whom the Bell Tolls* Hemingway foregrounds in Robert Jordan the consciousness of a revolutionary soldier, one whose political development is genuine but foreshortened, largely undoctrinaire and only partially formulated. Jordan's main political contribution stems from his military prowess as, metaphorically speaking, he again grows familiar with the 'the wind that blows through battle' (p. 184). Jordan, one notes, is an amateur although fairly sophisticated military historian with considered opinions on other men's wars from Agincourt onwards. He is presented, too, as having the strategic insight to recognise the Russian presence for what it really is, a military necessity. Jordan's psychology is demonstrably that of the soldier; he derives, for example, an arcane joy from the negation of combat, being fully able to blot out extraneous matters (p. 387). Intellectually too, Jordan apprehends the seamless nature of wars, the historical pattern that links Spain in the 1930s with America in the nineteenth century. To Jordan the Spanish War, as envisioned in the strike to capture Segovia, recalls other wars; Berrendo's beheading of the guerrilla band, for example, parallels incidents of scalping in the Indian wars (p. 331). By encapsulating the Spanish War within the resonances of wider American war myths Hemingway engaged a complex aesthetic problem.

Lacking the long-term political consciousness of such as Malraux and Orwell, he was faced with the formal problematic of portraying a war of ideas, and he tackled the problem by fitting an old-fashioned kind of war, the events leading to the blowing of the bridge, within a political framework, the education of Jordan. The location in the opening chapters reminds one more of the American Civil War than the Civil War in Spain and the terrain is described in a way that recalls the United States (for example, the quiet retreat of Pablo, with its campfire and corral, suggests a frontier outpost). Certainly the preparations the novelist draws upon, the preliminaries to the attack on Segovia, do not immediately suggest a machine-dominated war, Pablo's horses seeming to be more real than the occasional references to aeroplanes, troop movements and armoured cars. Politics and guerrilla warfare are equated in *For Whom the Bell Tolls*: in both, as Jordan observes, the important thing is to 'continue to exist' (p. 282) while preserving as many right principles as possible. This interweaving of politics, guerrilla warfare, and the learning which Robert Jordan acquires, ensures that *For Whom the Bell Tolls* is more ambitious, cerebral and formally complex than Hemingway's previous war writing.

Hemingway's narrative reinforces a tension between the underlying socio-mythical pattern of the novel and its overt ideological superstructure. The social myth is clarified by reference to Marcus Cunliffe's study *Soldiers and Civilians* (1969), in the section devoted to 'The American Military Ethos'. Professor Cunliffe projects three models of this tradition in the period extending from the Revolution to the

American Civil War, which he categorises 'Rifleman,
Chevalier, and Quaker'. Robert Jordan, in his independence
and guerrilla mentality, typifies the rifleman figure as outlined in this scheme. The reader meets potential chevalier
types also in the novel, in the more aristocratic and professionally disciplined fascist cavalry. The military bearing of
these men, uniformed in flowing capes, wearing fascist
insignia, and equipped with sabres, contrasts socially with the
more individualistic and revolutionary band of the unorthodox Pablo. As earlier suggested, the terrain recalls the
frontier and the Fenimore Cooper image of the rifleman:

> Ahead of them a horse whinnied in the timber and then,
> through the brown trunks of the pine trees, only a little
> sunlight coming down through their thick, almost-touching
> tops, he saw the corral made by roping around tree trunks.
> The horses had their heads pointed toward the men as they
> approached, and at the foot of a tree, outside the corral, the
> saddles were piled together and covered with a tar-
> paulin.   (p. 20)

Other events in *For Whom the Bell Tolls* which echo the Western
myth are the 'threshing' of the fascists (which parallels the
lynch-mob scene); the bridge-blowing incident preceded by
the attack on the outpost; El Sordo's fight on the hilltop, which
recalls Custer, and Jordan's final lone stand against the
oncoming troops (which is invested with ideological significance). These incidents are rescued from being clichés by
Hemingway's artistic tact. He selects details, for example, with
inventive aesthetic precision: this is evident throughout the
book and examples are numerous: Jordan, the leather-
stocking and freedom-loving man of action, for example,
taking care of his dynamite, 'each little cylinder wrapped
round and round with its two wires (the lot of them packed as
carefully as he had packed his collection of wild bird eggs
when he was a boy)' (p. 54); or the fascist Mayor, Don Benito,
plausibly attacked first by a man with whom he had been
engaged in a feud over the ownership of a piece of land –
these intuitions create rapport between writer and reader
and intensify imaginatively the political tensions at work in the
novel as a whole. Many of Hemingway's characters, too, are in

social terms remarkably acutely drawn. Anselmo, the loyal 'educated' Republican who hates fighting but overcomes his fear, represents one of these minor triumphs; Pablo is another. He is a psychologically interesting creation, a casualty of war who has been over-exposed to violence, which explains his inconsistent behaviour and psychopathic tendencies. One often admires the economy of the novelist's technique in presenting his characters – Lieutenant Berrendo, for instance, crosses himself after ordering El Sordo's men to be beheaded, a religious reflex that underscores his human credibility. In this he is similar to Ignacio of El Sordo's band, who, facing death, moves from quoting La Pasionaria to invoking the Virgin Mary. In both cases ideological gesture dramatises human response.

As has been suggested above, the problematic of fictionalising history, of giving fictive plausibility to historical events and people, is managed in an interesting way in *For Whom the Bell Tolls*. The epic sweep of the war in Spain is connoted by the wide range of characterisation, from peasants to brigade commanders, and by the use of set pieces such as El Sordo's fight on the hilltop, or the situation at Gaylords. Hemingway thus enables his reader to infer the ramifications of the war with geographical and sociological precision. The different theatres of war, ranging from the military HQ in fortified Madrid to the primitive locale of the guerrilla band, imply a war of movement and variety. The symbiotic nature of the Spanish conflict is also formally enacted by Hemingway in the construction of his narrative. An elementary example of this is the 'objective' balancing of atrocity stories, the killing of fascists by Pablo weighed against the rape of Maria and the murder of her father and mother. Other structural enactments of the political ethos of *For Whom the Bell Tolls* are the movements of the guerrilla band and the wider strike to secure Segovia. Both of the latter narrative events allow Hemingway to focus steadily and accurately upon the blowing of the bridge and its ideological and military significance. The bridge-blowing gains an almost ritualistic charge as a controlled and fashioned act of decisive momentum. The eventualities stemming from it are fictionally as multiform as Jordan's education, and the political and the military converge in aesthetic harmony.

Artists and intellectuals who had visited Spain, either as combatants or reporters, tended sooner or later to enter into profound disagreements. Carlos Baker has written of the attacks upon Hemingway made by former International Brigade friends such as Milt Woolff, Freddy Keller and Irv Goff.[3] The substance of their criticism was directed against Hemingway's disparaging references to Dolores Ibarruri and André Marty, together with Pilar's account of the loyalist massacre, in his Spanish novel. Perhaps the most formidable of these 'ideology boys', as Hemingway called them, was Alvah Bessie, who wrote a subtle analysis of *For Whom the Bell Tolls* in the *New Masses*. Bessie's own account of the Ebro campaign, *Men in Battle*, offers a valuable contrast to Hemingway's response to Spain and illustrates another facet of a political education gained in the Spanish crossfire.

In *Men in Battle: a Story of Americans in Spain* (1939) Bessie, a political activist who served in the Lincoln Brigade, capitalised upon his participation, in 1938, in the Aragon retreat and Ebro Defensive Campaign. He recalls in his memoir a meeting at the battlefront with Hemingway whom Bessie had previously attacked in print.[4] Ironically Bessie criticised Hemingway again immediately after the publication of *For Whom the Bell Tolls* and continued to do so over a decade later in *The Heart of Spain* when he wrote,

> We would particularly like to explain to the reader our reasons for the omission of work by Ernest Hemingway. It was felt that Hemingway's talent and the personal support he rendered to many phases of the Loyalist cause was shockingly betrayed in *For Whom the Bell Tolls* in which the Spanish people were cruelly misrepresented and leaders of the International Brigades maliciously slandered. The novel in its total impact presented an unforgivable distortion of the meaning of the struggle in Spain. Under the name and prestige of Hemingway important aid was thus given to humanity's worst enemies.[5]

Before *Men in Battle* was written, Bessie, who worked in a variety of occupations, had published *Dwell in the Wilderness* in 1935, and after Spain he was blacklisted because of his political affiliations.

Men in Battle posits the Spanish Civil War as an historical moment most effectively approached intellectually within a dialectical framework; the memoir tests out in a military context Marxist class theory, and its narrative is basically structured by a Communist perspective upon the Spanish crisis. Bessie's fundamental assumption, that Spain represented a momentous historical confrontation with fascism, vivifies his account by giving it an urgent polemical energy. The memoir's constant preoccupation with ideology offers the reader a recapitulation of the war perspectivised as a crucial political struggle to gain ascendancy within western political thought. The Spanish experience, as narrated in *Men in Battle*, transcends narrow political affiliations and takes on wider moral significance. Such an insight allows Bessie to focus more upon social relationships, which form the central thematic concern of the book. An instance may be noted when the narrator salutes the Spanish Republican flag, and finds within the emblem inspiriting semiological value: this emphasis upon fraternal relationships serves to indicate the imagery, structure and tone of Bessie's book; the pitch and melody of his prose celebrates the solidarity of the International Brigades and the Spanish peasants, members of the same idealistic family: 'Everywhere we were saluted with the clenched fist, the universal salute of the Popular Front, that seems somehow to signalise at once the lifted arm of international labour, the everlasting determination to be free, the strength of universal brotherhood' (p. 44). Written shortly after the war had ended, *Men in Battle* conveys as here in this passage the fervour of its author's commitment to the loyalist cause.

The collective heroes, the men in battle of the memoir's title, attract Bessie's admiration; these International Brigade volunteers exhibit through their conduct a high level of political consciousness, and are praised by the narrator as 'the first soldiers in the history of the world who really knew what they were about, what they were going to fight for'. Such men, Bessie polemicises, fought on the Republican side out of profound humanitarianism of spirit. The war attains the nature of a morality drama in such a rendering since the enemy represent a wholly pernicious social system, 'an evil power that would split man from man, brother from brother'.

Bessie's imagery once again relies conceptually upon the notion of a family threatened with dissolution rather than upon explicit dialectical formulation. Bessie frequently analyses the internal organisation of the International Brigades as a social model and approves the unhierarchical blend of discipline and democracy that is demonstrated. Their structure of command allows freedom of dissent while maintaining military efficiency (incidentally a wholly radical principle of military organisation nowhere else encountered in American war literature):

> It was understood that soldiers would obey their officers' commands in action: question them later. And therein lies the distinction that made this army unique in military history. For while certain manifestations of individualism had to be restrained in the interests of unified action, every soldier retained the right to question his command, his officers and commissars, and to bring his grievance to the attention of his fellow soldiers and his superiors. This was done in an organised and democratic fashion through the medium of the political meeting, for this was a political army first to last. (p. 54)

Men in Battle opens with the Republican victory at Teruel, which provided an impetus to the men training at Tarrazona training base. Training Bessie regards as an educative and programmatic indoctrination which should inculcate the overriding corporate lesson that the individual needs to submit part of his individuality for the common good of the loyalist army. Progressive and politically developed troops with the cause of the movement at heart, he argues, will come to understand the need for 'self-integration' in a collective cause.

Bessie frequently examines the motives of the men who came to Spain out of choice to fight for a principle they could easily have ignored. Against the background of growing international crises, and prompted in many cases by their distaste for a monolithic American state which seemed to neglect the welfare of the socially deprived while favouring the interests of capitalists, such men out of conscience left their families and many never returned to them. Bessie analyses his own motivation, and concludes that attitudes of selfish individualism, long ingrained in him, now proved morally inadequate as the foregrounding of self ignored wider social realities. The assets Bessie gained from the war in Spain allow him to dismantle an earlier middle-class life-style and to move towards the 'construction of a life ... geared to other men and the world events that circumscribed them'; he expresses his own rationale in these idealistic terms:

> Men went to Spain for various reasons, but behind almost every man I met there was a common restlessness, a loneliness. ... I knew, about myself, that the historical event of Spain had coincided with a long-felt compulsion to complete the destruction of the training I had received all through my youth; to achieve self-integration, and to lend my individual strength (such as it was) to the fight against our eternal enemy – oppression. ... It was necessary for me, at that stage of my development as a man, to work (for the first time) in a large body of men; to submerge myself in that mass, seeking neither distinction nor preferment (the reverse of my activities for the past several years) and in this way to achieve self-discipline, patience, and un-selfishness – the opposite of a long middle-class train-ing – and the construction of a life that would be geared to other men and the world events that circumscribed them.   (p. 81)

Starting from such collectivist principles, the men of the International Brigades, in Bessie's view, possessed an ad-vanced political education compared with that of the soldiers of conscript armies. Bessie's commander in his section of the Abraham Lincoln Battalion upholds this social morality through his exemplary and serious conduct (and with poetic justice 'much resembled the young Lincoln'). Jordan, in *For Whom the Bell Tolls*, sceptically referred to the puritanical quality of International Brigade Communism, and Bessie's work seems, on occasions, to exhibit likewise what is almost a religious intonation. His myth of the left thus incorporates its own principle of reification, lacking the imaginative and linguistic resources of an outstanding socialist artist such as Brecht or Solzhenitsyn.

When he remembers his fellow soldiers his account loses all traces of narrowness. The portraits in *Men in Battle*, such as that of the twenty-four-year old Aaron, who dies after being blinded, are of unsung proletarian heroes supported by their families at home – labour organisers, militant students, social misfits, the fighters in civilian life. These portrayals give the book an authentic interventionist spirit, as Bessie reveals himself to be passionately involved in the material and political emancipation of his fellows. As he himself accepts that men can co-exist fraternally, Bessie convinces the reader that he consequently understands what his comrades chose to die for. Their deaths, he suggests, had significance, unlike the futility of deaths in previous wars:

> For it is love alone that can, for even a moment of time, give you the illusion that you are not alone, penetrate your loneliness; separate it from you for that moment. And you are afraid that you will die without that love; you are not just afraid to *die*. And this is the meaning of it all (the people's war); these men behind these fragile rocks, these men whose flesh is torn to pieces by the hot and ragged steel; they could not accept their death with such good grace if they did not love so deeply and so well – were not determined that love must come alive into the world. What other reason could there be for dying? What other reason for this blood upon your hands?   (p. 292)

It is these humanitarian insights, eloquently phrased, that make *Men in Battle* more than a propagandising memoir. Bessie has deliberately rejected a literary prose style because he prefers instead to aim for a popular readership. He concentrates most effectively upon men under stress, like 'Emilio Marin, the Puerto Rican with the dark flat face with the stick of wood he held between his teeth to prevent them from chattering, to prevent him from biting his tongue when the planes came over'. Bessie juxtaposes these objective observations of soldiers in action with a broader narrative of the campaign, describing how Tarragona was bombed and Italian fascist troops reached the sea at Vinaroz below Tortosa, cutting loyalist Spain away from Catalonia.

Certain aesthetic problems are raised by the overtly ideological nature of *Men in Battle*. At times Bessie seems, in his preoccupation with politicising events to miss their larger human significance. An instance of this occurs when a captured fascist pilot had been smashed in the face by his loyalist captors. Bessie reflects 'we all agreed that while this may have been humanly understandable, it was politically incorrect'. The reader detects a certain clinical detachment in the positioning of Bessie's adverbs 'humanly' and 'politically'; and the prisoner seems to be regarded more as a political cipher than as a human being. Bessie is also prone to idealise the aspirations of the indigenous population and to overstructure the responses of his readers in a rather schematic way. An example of this kind of prescriptiveness is his attribution of profound significance to common happenings; such as when a Spanish girl, singing flamenco, is apotheosised as representing 'the voice of an entire people crying for freedom and for human dignity' (p. 329). The heightened rhetorical prose describing the girl's singing contributes to the formation of an unwarranted aura of mystification. With a working-class readership in mind such an explicit and didactic mode is perfectly legitimate as deployed, for instance, in Robert Tressel's English socialist novel *The Ragged-Trousered Philanthropists*, but one sometimes detects in *Men in Battle* a sentimentally utopian interpretation of situations in the war. Bessie at such times desires to instruct and proselytise, in order to persuade his readers of the full Marxist implications of events. This impulse towards prometheanism, though, supplies the strength also of *Men in Battle*, its interventionist social energy. For example, the young Spanish soldiers, who eventually come to dislike the Internationals, because of their own nationalistic pride, must learn that the holding operation they are engaged in adumbrates a wider class struggle of world dimensions; only through unity and vigilance, Bessie infers, will there be success against fascism: 'They were beginning to learn what the fight was all about. They did not know as surely as the international soldiers that this was a fight from which you could never run away, but they were learning' (p. 325).

Men in Battle renders an informative and authentic account of the Abraham Lincoln Brigade in action. From the exhilaration in which the book opens, through the first shock of combat and up to the Ebro defeats, Bessie reports often through painstaking use of detail the collective experiences of the Lincoln Brigade soldiers. The individuality of *Men in Battle* inheres chiefly in the undoctrinaire stories of these men. It is the tribute Bessie pays to his comrades, workers turned soldiers, that remains in the reader's mind when other aspects of *Men in Battle* are forgotten. The least narcissistic of heroes, they died for their fellow-workers. To these men, whether Lincolns, MacPaps, British or others, Bessie dedicates his book:

> For never before in the history of the world had there been such a body of men – a spontaneously gathered international volunteer army, drawn from every stratum of human life and every human occupation, handworkers and professionals, intellectuals and farmers. The very existence of this army, that had played so crucial a role in this Spanish war, was the guarantee of international working class brotherhood; the final proof that those who perform the work of the world possess a common interest and an identical obligation. It was the living embodiment of the unity that exists between all men of good will, whatever their nationality, their political or religious conviction, or their way of making a living on this earth. Every occupation, every colour, every nationality, these men had fought and died with each other; their roster was the roster of mankind.   (p. 343)

Men in Battle offers an interesting contrast with later novels which narrate the Second World War fight against fascism. Rarely does a Second War novelist exhibit the passionate idealism of Bessie. History, of course, had shown Bessie's cause, in Spain at least, to be a defeated one, and later novelists generally found the American army less democratic in spirit than the organisation of International Brigades. The victory of democracy witnessed by Hayes and Burns, if we may judge from their fiction, did little to advance the cause of the brotherhood of men which was anticipated in *Men in Battle*. Bessie's memoir recreates a historical moment with celebratory energy and communicates the spirit of comradeship that was kindled among the excesses and cruelties of the Spanish Civil War.

7 Second World War Fiction: Alienation and Group Identity

STUDIES IN ALIENATION

Norman Mailer's war novel *The Naked and the Dead* (1948)[1] offers an instructive visionary 'node' for comparison with the cluster of First World War novels discussed earlier in this book. The first encounter of Dos Passos, Cummings, Stallings and Hemingway had resulted in initial recoil translated, after aesthetic assimilation, into work of considerable artistic buoyancy, fiction which displayed impulses towards renewal and reconstruction. Hemingway pared down language and concretised experience formally; Cummings in *The Enormous Room* eulogised individuals who themselves incarnated regenerative metaphors; Dos Passos, through John Andrews's aesthetic spirit of inquiry in *Three Soldiers*, searched for a meliorist and progressive genre of fiction; Laurence Stallings's pacifist trajectory, his hero's determination to prevent 1914 from ever happening again, generates another powerful counterforce to war. The novels of these First War writers exhibit, as a common basis, a faith in the potentiality of the hero to perform significant morally affirmative acts: Frederick Henry, John Andrews and Richard Plume are all essentially good men. In Mailer's *The Naked and the Dead* the reader meets a very different situation and finds it hard to sympathise much with any of the major figures in the novel. Indeed, a plausible case can be advanced that not a single actively good man emerges throughout *The Naked and the Dead*; Cummings and Croft are clearly fascist in mentality; Hearn is incapable of moral decision; Martinez contributes to Hearn's death when he could have prevented it; Conn appears boorish and callous; Dalleson incompetent and self-opinionated; Red Valsen cynical and antipathetic towards officers; Brown weakly influenced by others and seeking self-vindication; Ridges hypocritically religious, since he sees no wrong in killing heathen; Goldstein is himself prejudiced; Wyman glory-seeking; Dove stupid; Gallagher a racialist who hates students and Jews; Polack without principle and totally disillusioned; Stanley passive and ineffective in carrying through his opposition to Croft. None of these characters seems capable of taking the kind of redemptive and positive action that Frederick Henry did in negotiating a separate peace or, like John Andrews, of making a noble aesthetic gesture. History had, of course, intervened and interpolated the years of the Boom and Depression, the growth of fascism, Spain, Auschwitz, the dropping of the two atomic bombs and the beginning of the cold war with the Soviet bloc. Spain, too, had demonstrated clearly both the necessity to abandon pacifism and also the organisational, ideological and strategic problems that needed to be solved before political idealism could be fully implemented.

In *The Naked and the Dead* no significant personal or social affirmation seems possible; marriage and the redemptive power of love, for example, are discredited throughout the novel: many of the major characters have suffered marital discord; Croft has been unfaithful to his wife and she to him; Cummings describes his wife as a bitch; Red Valsen has abandoned Lois; Polack, who has been seduced by a woman when a boy, regards all females with suspicion, and Hearn desires women merely as sex objects (in the account of his past life, marriage, portrayed through that of his friends and of his parents, is shown to be a materialistic and unfulfilling relationship). We have travelled a long way from Richard and Esme Plume, who comfort each other, and from Frederick Henry's responsible attitude towards Catherine Barkley. A series of other striking differences of attitude between Mailer's work and the earlier novels may be observed. A key one is the response displayed by characters towards the enemy: Dos Passos's characters generally show a reverence for the enemy nowhere paralleled in Mailer's; even the gentle Martinez prods a dead Japanese in the genitals and bodies are looted unceremoniously. The prevailing attitude in the novel adopted by its characters towards the Japanese seems to be that they are hysterically bent on ritual immolation.

In the earlier work of Dos Passos, collectivist action, interventionism or revolution was often considered a creative possibility for remaking society upon a more humane and egalitarian model; in Mailer's work Hearn experiences profound dissatisfaction with both the Communist Party and with syndicalism and trade-union organisation: the Communist Party he observes to be dominated by sterile theorists, and his labour companions, once a union is formed, refuse to strike. Left-wing politics, therefore, seem to offer little hope of disproving Cummings's conviction that 'History [is] in the grip of Right' (p. 334). Acts of individual revolutionary significance are discountenanced by the history of the Spanish Civil War when Hearn comes after reflection to realise that revolutions are no longer carried out by committed activists but by mechanised armies. Hemingway's Frederick Henry in *A Farewell to Arms* capitalises upon comradeship as a countervailing force to war, and he finds consolation in the dignity of Count Greffi and in the decency of both Rinaldi and the hotel barman who supplies him with the boat to escape with Catherine to Switzerland. In Hemingway, too, the Winchester-on-the-wall tradition of the frontiersman is in some measure reaffirmed in the self-reliant conduct of Frederick Henry and Nick Adams, but in *The Naked and the Dead* this becomes transmuted through the actions of the murderous Westerner, the Texas National Guardsman Croft, into perverted and sadistic blood-lust. The potency of art to reform, earlier encapsulated in John Andrews's serious aesthetic and moral gesture at the end of *Three Soldiers*, is also invalidated in *The Naked and the Dead*. Literary culture is treated only in relation to Hearn's dilettantism or Cummings's Machiavellian self-education. Earlier heroes, too, had found talismanic power in nature, but Croft reverses this tendency by squeezing the throat of a bird with an almost sexual pleasure (p. 448). Religion is likewise mocked as a moral code through the hypocrisy of Ridges and in the abortive sacrifice made in carrying Wilson; God behaves like a 'practical joker' in allowing the wounded man to die after such strenuous efforts have been made to keep him alive. Finally, earlier novelists such as William March, Humphrey Cobb, Dalton

Trumbo or Thomas Boyd had observed residual social energy in the working classes, yet the proletarian characters in *The Naked and the Dead* are, in the main, possessed of no special insights.

The process of osmosis discussed in philosophical debate by Cummings and Hearn (pp. 247–9), whereby America becomes infused by the historical moment and transforms fascism into kinetic energy, thereby releasing stored potential, provides the ideological framework for *The Naked and the Dead*. In such a dialectical formulation, which is not countered within the novel by any forceful opposing argument, the American army provides an effective model for future social organisation. Cummings's scheme has the value of being systematic and theoretically complete, and also gains from being cogently articulated. The General has undergone a rigorous course of self-education and has read in a variety of disciplines. His projections and analyses are not challenged or invalidated by the dénouement of events, merely interrupted in their course of evolution. Basically Cummings theorises that power élites will control the destiny of nations and will operate through strict social stratification; a 'fear ladder' will ensure that the hierarchy functions both to repress individuals and to encourage them in turn to repress their own social inferiors. Cummings postulates a Nazi century; the tormenting of Roth and Gallagher's intense hatred of Jews, together with the class divisions between officers and men, seem to internalise within *The Naked and the Dead* the triumph of Cummings's Hitler-like aphorism 'the only morality of the future is power morality' (p. 277). The Americocentric future, he argues, will be a fascist-dominated historical phase.

In Cummings's perspective social evolution may be likened to a condition of war. His vision confirms Valsen's apprehension of Croft's military usefulness as a sergeant: 'That Croft, what a baby. A hood. It was the kind of guy you needed. A sonofabitch' (p. 511). *The Naked and the Dead* as an imaginative environment seems designed for the dominance of men such as Cummings and Croft. The General, for example, thinks in the manner of an intellectual 'hood' when surveying his battle organisation; he gloats over 'thousands of men' deployed under his command, troops charged with America's energy which had 'become kinetic and it would not be reversed'. In such a mechanistic system a rifle is spiritualised 'an extension of man's power', and Cummings likewise apotheosises the machine. When he visits a gunner to supervise the firing of a howitzer this logic is turned into a rhapsodic epiphany of war; Cummings sees into war's primitive psychological justification:

> The war, or rather *war*, was odd, he told himself a little inanely. But he knew what it meant. It was all covered with tedium and routine, regulations and procedure, and yet there was a naked quivering heart to it which involved you deeply when you were thrust into it. All the deep dark urges of man, the sacrifices on the hilltop, and the churning lusts of the night and sleep, weren't all of them contained in the shattering screaming burst of a shell, the man-made thunder and light? . . . He felt cleaned in an acid bath, and all of him, even his fingertips, was prepared to grasp the knowledge behind all this. . . . All of it, all the violence, the dark coordination had sprung from his mind. In the night, at that moment, he felt such power that it was beyond joy; he was calm and sober.   (pp. 477–8)

Cummings, one of the most impressive creations in Second World War fiction, attains insight here into the archetypal bestiality of war, its atavistic power to strip away the complexities of modern life and to plunge the soldier back to the prehistory of man as a species. Such a vision acts for the General as a purifying intuition which cleans his spirit of routine and tedium. Passages in Mailer's novel like this revelatory awareness of Cummings seem appropriate to dramatise the global scale and atomic energy of the Second World War.

Lee S. Halpin, in discussing the American liberal response to the war, has argued that few writers 'could give up the assurance of civilisation's inevitable power to civilise' and chose to employ in their work instead the first war metaphor of 'good men under the heel of institutional power'.[2] The potency of Cummings as a character, and it is true of *The Naked and the Dead* as a whole, is that fascism is imaginatively apprehended at every level and dramatised as a working system of social control. Such a fictional logic informs *The Naked and the Dead* throughout.

This clearly emerges, structurally and linguistically, through the novel's concern with violence in thought and action, above all epitomised in the callous shooting of prisoners. The death of Hearn supplies another prominent example; Croft callously plans the lieutenant's death, instructing Martinez to remain silent and withhold information from Hearn that the Japanese are still guarding the pass. The 'fear ladder' induces Martinez to obey Croft's orders and Hearn is pointlessly killed, ostensibly because he threatens Croft's dominance of command over the platoon. After Hearn's death, Wyman attempts to bridge the communication gap between himself and the dead officer by referring to him as 'a good guy'. Red, who has shortly before declined to accept Hearn's offer of promotion, refutes Wyman's suggestion, 'They ain't a fuggin one of those officers is worth a goddam' (p. 511). Red's statement sways Minetta, who likewise concludes, 'They're all bastards.' The reality of Hearn's death, its human significance, is thus dissipated by his posthumous incorporation into the ranks of the hated officer class. This kind of prevailing nihilism, carried through the novel's unity of tone and language, is also expressed through the soldiers' maxims: 'it's all bloody noses'; 'it never turns out as you want it'; 'everybody loses'; 'win or lose, it's all in the cards' or in Minetta's vision of omnipotent destruction, 'everything is smashed all over the world'; the 'shattering gyre' of the war has deprived the troops of any individual control over events; they represent, as Cummings envisions them in his game of chess with Hearn, mere pawns. Such intuitions, of a deterministic and dehumanising nature, are augmented in *The Naked and the Dead* by other fictional devices.

The feelings of many characters seem unbalanced; for example, although the reader understands the exhaustion of Cummings, he is likely to find it difficult to believe that the General is so warped by command that he waits for Hearn to pick up a cigarette that the latter has defiantly dropped, with latently sexual excitement (pp. 273–9). Mailer's novel demonstrates the energy of negative emotions, of loathing, violence, disgust, parasitism and prejudice. A hint of the macabre side of this vision, its necrogenic undertone, is provided by a pattern of imagery related to sores, putrefaction, and bodily decay, as when the novelist writes of Hearn, 'He felt like an insect crawling through the entrails of a horse' (p. 263). *The Naked and the Dead* has much of this symbolism derived from the bowels and the mortuary. Here again, as an example, is Mailer's analysis of Hearn's feelings on another occasion: 'He felt as if an immense cyst of suppuration and purulence had burst inside him, and was infecting his blood stream now, washing through all the conduits of his body in a sudden violent flux of change' (p. 280). The imagery noted here confirms the arcane impression that the reader receives of *The Naked and the Dead* as a moral fable designed to exhibit the regressive tendencies of men at war. Locale plays an important role in this context as also do narrative patterning and structural irony.

The territory initially has the properties of a magical island, 'it was a sensual isle, a biblical land of ruby wines and golden sands and indigo trees', but this cannot last and Anopopei changes into a place like the surrounding 'black, dead' ocean; 'it was cold, implicit with dread and death' (p. 384). Rather in the manner later employed by the English novelist William Golding in *Lord of the Flies*, the island transports the men away from any vestiges of urban civilisation, away from the cultural associations of Europe, and places them near to the elemental jungle and primordial ocean. The disgusting atrocities committed by the Americans seem to be thrown into relief by the novel's terrain and environment etched in by the aura of the tropical rain forest. As far as narrative development is concerned, *The Naked and the Dead* utilises a rather heavy handed thematic pattern of reversal, most apparent in the way both Croft's patrol and Cummings's sophisticated strategy prove irrelevant to the outcome of the military engagement fought on Anopopei; the inept Dalleson finally gains the glory of victory through the mistakes of the enemy. Such a structural movement towards peripeteia seems to enforce in rather laboured fashion the two philosophical nodes of the book, that men are playthings of fate, and to achieve anything worthwhile by war is like going to a brothel to cure venereal disease.

When reviewed overall, the milieu of *The Naked and the Dead* connects the war situation with that in peacetime through the rather clumsy linking device borrowed from Dos Passos's 'The Time Machine'. This technique aspires to create a Tolstoyan sweep from peace to war, to enable the reader to understand the psychological motivation of the characters and to increment the authenticity of the narrative by relating in epic fashion the events on Anopopei to those in the United States before the war. In the case of Hearn the Time Machine plays a crucial role in enabling the reader to understand the origins of the character's alienation, his descent into *nada*. Robert Hearn, even at an early age, is described as a 'cold fish' who does not pull his weight and is accused by a friend of not trying hard enough during competitive youth activities (p. 285). As a young man he abandons the discipline of science, turning instead to the study of literature in a rather desultory fashion. After leaving college, his attempts at rebellion prove abortive, since he rejects the option of volunteering for Spain and fritters his time away in the job of junior editor and publisher's reader which he finds unsatisfying. Because of his political interests in left-wing activity he joins a union as labour organiser, although the same inevitable disillusionment follows as when he flirts with Communism but abandons it, believing it to be an ideology invalidated by its disciples at grass-roots level. It is to Hearn's credit that he rebels against his father's ultra-materialistic values and decides to resolve his difficulties independently. However such a stance leaves him vulnerably isolated as a radical intellectual without a party or any firmly-rooted ideological position. Hearn enlists before Pearl Harbor, rising eventually to the rank of *aide-de-camp* to General Cummings. Mailer treats Hearn subtly in depicting his intellectual disorientation; the lieutenant's vaguely liberal sentiments stand little chance against the dialectical completeness of Cummings's fascist logic, and Hearn's vacillating sensibility allows him to be easily outmanoeuvred by the single-mindedness of the General.

The tragedy of Hearn ultimately relates to his gradual increase in self-awareness and his apparent commitment to action, both of which are unrealised because of his premature death. Shortly before he dies Hearn asserts his faith both in the continuance of liberal principle as a counteractive creed to fascism and in the need for action, when he half-humorously acts out in his imagination the role of political assassin, instrument of vengeance in eliminating prominent American fascists. He also confesses to himself his own 'shoddy motive', that he, too, like Croft and Cummings, desires the psychological stimulation of military command (p. 488). Hearn has been shaped irrevocably by his class origins; he cannot establish rapport or forge a liaison with the enlisted men, neither can he stomach the ethics of his own officer class. Such an isolated position confirms his alienation; instead of gaining promotion in the company of officers, he dies in confusion betrayed by enlisted men. Hearn's anxiety is emblematic of the interest in the theme of alienation displayed by Second World War novelists; this chapter will consider other works which are substantially preoccupied with loss of self and the chapter will later examine ways in which contrasting novels demonstrate the achievement of group identity.

Stanley Cooperman, in comparing First World War writers with those of the later conflict, has particularly singled out John Horne Burns as illustrative of 'metaphysical' disillusionment, the 'sickness unto death':

> a World War II writer like Burns, far from being proud of his 'nothingness' could only suffer a sense of failure in his own alienation from a cause to which he still assented; this is in direct contrast to men like Cummings or protagonists like Andrews, for whom negation itself meant the assertion of alternative values. It is in Burns rather than in Dos Passos or Boyd or March or any World War I writer, that one finds the deepest realisation of nada – a spiritual nothingness without alternatives.[3]

Cooperman speculates that the First World War 'negation was corrective rather than existential', and writers could turn to 'exits' and alternative value systems to reverse the destructive nihilism of war itself. Cooperman's interesting proposition seems to be truer if applied to the work of Alfred Hayes than to that of Burns himself.

Hayes's *All Thy Conquests* (1946) and *The Girl on the Via Flaminia* (1949) explore fictively the American occupation of Italy, taking in the theme of liberation and the interaction between liberators and liberated. The former book is a frame novel or collection of loosely related short stories, a genre particularly popular with such Second World War novelists as Burns or James Michener, and a formal enactment of the alienation of both the liberators and the native population (the genre focuses upon disconnected lives, people whose consciousness is fragmented and whose situations rarely impinge in communal activity). *All Thy Conquests* presents a depressing composite picture of both the American troops of occupation and the Roman population. The novel's thematic structure reinforces the overriding impression of disjointed lives thrown out of harmony by war. Occupational upheaval forms the basis of one story where a zestful barman, Giorgio, loses his job and is reduced to penury, his family humiliated; sexual exploitation is dramatised through the experience of Carla, a young Italian girl made pregnant by a married GI who abandons her; aristocratic degeneracy supplies the subject-matter in Hayes's account of how an Italian homosexual marchese faithlessly betrays his father-in-law, formerly a fascist collaborator. Hayes's vision communicates a panorama of collective depravity and alienation, a Rome ravaged, without ideals and without a supportive indigenous culture. The reader of *All Thy Conquests* or *The Girl on the Via Flaminia* may feel that Hayes over-prescriptively attributes negative values to the American army of occupation. The situation narrated in *The Girl on the Via Flaminia* treats the novelist's basic war theme, the GI who conspires by his casual indifference to degrade an innocent Italian girl. Hayes, unlike Burns, finds no significant idealism in the Italian population; frequently he portrays Italians as procuresses or lethargic men supported by their women. Antonio, a former Italian soldier, articulates a principal criticism of the army of liberation when he registers disgust at the impotence and collusion of his fellow countrymen in the face of American assertiveness; to him Americans are drunks who elbow Italians into the roadway or vandals who scrawl on the walls of the Colosseum. Hayes's novels lack an imaginative centre of self-generating energy capable of acting against the prevalent moral devastation; his fictional environment offers the reader no prospect of escaping from the value collapse of war. The sombre perspective of his fiction is summated in the confused insight of his unheroic GI Robert as he muses on the issue of who is 'responsible' for Lisa's degradation. Hayes's fiction leaves the distinct impression that the irresponsible American army wreaks as much spiritual havoc upon Italy as the former fascist regime.

Whereas Hayes's two novels enact no alternative value system to the American ethos of materialist exploitation, John Horne Burns in *The Gallery* (1947) creates Italian characters who respect the principle of 'individuality, consecrated and unselfish' and thereby may defend themselves against the encroachment of mass consumer values. J. P. Diggins, writing of Burns's romantic Italophilism, has observed that 'by depicting his own culture as devoid of moral order and by projecting an idyllic portrait of Italy Burns's *The Gallery* gave to the generation of the forties what Hemingway's *A Farewell to Arms* gave to the generation of the twenties, a literary statement of the loss of innocence'.[4] *The Gallery* portrays fictionally the lives of the inhabitants of the Galleria Umberto in Naples occupied by the Allied army of liberation in 1944. Like Hayes's *All Thy Conquests*, Burns's novel comprises a series of portraits of individuated lives, foci intended to recreate correlatively the diverse life patterns of a war-torn city. The formal structure of the novel has been commented on by John Aldridge who has noted the discordance between the Promenade sections of the novel, where the author–narrator reflects upon his experiences and meditates about the quality of life he perceives, and the portraits of Americans and Neopolitans.[5] It is likely that the disunity noted by Aldridge implies the novelist's inability to transcend the vision of alienation at the heart of his fiction.

The Gallery postulates two alternative and conflicting concepts of civilisation; one the resonant Old World culture embodied in the Italo-North African life style which manifests itself in the 'sweetness' and 'discipline' of Italian architecture, and, conflicting with this admirable way of living, the money civilisation of the contemporary world symbolised by such American characters as Major Motes. The great military achievements and industrialised energies of the United States, the axis of Allied victory, fail to counteract American soullessness in Burns's fictional pattern. His narrator, who often speaks in a tone of passionate emotion, totally rejects the capitalist values of American culture, although the novel particularises decent and humane individual GIs such as Michael Patrick, the central figure of an early story. Burns's narrator, presumably articulating a point of view close to the novelist's own, explicitly disavows American idealism as spurious and raises for the reader a kind of aesthetic problem frequently encountered in *The Gallery*. Such overtly moralistic diagnosis seems to be cultural sociology unassimilated into the fictional current of the narrative:

> I remember that my heart finally broke in Naples. Not over a girl or a thing, but over an idea.... I found that outside of the propaganda writers (who were making a handsome living from the deal) Americans were very poor spiritually. Their ideals were something to make dollars on. They had bankrupt souls. Perhaps this is true of most of the people of the twentieth century.... (p. 156)[6]

The narrative development of *The Gallery* reinforces this insight and, for Burns's narrator, the war takes on the specific nature of social catalyst, outlining in clear profile the process of degeneration undermining modern acquisitive societies. He theorises beyond this that ideological confusion as witnessed in the conduct of individuals implies more than a temporary deracination generated by military campaigns; it points to a more important underlying reality, the collapse of Americanised civilisation:

> the war was supposed to be against fascism – not against every man, woman, and child in Italy.... But then a modern war is total. Armies on the battlefield are simply a remnant from the old kind of war. In the 1944 war everyone's hand ended by being against everyone else's. Civilisation was already dead, but nobody bothered to admit this to himself. (pp. 156–7)

What his narrator indicts as the 'deficient moral and humane sense' of the United States as a nation is exhibited in the portraits of several of the American characters presented in the novel as loci of values. Louella, an American woman volunteer, demonstrates through her conduct the omnipresent 'Hollywood ethics' and 'plastic and chrome' façade of American culture. Ironically she regards herself as the inheritor of the pioneer woman tradition, a self-projection in-

validated by her defunct moral awareness: she refers con-
temptuously to Italians as 'greasers', commends the practice
of black-marketeering as 'business acumen' and works herself
up into a disproportionate 'sweat of empathy' for young
American fliers, whom she pampers in a grotesque parody of
maternalism. In addition to the treatment of such individuals
as Louella, Burns delineates collective portraits, exemplified
in the inwardly lonely homosexuals who inhabit Momma's
bar. *The Gallery* effectively evokes the tinsel gaiety of Allied
soldiers, the undercurrent of despair and madness beneath
the forced spontaneity induced by alcohol. The GIs are shown
to lack any profound shared communal links and to live instead separate lives moulded by a frenetic feeling of humanistic loss. As closing time begins to approach in Momma's bar,
the illusory unity of the soldiers begins to fragment, and
restlessness and artificiality break through to the surface. The
American soldier, epitomised in Captain Motes of 'The Leaf',
is presented as essentially an onlooker, spiritually confused
and incapable of genuine participation in life's feast.

Burns's novel, unlike Mailer's, reveals little concern with the
class divisions consequent upon military rank; his gallery of
misfits includes enlisted men and officers like Motes, one of
his most interesting creations. Motes, by his directionless life-
style, echoes the hysterical tempo dramatised by the lost souls
at Momma's bar. A Southern officer, unhappily married, he
turns into a cold, withdrawn spectator of life, a spiritually
sterile man who is potentially homosexual. Being such a re-
mote and miserable figure, he falls easy prey to flatterers, and
attracts similar unpleasant sneaks and bullies such as the re-
pulsive sycophant, Stuki. In Burns's most characteristic manner the reader is offered a metaphor for the United States
army and ultimately the American way of life, a group of
spineless and immature officers engaged in chicanery and
self-seeking. Motes and Mayberry, another of the censors, are
racists, like Louella; they liken the situation in Italy to that in
the Southern states of America, and believe, 'All Europe and
its parasitic population are obscene – like the nigras' (p. 103).
The dualism of *The Gallery*, its tendency to polarise two potentialities for cultural development, may be conveniently
examined by contrasting such degenerate figures as Motes
with the Neopolitan reverence for custom and ceremony. The

Americans reveal themselves to be incapable of living in the manner of Giulia, an Italian girl and the heroine of the novel. On the contrary, the GI, who is presented as racially prejudiced or sexually perverted (on one occasion the reader observes a couple of American soldiers planning to deflower two Italian girls of about eleven and twelve), destroys life. The story 'Queen Penicillin', which treats the end result of gratuitous sexual exploitation, venereal disease, suggests the prevalence of deep psychic pollution, and infers Burns's distaste for the conduct of well-bred American boys, who believe they are released, in the war zone, from obligations of social decency. Political liberation has ironically turned into harmful sexual promiscuity.

Traditional cultural values prevent Giulia from descending into prostitution like many of the Italian girls in the Galleria Umberto. Because of the principles to which she clings, she discovers inner moral resources which enable her to withstand the chaos around her. In this she contrasts with Louella, the American girl whose veneer of compassion appears to be synthetic. Giulia has a major advantage over Louella, the narrator implies, in that she has a cultural inheritance which permits her individual dignity; she draws for guidance upon 'standards of honour passed down through generations of Italian mothers' and consequently 'saw the purpose of her training, to be an Italian girl of softness and dignity' (p. 142). When she meets an American officer whom she comes to love, she insists that he conform to the stylised rituals of Italian courtship, for the 'traditional functions of duenna, cisisbeo and arbiter' shored up family life against the repercussions of wider economic and social collapse. For the reader of Burns's fiction, unlike that of Alfred Hayes, Italian life through the power of such idealism holds a moral excellence from which Americans, if percipient, could learn. Burns's vision, although profoundly anti-American, does not therefore lack affirmation. His travelogue subject matter in the Promenades also offers the reader a poetic recapitulation of the bustle and confusion of the Galleria.

The aesthetic vibrancy and sophistication of Italian culture drew many American Second World War writers to perceive in it an alternative milieu to that of war, probably the most famous war novelist of all being Ernest Hemingway whose

study of alienation set in Venice in the figure of Colonel
Cantwell presents a character whose apprehension of the
Second World War is in the nature of a swan-song. The sick
Colonel, aware of his mutability, apprehends the Second
World War as a last strand in the pattern of previous wars; the
war becomes less of a forward-moving historical event than a
dying fall. Cantwell's despair stems from his military career,
the horrors he has witnessed having separated him spiritually
from his fellow men and contributed to the Colonel's apprehension of *nada*.

Frank Ross has discussed a new type of hero in twentieth-
century war fiction, the soldier with a sadistic streak, whom he
describes as an 'assailant–victim'.[7] Lieutenant Henry of *A
Farewell to Arms*, who cold-bloodedly condones the shooting of
one of his own side for disobeying orders and is later himself
victimised at Caporetto, is such a type, as is Chrisfield in Dos
Passos's *Three Soldiers*, Gray in Faulkner's story 'Victory', and
Croft in Mailer's *The Naked and the Dead*. Colonel Cantwell of
Across the River and into the Trees seems as much an assailant–
victim as these others: for example, the reader learns of a fight
he had with two drunken soldiers when he savagely attacked
them because they whistled at his girl, and, in the role of
victim, he appears indisputably a casualty of war, a dying and
embittered man. The difference between Colonel Cantwell
and some of his prototypes, is that Hemingway *convinces* us of
a plausible reason for the Colonel's apparent sadism. Whereas
in *A Farewell to Arms* the shocking incident where the deserter
is shot is quickly passed over without comment by the narrator, Frederick Henry, and thus psychologically unsubstan-
tiated, in *Across the River and into the Trees* Hemingway portrays
a sick man who may legitimately be expected to behave irra-
tionally and brutally at times. Cantwell has endured many
horrifying experiences, as when the regiment he loved was
decimated, and he suffers from wounds which make it imaginatively appropriate that he should, on occasions, wish to
vent his anger on others for no apparent reason. The Colonel
has to purge his past by revealing his traumatic experiences to
Renata, partly in a confessional tone, and thereby he finds
release from his chaotic memories. His suffering is made
more bearable when the young girl shows that she understands his problems and returns his love, and thus she pro-

vides the means of his absolution. Colonel Cantwell's confessional way of talking, which opens to the reader the immense flaws in his character, also offers a means of enlisting the reader's sympathy and developing the tragic potentiality of the novel.

Across the River and into the Trees displays close affinities with several earlier American war stories; it recalls Faulkner's *Soldier's Pay* whose central figure, Donald Mahon, has been, like Colonel Cantwell, irrevocably scarred by war and who also dies with considerable dignity. Faulkner's hero is betrayed by his fiancée, and a similar betrayal is at the core of a fine story by Laurence Stallings called 'Vale of Tears' published in *Cosmopolitan* of May 1931. Where this story parallels *Across the River and into the Trees* is in the contrast between the wounded hero and his exceptionally beautiful girl. Both writers describe the wounds of their heroes with precise realism: their girls contrapuntally affirm life, health, and beauty in a universe of pain and death. Renata in *Across the River and into the Trees* similarly represents physical perfection, contrasted with the Colonel's physical deformities.[8] All three writers, Faulkner, Hemingway, and Stallings, place their heroes in the post-war situation, although the horrors of combat are introduced into their stories by means of flashback techniques. (The hero of Laurence Stallings's novel *Plumes*, Richard Plume, is a fictional creation in American literature who resembles Colonel Cantwell in his preoccupation with his own wounds, and Stallings, like Hemingway, was himself severely wounded.)

Hemingway's protagonist differs from the heroes of the other two stories in being still physically active up to the time of his death; Donald Mahon lives on as a silent invalid, and Stallings's hero only as a bed-ridden cripple. Cantwell, the 'busted' general, remains defiant of military authority, continuing to display a contempt for bureaucracy which has contributed to his demotion. Hemingway created a complex figure in Cantwell who is ostensibly a man without self-pity, continually on the offensive against melancholia. This attitude of attack represents ironically a defensive shell, unknowingly adopted; underneath it the Colonel feels in a state of emotional stress, a man who has cracked-up because of what war has done to him. It is the obsolescence of the Colonel that moves the reader, as Cantwell seems only half-aware of his own redundancy, a pugnacious individualist in an age of bacteriological warfare. He conceives of himself in varying terms, which reflect his egotism: he imagines himself, by turns, to be a general who criticises his peers such as Eisenhower or Patton, and a humble colonel with a conscience, the 'lowest thing' on earth, a common infantry soldier. Such a changing focus of self-definition is augmented by his unpredictability, his moodiness, and his 'wild-boar truculence' (p. 65) that makes him act unkindly towards others. All of these defects are understandable, and they are exonerated when the reader considers what the Colonel has been through, his 'great sorrow', when other men's orders resulted in the deaths of many of his fellow soldiers. The Colonel's vituperation and his occasional infantile and vulgar behaviour represent fictionally the appropriate actions of a man living on drugs, who has been destroyed by what he refers to as his 'sale métier', and who wakes up at night sweating, a victim of neurasthenia. He feels bound to suffer, for, allied to his physical disabilities, he has inherited a mental burden, because he has accepted sole spiritual responsibility for losing three battalions in combat through decisions which were not his own.

Hemingway, possibly not always fully aware of the nature of his achievement, allows the reader to see beneath the surface of Cantwell's mind. The novelist pours into his creation a mass of contradictory, unresolved, and unassimilated textual inferences, and these verbal inconsistencies and apparently irrelevant happenings contribute to the semantic autonomy of the delineation. The novel reminds one, in some ways, of Samuel Richardson's *Pamela*. The central figures in both novels are made to behave contrary to their intentions, and are characters whose true state of mind may only be implied from the paradoxical and contradictory terms in which it is delineated. The young servant girl, Pamela, is unaware of her true marital aims, and the modern reader must often treat what she does and says with scepticism, and a corresponding ambiguity motivates Colonel Cantwell. The dualism, in the Colonel's instance, derives from the desperation of his predicament. He ritualises experience, only half-realising his obsolescence, and tries to avert the implications of his perilous condition. He has lost his grasp of the present and, consequently, tries to cling on to what for him represents the good and the true. Hemingway thus suggests the shifting unease of the Colonel and his fear of death. The trivialities of Cantwell's mind, his over-concern with good taste, his love of ritual, and his oblique self-comparisons with heroes of the past and present, imply his psychological confusion. Hemingway, through Cantwell's references to fictional and historical figures such as Richard the Lionheart, Lear, Othello, Stonewall Jackson and Marshal Ney, makes the reader aware of human unfulfilment. Cantwell is as unlike these legendary figures as any man is, and yet his tragedy, that of a sick and dying man, is similar to that of the real Stonewall Jackson or George Armstrong Custer.

If the Colonel's wounds, which are frequently referred to in the story, marked for him the onset of maturity, they also signified the end of his personal 'immortality'. *Across the River and into the Trees* would be more adequately described by the title of Faulkner's *Soldier's Pay*; for Cantwell has received his payment. His self-styled 'triste métier' has familiarised him with death, and his trade, 'the killing of armed men', has left him a pathogenic wreck. In the face of his own approaching end he retains only his 'bad dreams' as a soldier to fall back upon. His 'soldier suit' will not protect him against his illness, and so he clings onto a code of behaviour and philosophy suitable only to war time (p. 180). The Colonel, uniquely battered and frustrated, is fictionally the end product of the two world wars, a psychologically and physically destroyed character, the emotional equivalent of a boxer who continually relives his fights.

Cantwell's memories of war are presented with the authenticity and the personal bias of a general's memoirs. The Colonel's opinions on military life are delivered from both the standpoint of authority and that of the common soldier, and these wryly alternating reflections upon war supply the source material for the interplay of military themes in *Across the River and into the Trees*. The Colonel has very definite views about generals, both contemporary and of the past, he lambasts war profiteers, army career diplomats, military journalists, and the 'organisation man' at army HQ: he admires the common soldier, but is paradoxically impatient towards Jackson, his aide; and he reacts surprisingly sympathetically towards the enemy. The reader is made aware, at every twist and turn, of the Colonel's thoughts, of the military cast of his mind, an impressive imaginative achievement. When Cantwell interpolates his private theories, recollections, and anecdotes about war into almost every facet of his conversation the reader feels that the fictional Colonel has the authenticity of a 'busted' general who behaves as if thoroughly obsessed with his career and with guilt for the deaths of his men. These comprehensive military reflections scattered throughout *Across the River and into the Trees* are the equivalent of the 'political' discourses in George Orwell's *Homage to Catalonia* or his *1984*; Orwell presumably felt that in both cases these political interpretations were fundamental as they threw into relief the main events of the narrative; it may be argued that Cantwell's speculations about military life similarly impede the narrative, but this denies the basis of Hemingway's technique. The Colonel is necessarily a war bore: when he, for example, relives an old campaign or fulminates against a bureaucratic officer whom he calls a 'pistol-slapper' he reveals, in the process, much about himself. The mind of Colonel Cantwell is represented as being totally conditioned by the past, has no future, and very little present. The actual events of the story are narratively sparse; and they are set into the wider context of the ex-general's career; thus everything in the story is ordered in relation to Cantwell.

Because the events of the novel exist in relation to Cantwell's psychological condition, the Colonel's military attitude is extended into a metaphor for life in general. Upon this conceit the novel turns, and all aspects of conduct and behaviour become militarised. For the Colonel civilisation pivots upon war, the present represents a continuation of past wars, and the terrain is peopled with imaginary soldiers. Hemingway surrounds the Colonel with martial imagery, so that even Renata's love becomes 'armour'. This provides a fictional explanation of the apparent absurdities that litter the novel and have aroused the wrath of Hemingway scholars, seeming to be elements of self-parody or posturing. They *are* gestures, frequently empty ones, without grace of execution, and it is fictively appropriate that they should be so. It is a sign of the Colonel's condition that a bathroom should be transformed into a 'defensive' rather than an 'attacking' one

(p. 111), that he should have his 'flanks' covered in a bar, that when he walks to meet his girl he synchronises his watch as if going on a military operation; this is plausibly the way the reader would expect a dying ex-general to act. The Colonel's eyes are once likened to the 'hooded muzzle' of a tank's gun which shows that Cantwell has become himself a mindless weapon of war; like Marlowe's Faustus he has exchanged his soul. In return he has witnessed phosphorised German corpses eaten by dogs, and he is haunted by the death of his brother Gordon, possibly by deliquescence or as food for land crabs. It is not hard to understand how Cantwell has reached the situation where he believes only in the 'occasional' bravery of man which is a 'mystery' and in 'the act of presence' a man makes for a woman in lovemaking.

Some of the ambiguities in Colonel Cantwell's character stem from the contradictory impulses that seem to have motivated his creator. Hemingway, by temperament a descendant of the American volunteer, the continuum that stretched from the Minuteman at Lexington and Concord, through the Kentucky Rifleman at the Battle of New Orleans to the Ambulance Drivers in France and Italy, was at heart an amateur of war, paradoxically opposed to institutionalised militarism. In creating an authority figure, like the ex-general, Cantwell, Hemingway draws upon many of his own military theories (interestingly, Philip Young has testified to the extensive library the novelist possessed of books on military history and strategy).[9] Cantwell, by means of a wealth of accumulated textual details, is presented as a thoroughly convincing fictional ex-general, but, unlike Mailer's General Cummings, who enjoys the abuse of power, Cantwell feels schizophrenic about his own high rank and prefers to think of himself as a common soldier.

The ex-general thus subsumes two diametrically opposed facets of the American military ethos, a hostility towards professional soldiery and its antithesis, an involvement in the mystique and dignity supposedly conferred by war. Professor Marcus Cunliffe, in his study *Soldiers and Civilians: the Martial Spirit in America, 1775–1865*, explores this clash up to the end of the Civil War. Cantwell epitomises the further development of this tradition, since he reveres military élitism, manifested in the group of veterans that comprise the Order of Brusadelli, and yet reveals himself to be anti-militarist in the disparaging attitude he displays towards the military overlords who are his superiors. In this psychological ambiguity Cantwell acts as an American archetype. Writers, at least from Whitman onwards, have exemplified the dichotomy: while hating war, and, presumably, peace-time armies, they have found the idea of enlisting as a volunteer in war-time compulsively attractive; the list of names is impressive, and includes such as Alan Seeger, Joyce Kilmer, Robert Sherwood, Dos Passos, Cummings, Stallings and, of course, Hemingway himself – all were perhaps initially magnetised by what Professor Cunliffe has called the potential triumph of 'spontaneity' over 'premeditation', the belief that in war an American is, in some arcane way, ennobled and purified, enabled to transcend the narrow limits of his nationhood.

Cantwell's traumatic experiences develop in him an awareness of the cycle of life. His psychological mutilation becomes an agent of understanding and contributes to the incremental unity of the book. The Colonel, like the crippled duck he uses as decoy, has no biological choice, for he recognises that 'He who dies on Thursday does not have to die on Friday.' This mature cognisance that there is a system, biologically ordained, in which man has his place enables Cantwell to contemplate his own death in transcendental terms and to reflect upon it as a contribution to the beauty of terrain:

> They passed the long line of boats in the slow canal that carried water from the Brenta; he thought about the long stretch of the Brenta where the great villas were, with their lawns and their gardens and the plane trees and the cypresses. I'd like to be buried out there, he thought. . . .
> For a long time he had been thinking about all the fine places he would like to be a part of. The stinking, putrefying part doesn't last very long, really, he thought, and anyway you are just a sort of mulch, and even the bones will be some use finally. I'd like to be buried way out at the edge of the grounds, but in sight of the old graceful house and the tall, great trees. I don't think it would be much of a nuisance to them. I could be a part of the ground where the children play in the evenings, and in the mornings, maybe, they would still be training jumping horses and their hoofs

would make the thudding on the turf, and trout would rise
in the pool when there was a hatch of fly.   (p. 35)

Such a passage works redemptively to suggest an elemental
process of regeneration.

The novel's coherence derives in part from the fictional
strategies that Hemingway deploys, and these are mainly
consequent upon the narrative technique, which recalls that
of interior monologue, as Peter Lisca has analysed in an
interesting criticism of the novel.[10] An example of these new
strategies, which Lisca discusses, is the subtle use of thematic
metaphors as extensions of the Colonel's consciousness. The
lonely and homeless soldier, the exiled international man, is
thrown into relief by these images of his condition. Cantwell,
whose only 'fatherland' derives from the salvation of sex, is
profiled against the stark game marshes where magnificent
ducks are ensnared by treachery. The narrator absorbs him
into other symbolic structures that measure the hiatus between human aspiration and the actuality of existence.
Cantwell, the Napoleonic figure, the prematurely old soldier,
wearily grappling with an imagination diseased by war,
meditates with humour in the fish market upon the shrimps
and lobsters that like himself await their 'immortality'. Here
his intuitions are near to poetry. He celebrates life in the
empathy he reveals with these creatures, and objectifies his
own fate; thus his own mind has passed beyond suffering and
he attains tragic stature:

> A market is the closest thing to a good museum like the
> Prado or as the Accademia is now, the Colonel thought.
> He took a short cut and was at the fish-market.
> In the market, spread on the slippery stone floor, or in
> their baskets, or their rope-handled boxes, were the heavy,
> grey-green lobsters with their magenta overtones that
> presaged their death in boiling water. They have all been
> captured by treachery, the Colonel thought, and their claws
> are pegged.
> There were the small soles and there were a few *albacore*
> and *bonito*. These last, the Colonel thought, looked like
> boat-tailed bullets, dignified in death, and with the huge eye
> of the pelagic fish.

They were not made to be caught except for their voraciousness. The poor sole exists, in shallow water, to feed man. But these other roving bullets, in their great bands, live in blue water and travel through all oceans and all seas.

A nickel for your thoughts now, he thought. Let's see what else they have.

There were many eels, alive and no longer confident in their eeldom. There were fine prawns that could make a *scampi brochetto* spitted and broiled on a rapier-like instrument that could be used as a Brooklyn icepick. There were medium-sized shrimps, grey and opalescent, awaiting their turn, too, for the boiling water and their immortality, to have their shucked carcases float out easily on an ebb tide on the Grand Canal.

The speedy shrimp, the Colonel thought, with tentacles longer than the moustaches of that old Japanese admiral, comes here now to die for our benefit. Oh Christian shrimp, he thought, master of retreat, and with your wonderful intelligence service in those two light whips, why did they not teach you about nets and that lights are dangerous? Must have been some slip up, he thought.   (pp. 192–3)

It is significant that even in this passage military imagery is functional as the Colonel is depicted comparing the shrimp with a 'Japanese admiral', and praising it as a 'master of retreat' whose 'intelligence service' was unfortunately inadequate. After the shoot, dead ducks are also conceived in martial terms: 'They were laid in groups that were never of the same number. There were a few platoons, no companies, and, the Colonel thought, I have barely a squad.' This consistently military ambience of *Across the River and into the Trees* creates the quality of *Gestalt*, and may be a factor in the 'calculus' that Hemingway believed he achieved in the novel. It is probable that, as Peter Lisca has suggested, critics have brought to the book a set of assumptions narrowly based on the novelist's earlier canon. *Across the River and into the Trees* remains an under-rated novel: it possesses a complexity inhering in the interaction between its verisimilitude and its more symbolist and poetic qualities. As a study of failure and *nada* it has at times a tragic intensity. Although not, as the novelist is reputed to have once thought, his best novel, it represents an admirable attempt to write in what for Hemingway was a radically new fictional mode.

GROUP IDENTITY: COZZENS, JONES, HERSEY

In our previous discussion of Second World War fiction the most characteristic of all fictional creations is probably Norman Mailer's Robert Hearn, the confused intellectual who loses both his moral and social bearings in what the narrator describes as 'the isolation of the army'. Hearn cannot establish creative rapport with his platoon, despite his former left-wing idealism, and he has severed his connections with the prosperous officer class whose conduct reminds him of the materialist ethos of his father's family. The reader of *The Naked and the Dead* is assailed by the novel's prevailing nihilism; little spiritual or social affirmation seems possible in an environment dominated by such proto-fascists as Cummings and Croft. The novels of Hayes and Burns also reinforce the metaphor of the individual's descent into spiritual *nada*, since the American army, by its degenerate practices, shows little moral concern for the indigenous population that it should assist. Hemingway's *Across the River and into the Trees* completes the totality of nihilistic statement through its more metaphysical study of Colonel Cantwell's descent into *nada* which derives from his traumatic military experiences.

In the remaining analysis of Second World War fiction an attempt will be made to locate, in three novels, *Guard of Honour*, *From Here to Eternity* and *The Wall*, a preoccupation with group identity as a significant fictional theme. *From Here to Eternity*, for example, provides an interesting contrast with *The Naked and the Dead*. In Jones's novel many of the negative forces that lead only to despair in Mailer's translate into a positive impetus towards rebellion. Prewitt, Jones's hero, transforms the philosophy of psychic aggression (manifested in Mailer's Cummings) and physical violence (the mainspring of Croft) into affirmative revolt. The hatred of officers, too, so sickeningly demonstrated in Mailer's novel when Hearn is insulted verbally by his platoon, after his unnecessary death, contributes in Jones's novel towards the formation of a constructive impulse which binds the enlisted men together. The values of the political hobo, discarded by Mailer's cynical Red Valsen, motivate Jones's Prewitt whose elementary intimations of social reconstruction validate his own defiant death. An alternative trajectory towards group belonging, manifested in the collective humour of Jones's soldiers when directed against the ubiquitous 'them', may be traced in Gould Cozzens's very different army novel, *Guard of Honour*. Cozzens's novel endorses the viewpoint of the army executive. (A similar concern with the solidarity and standards of the officer class may be noted elsewhere in Second World War literature: in William Wister Haines's flag-waving play, *Command Decision*, for example, where the army is conceived of as a 'receivership' for the failures of the people, and senior officers accept a consequently onerous institutional responsibility. Herman Wouk, too, in *The Caine Mutiny* and *Winds of War* later, and James Michener in *Tales of the South Pacific*, celebrate and uphold the competence of the élites directing the forces' administrative hierarchy.)

A difference of emphasis characterises John Hersey's subtle work, *The Wall*. The title of this novel may be read ambiguously to refer either to the wall erected by the enemy to contain the Jewish inhabitants in their ghetto or as referring to the psychological wall behind which the oppressed people ultimately defend themselves. Formally, too, Hersey's novel confronts the historical situation of the Second World War in an interesting way; the novel's bulwark solidity enacts the resistance of its characters, their underground tunnelling. Hersey's massive accumulation of detail, purporting to be factual documentation, fictively conveys the actions of a stern collective purpose that will not allow itself to be broken. Hersey's fictional technique, which rests on the stratagem that the novel synthesises actual letters, an epistolary method often used by historical novelists in the eighteenth and nineteenth centuries in England, further suggests artistic integrity, a concern to be both accurate and just. Hersey exploits the illusion of reportage to depict the horrific and bestial nature of the Second World War. The 'documentary' firmness of *The Wall* contrasts with the genre of frame novels which infer alienation by their loose narration of compartmentalised lives. Conversely, the convention of verisimilitude in Hersey's novel is employed fictively in the cause of social commitment. The psychologically disturbing nature of the conflict provides Hersey in *The Wall* with the means of showing through synecdoche how a nation fights for ethnic survival. Thus stating the verities of the Second World War, Hersey's technique reveals considerable flexibility and points to the heterogeneity of formal approaches that were open to Second World War novelists and rarely capitalised upon. *The Wall*, through its aesthetic, creates the illusion of ideological stasis; in this ghetto, if the reader pauses and draws together all the significance of other theatres of combat, the distinctive meaning of the war is being dramatised. *The Wall*, like the other novels that are discussed in the remaining part of this chapter, substantiates the hypothesis that the Second World War as a fictional topic allowed the novelist to treat the matter of social regeneration and to pursue affirmatively collective experience that enabled the individual to transcend his alienation within a wider group identity.

Taken together, *Guard of Honour*, *From Here to Eternity* and *The Wall* delineate patterns of conduct and moral principle that enable the single man or woman to reverse the energies seeking to minimalise the individual's basic human significance. In the fiction of Jones, Hersey or Cozzens the reader encounters characters vastly different from Joseph, the hero of Saul Bellow's *Dangling Man* (1944). Joseph, a former Communist, naturally opposes fascism and believes that it must be countered by force, and yet he wishes to hold on to personal neutrality, willing to be 'a member' of the army and yet distinctively separate also, not 'part of it'. The novels now to be discussed briefly in this chapter, portray through their fictional structures and imagery characters whose positions have been reached by passing beyond Joseph's neutrality into some form or other of commitment usually of an unformalised nature. In Jones and Cozzens the principal characters are 'of' the army, conformist or non-conformist according to the reader's own point of view; and in *The Wall* belonging and transcendence accrue from courageous resistance to Nazi oppression.

Most of the Second World War novelists discussed in this chapter as a whole employed a loosely social realist fictional model, and few of the works examined reveal profound interest in aesthetic innovation. Such experiments as Mailer's Chorus, Patrol, and Time Machine or the popular frame novels do not demonstrate intensely energetic formal experimentation. James Gould Cozzens, a US army major in wartime, produced in *Guard of Honour* (1949) a novel broadly within this generic tradition.[11] Its narrative, pointing a three-day crisis at Ocanara, an Army Air Forces training base, depends upon a slender and harmonious plot dramatised through an accumulation of subordinately relevant fictional detail. Cozzens's prose seeks for urbanity of manner and repudiates the coarseness and army slang deployed by such novelists as James Jones or Norman Mailer in their attempt to recreate a plausible idiomatic rendering of service life.

Cozzens creates a panorama of the Ocanara air base, although his standpoint is selective, being angled consistently from the officers' point of view. In this he is the antithesis of James Jones, who firmly supports the enlisted men in *From Here to Eternity, The Pistol* and *The Thin Red Line*; Cozzens's brother officers, particularly the high-ranking ones, form a social élite whose conduct is governed by unwritten laws and whose lives are linked together by 'a sacred unfailing bond' (p. 373). Cozzens's novel renders a subtle study of army diplomats and men of action: the novelist narrates the ramifications of an internal political affair, evoked through the events of a few days which reveal considerable implications for the chain of command. An old officer shoots himself; there is a racial incident at the base; the commanding officer nears nervous exhaustion; and finally an accident occurs when parachutists die through carelessness.

Cozzens seems fascinated by the psychological motivation of bureaucrats, to whom his narrator appears sympathetic, in the workings of the army's large-scale organisation. One of the novel's principal motifs derives from the interplay between the administrative minds of such as Colonel Ross, and the active military mind, represented principally by General Beal. Ross, an ex-judge, mirrors the philosophy of conservatism in his attempts to impose order on the events which threaten danger to the status quo. He believes that he must protect the interests of his brilliant but erratic commanding officer, Major-General Beal, and control the racial disturbance that has arisen on the base. A group of negro fliers have been assigned to Ocanara, which precipitates colour prejudice, because many of the Southern officers wish them to be excluded from communal recreational facilities, including an officers' club. Ross tries to persuade the negroes to accept segregation, himself convinced that, as prejudice exists, it regrettably cannot be changed overnight and must thereby be complied with. He respects the professional expertise of the fliers, but limply accepts that their rights as men must be limited in the interests of army stability. Ross's constitutionalism, his belief in freedom and loyalty, does not, therefore, extend to the black minority, which suggests that his pragmatism is without a true sense of social responsibility. In his handling of the racial theme, widespread in Second World War novels, Cozzens, therefore, adopts a more compromising position than that of his fellow novelists. The novel seems unsympathetic towards the movement for racial integration enacted historically by the American legislature during the war years.

The overall philosophical consideration in *Guard of Honour* relates to the good of the serice, which Cozzens interprets in a different way from such as Jones and Mailer by reversing the generally derogatory post-Hiroshima attitude to the abstraction of military 'honour'. Cozzens's heroes, high officers such as Colonel Ross and General Beal, believe instinctively in the concept of 'honour', and liberals who discredit it as obsolete are 'somehow odd and unpatriotic'. Whereas in many Second World War novels epauleted officers are depicted as vicious or incompetent, in *Guard of Honour* they are portrayed sympathetically. In the class warfare that underpins many novels of army life Cozzens is iconoclastically of the right, which predisposes his narrator to view the army as an organism where each man has his appointed place and rôle, and where officers govern legitimately. This intellectual position does not prevent his narrator being critical of the deficiencies of individuals, but it ensures that the novel supports imaginatively the pyramid of power, which is 'the good old army way' (p. 374). In the last resort, Cozzens admires the 'brave old army team', although his narrator may joke about its limitations, which is why its lame ducks are exonerated. Excuses are made, for example, for the impatient and angry Major Post, who has only one arm, or for Lieutenant-Colonel Carricker, because he is a combat veteran. These men have served their country faithfully, and are the novelist's equivalent of Mailer's veterans such as Red or Croft.

Cozzens's novel glamorises 'the proprietary, paternal instinct of command', which covers up for its own, and which deplores spies, troublemakers, or informers, such as the radical Edsell, a writer in civilian life, who has become 'disaffected' enough to co-operate with the negro officers in their grievances. Through this support Edsell, it is implied, disloyally helps the enemy, since he disrupts the smooth working of the United States military. He is derogatorily referred to as 'a well-known sorehead' or an 'agitator' (p. 491), the kind of man who would be a hero to Irwin Shaw or John O'Killens: only a Cozzens or a Herman Wouk would regard Edsell's qualities unsympathetically.

The gentlemanly code, lightly referred to in *Guard of Honour* by Ross as 'the West Point Benevolent and Protection Society', seems to be intellectually appealing to Cozzens, whose narrator finds stimulation in the hierarchy's capacity to transform its workings into codes of loyalty. The high officers abide by common rules, and have a genuine familial regard for each other, as Bus Beal, the Old Man, or Jo Jo Nichols conceive of themselves wholly as a team. Although the fliers and their senior officers engage in promotion struggles and intrigue, their lives are dignified through their intuition of belonging to a community. That is why the novelist fastens on to the customs and rituals of the airmen, because such convention and ceremony shapes the daily life of the base and provides a traditional sense of continuity. It is implied that there is something positive and encouraging about being an old army man with a sense of clarity about one's place within the pattern. Even the dead pilots are 'not forgotten' and will not go 'unrevenged' while the living, for 'economical considerations', use the equipment they have left behind. The imaginative sense of interdependence, of command responsibility distinguishes *Guard of Honour*, setting it above other air-force novels, such as John Hersey's combat novel *The War Lover*. Ultimately Cozzens's sense of army mutuality is born out of this romantic admiration for authority.

As Frederick Hoffman notes,[12] the characteristic Second

World War novelist went to war in his formative years with almost no knowledge of normal life to reinforce his war writing; in this respect Cozzens's characters have a different experience. His principal character, Ross, is called to duty from a happy home life, and both he and Major-General Beal are portrayed in domestic situations, which extends their range as fictional creations. Whereas Mailer often creates characters who seem bemused and disorientated by the experience of war, Cozzens's characters successfully relate war to a scale of peace-time values. Mailer's device of 'The Time Machine' gives the impression of being a clumsy and artificial fictional technique to set the characters within their past history, which lacks the ease with which Cozzens's creations behave according to their past lives. *Guard of Honour* thus goes some small way to attaining a gradual social progression from peace to war.

Guard of Honour eschews egalitarianism, and its principal characters act deferentially towards vested interests since they wish to avoid debâcle and to preserve a sense of order, almost eighteenth-century in its fastidiousness. That is why Ross advocates tact and the practical politics of postponement on controversial issues such as racial integration. Cozzens's heroic characters are lucid and conscientious, frequently with self-imposed moral strictures, as in the case of Captain Nathaniel Hicks, who, after being reluctantly unfaithful to his wife, remains soured by the experience. Conduct, whether individual or social, must, it is implied, work for order and restraint if the alternative is not to be the sort of *nada* and cultural chaos that inform Mailer's *The Naked and the Dead*. Cozzens's heroes reject rebellion; they believe that, without authority, the army, like any other organisation, falls into anarchy. The structures of command provide security for them in the same way that society holds together through its corporate bonds. Unfortunately, as the instance of racial segregation illustrates, Cozzens's sympathetic characters do not always manifest the critical intelligence to engage social issues in a morally serious way. Cozzens's picture of army life, which excludes the viewpoint of the rebel, is as distorted as that of James Jones: whereas Jones's heroes detest officers, Cozzens's hardly acknowledge enlisted men. Both novels are ultimately out of focus and lack the social range of characterisation demonstrated by Norman Mailer in *The Naked and the Dead*.

Like Hemingway, whom he often resembles in his accentuation of physical power and in his avowed anti-intellectualism, James Jones is a prolific war writer, returning to the theme of soldiering again and again in his work. *The Pistol* (1959) and *The Thin Red Line* (1962) followed *From Here to Eternity* (1951), Jones's most impressive war novel, which exalts those who will not conform to the army's authoritarianism. The main thread of narrative in *From Here to Eternity*, set in Schofield Barracks at the time of Pearl Harbor, delineates Prewitt's, its hero's, rebellion and his defiance of his commanding officer, who tries to intimidate him into boxing. Jones himself, who was awarded the Purple Heart and twice reduced to the ranks, seems to have been something of a 'romantic revolutionary' like Prewitt. *From Here to Eternity*, written in a language drawn from barracks life, both celebrates and bemoans army life, stimulating Maxwell Geismar to write,

> The novel is correctly, if ironically, dedicated to the United States Army, and beside it, the war novels of writers such as Norman Mailer or Irwin Shaw are 'lit'ry' or derivative or simply lacking in the knowledge which James Jones has absorbed through his rebellious blood and bones.[13]

Jones's fiction seeks to imitate the artful simplicity of folk art and to dispense with undue intricacy either of form or language, since these are inappropriate for a novelist writing from the point of view of the inarticulate soldier. *From Here to Eternity* extends formally and thematically the genre of social protest fiction common during the 1930s, and it translates the former's class warfare into a military setting. Jones, in depicting the men's conflict with their officers, exposes the less salubrious aspects of army training, those that are rarely written about, such as life in the stockade or the whorehouse. The novel is exceptional for its protracted investigation of the abuses of military power, and for its fictional genre of realism. Its naturalistically rendered scenes of internal army violence are among the most brutal in Second World War fiction and are conveyed in a tone of genuine outrage.

If they cannot get a 'piece of ass' or arrange a 'shackjob' or a visit to Mrs Kipfer's whorehouse, Jones's soldiers are either gambling or reading comics. His novel takes a worm's-eye view of man, and his soldier's quotidian morality may be likened to that of the rooster, but, despite the blood, sperm and sweat his heroes frequently exude, Jones's men are imaginatively alive. They move stoically through a tough environment, and in the best of them, such as Prewitt or Maggio, according to Jones's narrator, survives the pioneer spirit, a disappearing element of the American tradition. Jones defends his 'straight duty' men with as much fervour as Cozzens his officers, and similarly excuses their short-comings; for 'everybody sticks the dog face'.[14] They fight each other, for example, merely because 'the real enemy is hard to find'. Jones's account of barracks life is the most intimately rendered of any American novelist. His narrative buttonholes the uninitiated reader with a mass of information; for example, when the narrator describes fatigues, he lists all of the duties the soldier must perform, down to that of emptying the officers' wives' menstruation pads out of the bins (p. 82). The reader also encounters 'the twenty per cent men', the regimental money-lenders, and accompanies Prewitt and Maggio on a 'queer hunting' trip where money is extorted from homosexuals. Little concession, as in Cozzens, is made to reticence: when Jones writes about the whorehouse he spares few details.

In the 'close comradeship' of the card game or the drinking bout the outsider or misfit sheds his loneliness, and the army becomes a 'multiplication' of one's identity, which gives the individual soldier a sense of permanence (p. 262).[15] Always on the lookout for evidence of nonconformity, Jones's narrator divides the soldiers of the 'Pineapple' army into 'jockstraps' and 'non jockstraps', the former asserting that they represent qualities of leadership, the latter disgusted at this method of getting on. Captain Dynamite Holmes, Prewitt's superior officer, himself seeking promotion, suggests that 'good athletics makes for good soldiering', and in his company the route to success is through boxing. Prewitt, a boxer of merit, who has inadvertently injured a man in the ring, will not box for the squad, although fully aware that, if he were to do so, he would be favoured by Holmes. The system of preferment enrages Prewitt and Maggio, and top sergeant Milt Warden, similarly 'wild and woolly', who rejects a commission because he hates the complacency of middle-class officers. Warden feels contemptuous of officers, who are either 'leather cavalrymen' like Holmes or blimpish professionals subsisting on private incomes.

In *From Here to Eternity* officers are depicted as either bunglers, scoundrels or neo-fascists, such as Sam Slater, whom Holmes admires. In one of the few intellectual discussions in the novel Slater outlines his theory of domination, which sounds curiously like the philosophising of General Cummings in *The Naked and the Dead*. Slater believes that the enlisted men must be broken, as no individualist can be allowed to withstand the tyranny of the officers, who govern through cruelty (p. 333 ff.). Each man has a 'degree of apprehension', which the superior officer must gauge and exploit to the army's advantage; the consequence of this theory is that rebels such as Prewitt and Maggio are driven to the Stockade. Here the recalcitrant individual is broken systematically, and humiliated both physically and psychologically. The Stockade chapters stand out as among the most memorable in the whole of Second World War fiction, and are imaginatively intended as a vindication of Prewitt's rebellious attitude, since they show in its clearest form the oppression of the enlisted man by the discipline of fear. Here the novelist makes his most profound affirmation of human endurance and heroism in his portrayal of the men of Number Two Barracks, the élite who defy their punishment and emerge undefeated. They absorb much physical punishment, like Maggio, disfigured by constant workings over in the 'Gym', or they may die, like Blues Berry, at the hands of the sadistic Fatso Judson, whom Prewitt later kills out of revenge. Jones rejoices in their solidarity, and in the tenderness and wisdom that their pointless physical pain induces. *From Here to Eternity* subversively commends the resistance of the outlaw soldier who stays true to himself (see Book IV, 'The Stockade'). The novel's viewpoint seems unwilling to apply conventional moral strictures, even in the case of John Dillinger, whose mental mutilation at Schofield prompted him to be revenged afterwards upon the United States as a whole.

Prewitt, the novel's hero, emerges as one of the outstanding creations in Second World War fiction. The events of his past life and his career in the army are complicated by irony, because temperamentally he cannot help behaving as 'a bolshie'. His refusal to bend is interpreted as arrogance by his superiors to whom he represents a threat, and eventually he alienates them completely. When involved in a fight with Ike Galovitch, a noted 'jockstrap', Prewitt is court-martialled, and refuses to save himself by informing the army authorities that his assailant carried a knife. His rebellion is therefore extreme, almost to the extent of being masochistic. His underprivileged background, which Jones narrates in a tone of grim humour, prepares us for his bizarre affection for a whore and for his ironic death when shot by his own side after deserting.

Towards women the narrator of *From Here to Eternity* adopts an ambiguous attitude. In the case of Karen Holmes the reader sympathises with her disillusionment, exonerating her infidelity on the grounds that her husband gave her venereal disease, but the novel seems to be more at home imaginatively in Mrs Kipfer's whorehouse. Mrs Kipfer chooses 'to do her bit towards total victory' after Pearl Harbor by keeping open for trade. Military metaphors are also used by Lorene, Prewitt's whore, to describe her decision to become a prostitute: she too conducts herself as one of the 'enlisted', and opens in business 'just like a grocer'. The majority of the soldiers in *From Here to Eternity* take a sexually predatory view of women and the women prostitutes naturally adopt an economic view of themselves. Violence supplies the chief yardstick for evaluating character in Jones's novel, providing a test by which men may measure themselves. Jack Malloy, an intelligent theorist, who reminds the reader of 'a latter day Robin Hood' or a 'twentieth-century Jesse James', does not shirk from punishment, but takes no more than necessary. In this he reacts more subtly than Maggio, whose insolence invites his beating up, thereby illustrating the criminal-hardening process. In the case of Bloom, one of the few unsympathetic portrayals of Jews in Second World War literature, lack of physical courage becomes a contributory factor towards suicide. *From Here to Eternity* seems to over-emphasise the dominance played by physique in army life: even the novel's minor heroes, such as Maylon Stark, reveal themselves to be capable of physical outbursts, or, like the hard-drinking, impassive Chief Coate, they are legendary athletes resting on their laurels. The most verminous characters, those such as Fatso Judson, use their strength to intimidate their own class.

From Here to Eternity narrates a pattern in which the enlisted man, through his own achievements, triumphs over all attempts to degrade him. Jones's prose conveys the novelist's intense egalitarianism, as, for example, the narrator describes Prewitt's genius for bugling, which takes on symbolic import through its powers of communion; such a passage, of considerable imaginative power, builds cumulatively, and indicates the linguistic vitality of Jones's novel. The extract refers to the playing of Taps:

There was no placid regimented tempo to this Taps. The notes rose high in the air and hung above the quadrangle. They vibrated there, caressingly, filled with an infinite sadness, an endless patience, a pointless pride, the requiem and epitaph of the common soldier, who smelled like a common soldier, as a woman once had told him. They hovered like halos over the heads of the sleeping men in the darkened barracks, turning all grossness to the beauty that is the beauty of sympathy and understanding. Here we are, they said, you made us, now see us, don't close your eyes and shudder at it; this beauty, and this sorrow, of things as they are. This is the true song, the song of the ruck, not of battle heroes; the song of the Stockade prisoners itchily stinking sweating under coats of grey rock dust; the song of the mucky KPs, of the men without women who come to scour the Officers' Club – after the parties are over. This is the song of the scum, the Aqua-Velva drinkers, the shameless ones who greedily drain the half filled glasses, some of them lipstick-smeared, that the party-ers can afford to leave unfinished.

This is the song of the men who have no place, played by a man who has never had a place, and can therefore play it. Listen to it. You know this song, remember? This is the song you close your ears to every night, so you can sleep. This is the song you drink five martinis every evening not to hear. This is the song of the Great Loneliness, that creeps in like the desert wind and dehydrates the soul.   (Ch. 15)

From Here to Eternity, as much as Cozzens's *Guard of Honour*, demonstrates imaginatively the potentiality of self-validation within the American forces. The familial group identity of enlisted men, and their collective rebellion against the officer class, suggests a coherent and proud life style. The next novel to be analysed, *The Wall*, examines how the historical crisis of the Second World War generated another kind of social awareness under the pressure of threats towards racial extermination.

John Hersey, in *The Wall* (1950), experiments in the documentary and pseudo-journalistic mode of war fiction. *The Wall* purports to be the journal of a Jewish man of letters, Noach Levinson, who interprets the story of the Jewish ghetto in Warsaw. Levinson, a member of the Jewish Council, the Judenrat, which governs the Ghetto, bases his narrative upon official records and personal experience. After the war the journal is supposedly discovered, having been buried to ensure its survival, and a selection made of its contents by a sympathetic editor. The archivist, Levinson, articulates the consciousness of the Jewish people in the ghetto through his own impressions of localised events. The novelist represents him to be a scholarly man who draws upon a wide range of reference material and who exhibits an immense knowledge of Jewish history and literature. The inhabitants of the ghetto, as seen in *The Wall*, change from apathy to militancy and from cowardice to bravery. Following this development, Levinson's account becomes gradually more 'febrile' as the conduct of the oppressed population grows more desperate and heroic. *The Wall* is the most prominent achievement of John Hersey as a war novelist, and, in the opinion of Maxwell Geismar, is one of the most important novels written during the 1950s.[16]

The Wall treats one of the great historical themes of twentieth-century fiction, the psychological results of massive racial persecution.[17] The Jews in the Ghetto initially contribute willingly to their own fate: they are ironically compelled to build a wall separating them from the other inhabitants of Warsaw, and thus are made to contribute to their own humiliation. Their Nazi oppressors try to break their spirit by enforcing the principle of collective responsibilty, and by using a technique of gradual degradation. The first responses of the

Jews produce confusion: some accept the situation almost with relief; others try to buy their way out of the ghetto; many try to escape their Jewishness by pretending to be Polish Catholics. Hersey confronts the scale of the tragedy by creating the illusion of historical documentation, and *The Wall* seeks to persuade the reader of its accuracy by its seemingly authentic command of detail. The novel appears to be thoroughly researched, and the novelist, by using frequent insets and asides, creates a painstakingly detailed recreation of ghetto life. Its characteristic features, such as black-marketeering, torture and psychological servility, are subtly drawn. Civilian inertia, though, slowly gives way to civil disobedience and finally to active opposition.

The effectiveness of Hersey's novel derives from its illusion of being non-fiction. Details are creatively exploited for the purposes of wider inference: children, for example, play a 'Resettlement' game which mirrors the way adults are shipped off to the death camp; a man who faces death disowns his wife, shouts he does not love her, and then chooses to die by her side; men live underground in bunkers, burrowing like animals; a baby is killed because its crying may be dangerous; a man betrays his mother and carries her off to be executed. Hersey's narrative chronicles the indifference of the rest of the world to the Polish Jews' struggle, describes the bitter and prolonged fight in all its phases, and movingly shows how people living in sewers and bunkers retain the ceremony and ritual of their faith. The novel includes a large number of characters, representative of the whole spectrum of Jewish life. They range from Levinson, the man of letters, to Stefan, the collaborator; despite the range of characterisation, the reader is likely to remember the more prominent of Hersey's creations, such as Berson, the defiant central character, who ultimately becomes proud of his Jewishness; Rachel, who transcends her apparent ordinariness and heroically supports the resistance movement; Rapaport, who intellectualises socialist thought; and Pan Apt, a merchant, who deserts his religion and family in order to escape. Characterisation principally supplies the fictional means of providing information and insight for the reader into the fight for survival and also humanises the intellectual and political dimensions of the conflict.

The war novel treats modern civilisation through the fictional attempts made by the novelist to order the larger experience of military conflict and to evaluate its human consequences. *The Wall* suggests the centrality of the genre through its thematic concern with mass death. Hersey reveals an intense interest in the exigencies of survival, and structures his fiction upon the dramatic outcome of the struggle for the continuation of the order and customs of Jewish life. His 'documentation' explores the divisiveness of Jewish political organisations and their internecine struggles, and fictionalises the evolution of Jewish resistance movements and underground organisation. In the face of these manifestations of defiance Jews are compelled to define their own racial feelings and to assert their own ethnic identity. Berson finds himself attracted by the 'meliorism' of the archive being buried; 'the belief implicit in it that man can learn from man's tragedies' (p. 382). The novel implies that war produces Jewish victory as well as defeat, and that the conquered people hold within them the capacity to withstand; thus the novel transcends individual alienation in suggesting affirmatively that a people may collectively learn from tragedy. The characters of the novel thus attain group identity.

The Wall suggests the importance of religious tradition in Jewish life. The novel demonstrates also how such continuity symbolises the survival instinct necessary to a people whose 'offence . . . was existing; they stood guilty of the crime of being alive' (p. 245). Hersey's novel celebrates the endurance of the Jewish people, their enterprise and energy as creators of wealth and builders of cities. This the narrative opposes as a value system against the illogicality of their Nazi oppressors, who give form to some of the twentieth century's most horrific words: those such as 'pogrom', 'genocide', 'liquidation' – what one has come with hindsight to think of as the vocabulary of Belsen. The archive itself manifests through its symbolism a defiant reaction to the obscenity of men and women being herded into box cars like animals. It embodies Levinson's humanistic credo: 'I believe in the simple, one sentence politics of humanity . . . the struggle of Humanity against anti-Humanity.' In this sense the role of the war novelist is epitomised in the scribbling of Levinson, since his creative achievement is to record and mime imaginatively the terror he shares with the victims of war. The war novel, like Levinson's archive, acts as imaginative record:

> Above all we must keep a record. Else how will the world ever know? It may not care when it knows; if there is apathy right here in the ghetto in Warsaw (and there *is*, my God!) . . . what will there not be for ever and ever, at the untouched ends of the earth, in Melbourne, in Rio de Janeiro, in Shanghai, in Chicago.   (p. 426)

The Wall appears to be a most effective work of historical reconstruction, and is written in a careful exact style which reveals little tendency on the novelist's part to rhetoricise. The prose, clinical and fussy, persuades the reader aesthetically that it genuinely represents the work of a theologian and historian. Hersey's technique of documentation, where the reader is barraged with statistics, dates, and minor details, also serves to defuse the emotion latent in the vast scale of tragedy: the facts by being toned down attain a detached quality of verisimilitude. The novel's fictional historiography, that it is a fragmentary and imperfect source book of a historian, contributes to our sense of *The Wall* as a modern historical novel, figures, lists, memoranda being in series pieced together. Hersey's technique sometimes irritates the reader by the seeming excess of non-contributory detail. The novel, for example, has a long-winded build-up, and might have begun more effectively with the erection of the wall itself instead of the novelist providing a mass of detailed background concerning the events leading to it. But the basic technique of gradualism does have compensations: it is helpful for the reader to have each entry of the archive angled from the viewpoint of a particular character.

Hersey was an important Second World War journalist, one of a line of fine reporters (instanced in such works as Steinbeck's *Once There Was a War* or John Gunther's *Inside Europe*); his contribution to the war novel drew upon his journalistic expertise in order to dramatise the scale of racial persecution, and to filter it through the consciousness of one man, Levinson. *The Wall*, despite its diffuse nature, remains an impressive book, almost anthropological in its study of ghetto life where 'nobility like corruption flourishes' under the intense

pressure of imminent death. The ghetto, like the concentration camp, has become one of the holy places of modern
literature. By not showing the degradation of the Nazi oppressors in close up – they are shadowy figures in *The
Wall* – Hersey focuses all the more intensely upon the Jewish
victims. The subject-matter of his novel dramatises the struggle of a community against the encroachment of persecution.
The symbol of the wall itself, with its associations of the Wail-
ing Wall, suggests that resistance can heroically be made
against such attempts to degrade a people or a racial minority.
In such a massive historical enterprise of preservation as that
undertaken by the Jewish population of Warsaw the pressure
of circumstance allows no time for the individual to descend
into *nada*.

8 Second World War Poetry: the Machine and God

Considered as an extended imaginative discourse, American Second World War poetry presents considerable difficulty for anyone seeking to map out a critical diagram or model. The diversity of war poetry, written by both civilians and combatants alike, resists facile survey or definition, and probably all that the critic can usefully achieve in an introductory study is to identify certain nodal points that seem to represent principal poetic configurations. Such an enterprise forms the substance of this chapter which treats war poets and clusters of war poems written directly upon the various facets of the Second World War, and seeks to outline, in consequence, an introductory theory of classification in order that the reader may approach the area with some preliminary guidance. The title 'God and the Machine' conceptualises the antithetical concerns of Second War poets; the chapter, as its analyses demonstrate, might equally aptly have been entitled 'Aesthetics after War', 'The Autonomy of Dream' or 'War as a Social Paradigm'. A broad consideration of Second World War poetry as a distinctive genre and public form opens the chapter, and this initiatory and generalised examination of the literary context and historical situation of the war poets is followed by detailed analyses of the work of individual poets and poems. An attempt will be made to construct a linking generic argument from such a plotting of intersecting poetic dimensions and matrices. The over-arching argument may be briefly introduced as follows.

The war represents in the work of many poets a further collapse of Christian–Judaic civilisation. This cultural situation is treated in poetry through a pattern of imagery dramatising the encroachment of technological warfare in which the machine, the creator of illusory aesthetic spectacle and the dispenser of death, expropriates many of the powers and functions traditionally attributed to God. The combatant, imprisoned like Randall Jarrell's 'boy in the bubble' (an analogy for the airman in the cockpit), suffers grave psychological harm, and only through dream release, visionary memory or psychoneurotic hallucination, or, as in Louis Simpson's poetry, through other modes of psychotic recreation, may the historical and human significance of the war be imaginatively apprehended. Linguistically and culturally, the war poet, to borrow Howard Nemerov's phrase, supplies through his metaphors a guide to the ruins.

At the advent of the Second World War American poets as a group were firm in their ideological commitment to defeat fascism, the social evils of which were copiously treated in literature: such works as Sinclair Lewis's *It Can't Happen Here* (1935) or Edmund Wilson's *To the Finland Station* (1940) demonstrate the energetic repudiation of fascism by the American liberal intelligentsia. The historical contrast with the unpreparedness evidenced in the situation of Seeger and Kilmer over twenty years earlier could hardly have been more striking. This may be illustrated in poetry by the disappearance of the literary trope of the soldier abroad represented as heroic crusader. Such naive stereotyping had vanished forever, and the infantryman or airman had evolved imagistically into a type symbolic of loss and deprivation. Louis Simpson's child-like soldier, abandoned by his officers, offers a central metaphor for the Second War poet's projection of the soldier's situation or Randall Jarrell's imprisoned airman, whose fate Jarrell encapsulated through the image of the 'boy in the bubble'. Another spokesman, the young man of 'Losses' also by Jarrell, suggests the central poetic voice of the Second World War: this youth communicates an aura of psychological disorientation as he follows orders in burning exquisite cities recently learned of in school. The recent past of warfare had been so thoroughly assimilated that the poet, such as Shapiro or Ciardi, who spoke of the continuity of war as a contingent social reality could assume that his educated readers shared his own dislike of patriotic rhetoric. Although some poets, such as Walter Benton, satirised the language of propaganda, this tradition of anti-war writing was by and large so well established that its potentialities had been exhaustively exploited earlier by such men as Cummings. This common ground between poet and reader, the shared dislike of war, presented civilian poets with the opportunity of writing of war with a conviction and authority that non-combatant writers of twenty years earlier did not possess, as a sequence of fine poems by such poets as John Berryman, Robert Lowell, Marianne Moore and Allen Tate clearly proves. (Interestingly, the mass media's coverage of the war in Vietnam also generated a vigorous poetic response from such civilian poets as Denise Levertov and Galway Kinnell.)

The most typical Second World War poet wrote like John Ciardi, in an ironic and slightly self-mocking tone. The new war poets often wrote from a common standpoint of subversive irony, as if, like Ciardi, they were preparing their own fatuous epitaphs just in case (see Ciardi's poem 'Elegy, Just In Case'). This intellectual fifth-columnism, directed not against the opponents of fascism but at the poets' own propensity to adopt heroic postures, obliges them to harden their work with a surface of unbelief so that the creeds in which they believe, notably the integrity of the individual and the continuance of political freedoms under the aegis of a democratic social order, remain mediated, subsumed under the tonalities of a language suggestive of provisionality and doubt. Second War poets often regard the military conduct of the war with considerable scepticism, which translates artistically into verse forms and linguistic expression communicative of detached observation. The plain colloquial style of poetic expression, which owes much to the influence of W. H. Auden, formalised this tentative exploration of social values. For example, several poets, notably Howard Nemerov, Richard Eberhart and Karl Shapiro, deployed an imagery suggestive of theological inquiry, and envisioned a total value-collapse in a war-weary world, dominated by scientific materialism and presided over by an apparently indifferent deity. The poetic treatment of the Second World War displays a propensity towards cultural diagnosis. Aesthetically this manifests itself in the cerebral nature of much war verse: the major thematic preoccupation alluded to above, the analysis of how organised religion failed to prevent the recurrence of war, confirms the poetic impetus to examine social processes (a theme explored at roughly the same time in prose by T. S. Eliot in *The Idea of a Christian Society*). Other poets, such as Allen Tate, relate war to developing historical forces, and evaluate the social determinants of the present conflict from the perspective of the past. Of course, poetry is not cultural sociology, and such short-hand formulations of the critic cannot do justice to the textures and nuances of poetic language, yet it is helpful to note the intellectuality of Second World War poets compared with their predecessors of twenty years earlier. Poets seemed prepared to draw in their verse upon a philosophically 'balanced' vocabulary and not to over-react, poetically speaking, to the war's barbarism.

Jarrell, Wilbur, Lowell, Ciardi, Nemerov, Kunitz, Stauffer, Shapiro, Simpson, the conscript generation of poets referred to in Karl Shapiro's *To Abolish Children and Other Essays* (1968), were conspicuously erudite. They had begun to write, as young men, calling upon their academic backgrounds, and most of them returned, after the war, to posts in universities or colleges. The first-hand experience of war of these writers, except the pacifist Lowell (who had himself unsuccessfully tried to enlist before his imprisonment in protest against Allied bombing), was inevitably modified by their intellectual interests. Shapiro writes revealingly of his fellow poets,

> our generation lived through more history than most or maybe any. We lived through more history even than Stendhal, who fell, as he says, with Napoleon. We were reared as intellectuals and fought the Second World War before it happened and then again when it did happen. . . . None of my generation were war heroes that I remember. . . . In a sense we waited out the war in uniform. . . . Unlike the war poets of the First World War, who never recovered from the experience, our generation did. We inherited an historical perspective which was denied our fathers. . . . The war was of secondary importance to us even when we were part of it. . . . Our poets became the university poets. But the tragedy of our generation – and I believe it is the tragedy – was that our army never melted away. It remained, it grew bigger, it was more and more over the world.[1]

The historical perspective that Shapiro outlines here shaped the initial response of the poets towards their experiences. In place of the strident idealism of Seeger and Kilmer, Second World War poets responded more rationally to the political and social upheavals of war. W. R. Brown, a postgraduate Scholar of the University of Michigan, has identified this tendency when he suggests that the 1939–45 poets tended to employ philosophical lines of inquiry to explore the infra-structures of the war.[2]

One notes a common bond between poets who felt themselves to be psychologically altered by their participation in the war: such a feeling of irrevocable experiential change finds articulation through the soldier's statement in John Ciardi's 'Inscription for a Soldier's Marker': 'War made me and outlived me – The bone skills of a conscript generation shaped me from blood.' It was a self-projection, of a posthumous existence after the war's end, that motivated much war poetry. Karl Shapiro, writing autobiographically in 'Recapitulations', also dramatises the meaning of such an experience, believed by the participant to be so profound that life afterwards was haunted by memories and half-formulated visions of war:

> It was the death he never quite forgot
> Through the four years of death, and like as not
> The true death of the best of all of us
> Whose present life is largely posthumous.[3]

In essence, these lines crystallise the imaginative significance of war for the combatant poet. The veteran who is also a poet capitalises upon his memories of battle, and thereby taps a recurrent poetic source. Many of the poets to be considered in this chapter return again and again in their poetry to investigate, through a variety of metaphors, the destructive potential of machinery. For example, John Ciardi and Robert Glenn Price, who both witnessed the American bombing raids at Saipan, try to offer a poetic consciousness of such mechanised devastation. The imaginative treatment of weapon systems and their strobic generation of a deceptive beauty of motion offers a method of examining the poetry of the Second World War.

Randall Jarrell has emerged as the most permanently interesting of those American poets who wrote extensively of the Second World War. His poems treat a comprehensive range of military activities and personnel, as well as those civilians, especially children, who suffered as a consequence of war's social upheaval. Jarrell's preoccupation stems from a historicist base; his subject-matter and rendition attempt to link the reader to actual historical situations and precise geographical pressure-points such as Haifa or Melanesia or a particular concentration camp in the Prussian forest. Jarrell's war poetry frequently employs the modernist device of the mask, and many of his poems either purport to be the soliloquy of a single person, as in 'Eighth Air Force' or the narrative observations of a well-placed witness as in 'Transient Barracks'. The locale of his poetry incorporates a wide angle. In the British edition of his *Selected Poems* (1956) his war verse begins with a section entitled 'Bombers', which concentrates upon the American Eighth Air Force, its barracks and personnel; this section leads on to 'The Carriers' – as its title suggests, concerned with the airman at sea; other following sub-divisions are 'Prisoners', which examines both American and German prison camps, 'Camps and Fields', taking in base camps and target ranges, 'Children and Civilians', moving from Odessa to Scotland, and, finally, the reprise, 'Soldiers', which reverts to the United States in ideological recapitulation.[4]

At the heart of Jarrell's poetry the airman represents through his situation the primal condition of war. In addition to the fighter pilot, gunner or bomber, two other human images recur in interrelationship, the prisoner and the child; taken together, the situation of these three figures, the airman, the prisoner and the child, provides analogues or a system of parallels for the precise historical nature of warfare, its political energy and its technological demonstration of naked social power. Two opening poems in *Selected Poems* through their metaphors rehearse Jarrell's preoccupations. In 'Eighth Air Force' the thoughtful speaker soliloquises upon the role of his comrades and interrogates their values. Ambiguously their conduct reflects the paradox underlying the war against fascism: the airmen behave, in generic essence, as 'a wolf to man'; they are 'murderers'; as a species of hired assassins 'Men wash their hands, in blood, as best they can' (p. 157). Contrariwise, the narrator recognises the criminal scapegoating process that socially exploits them as instruments, because they are also agent-victims, frightened, child-like and even (according to an overriding equation, it is implied, which prefers 'democracy' to fascism) 'just' men.

Hinted at in 'Eighth Air Force', the image of entrapment provides, in 'The Death of the Ball Turret Gunner', Jarrell's most concentrated analogy for the war's reality in relation to the practitioner airman. In this poem the airman, speaking from beyond death, dramatises his fate; he begins life as a child, trapped in his mother's womb, but also as a prisoner encased in fluid. Life in war extends the metaphors of the child's evolution from the embryo into a counter state of imprisonment, the bubble of the aeroplane cockpit, Jarrell's central image of war. The boy in the plexiglass dome parallels the organism growing sexually in the mother's womb:

> From my mother's sleep I fell into the State,
> And I hunched in its belly till my wet fur froze.
> Six miles from earth, loosed from its dream of life,
> I woke to black flak and the nightmare fighters.
> When I died they washed me out of the turret with
>   a hose.   (p. 158)

Jarrell's poetic impulse towards concretisation, his fusion of intellect and directed passion, resists stereotyping, and the suggestion of mystification, of trans-historical or metaphysical vagueness, accruing from a voice speaking out of death, are flatly dismantled by the precision of his concluding line. War's reality is pinned down by the detail of the pressure-gun steam hose, again washing out the amniotic-like fluid. The ramifications of the imagery, with its suggestions of a new kind of birth into death, of abortion, of 'the State' of elemental biological war, are brought down to earth. Even the 'wet fur' mentioned is grounded in fact, as it refers to the airman's wired fur flying jacket: the flier becomes thus, objectified, a shivering wet animal yet also an instrument of technology. The 'turret' recalls the child's toy castle but is, in reality, an execution chamber.

'Losses' and 'Transient Barracks' further point up the

complexity residual in 'The Death of the Ball Turret Gunner'. Every generation of soldiers presumably subjectivises its own collective identity, believing its situation to be different from that of its predecessors. 'Losses' expresses in its narrative 'we' a clear statement of despair intended to mark the confused awareness of those 1944 pilots who died in combat or training without experience adequate to measure the significance of their deaths. 'We died like aunts or pets or foreigners', the persona reflects, unsure of the morality of his conduct in burning cities learned about in school. Significantly, this poem, like many of Jarrell's (and of Louis Simpson's, to be discussed next in this chapter), also evokes dream and waking-sleeping as psychological referents of war; the narrator dreams of cities and death:

> But the night I died I dreamed that I was dead,
> And the cities said to me: 'Why are you dying?
> We are satisfied, if you are; but why did I die?'
>
> (p. 160)

The unexceptional, unmerited nature of combat death carries over in 'Transient Barracks' to the airman's life of waiting in dread. The flat casualness of this poem with its documentary slowness again implies that reality has become more difficult than ever either to evaluate or to perceive.

Like 'A Pilot from the Carrier' and 'Pilots, Man Your Planes', 'Siegfried' (pp. 163–5), deflating the Wagnerian overtones of its title, deploys the contradictory imagery of tension found in much of Jarell's poetry concerned with the experience of combat. The boy pilot takes on a multiplicity of roles, seeming to be both 'actor' and 'watcher' in his guilty foreknowledge. These three poems re-enact the multiform perceptions of the flier engaged in a separate dog-fight, cut off from normal gravity and subjected to a radical new series of perceptions. His sight vision depends upon his neo-aesthetic stasis, a dream-like state of control that enables him to dispense 'death under glass' and 'switch' on steel that produces flowers of fire. The illusion of being framed inside an infallible magic glass masks a considerable irony. The helpless boy seems to attain the actual properties of his 'machinery of death', the sophisticated aeroplane. The glass and the fuselage become spiritualised, an extension of himself, a humanised skin of steel. The boy under the bubble represents, in his solitary state, the modern nuclear warrior, the technician–scientist, the skilled artificer of weapons control. Jarrell, in the conclusion of 'Siegfried' reverses skilfully the earlier aura of invincibility he has evoked by transforming the action from the sky to the operating theatre; here the magic glass is now the theatre lights and the wire of the airman's jacket translates into the wired artificial leg. The airman's earlier intuition in 'Siegfried' of shell splinters, statistics and bomber patterns, has been turned upon himself; he has not, as he formerly wished, reverted to his natural state, before war, 'let it be the way I was', instead, like Richard Plume, the engine he wears mechanises his former leg. The system of weapons have taken the flier completely over, making him truly 'different, different'; he has 'tasted' now his own blood, and is spiritually and literally grounded. His system of locomotion has been altered irrevocably from a biological one to a mechanistic.

In 'A Pilot from the Carrier' (p. 166) the prisoner, child, airman analogues are overtly fused. The wake of the ship becomes 'a child's first scrawl', the wings blaze 'toy-like', the carrier's smoke recalls the genie of Aladdin's lamp. The airman, though, is trapped, being initially 'strapped at the centre of the blazing wheel' as if in the electric chair. One recalls the mythopoetic image of the airman in Faulkner's short stories, depicted as an archetypal fallen angel, when reading Jarrell's poem of despair. Jarrell's airman, imprisoned in the canopy of the cockpit or hunched in the belly of the green plane, remains locked in, buckles in his groin, trapped and estranged, assailed by fire and tracer bullets. Far from being an aesthetic experience, the perception of a 'pure smear of flame' for Jarrell's pilot, signifies another, blind, black hemisphere. The pilot stays permanently trapped, 'turreted and bucketed with guns', clasped by the parachute or the torpedo fish, incarcerated by the warships' tanks, a victim of 'the bubble, Hope', which explodes only to increase his agony. His exits are existentially blocked by the hardware of battle.

Rarely does the reader detect a hint in Jarrell's poetry of any affirmative outgrowth of war. Even in 'The Dead Wingman' the loyalty and sense of responsibility one flier feels for another seem nullified by the poem's nihilistic conclusion. Expressions such as 'no sign' or the stark negative 'no' are marshalled in 'The Dead Wingman' to connote the futility of the pilot's questing dream in which he searches for his lost wingman. Another expression used chorically in syntactic repetition is 'stubborn', which suggests the way the flier persists in his task, unwilling to give up, and thus his action becomes analogous with those who search in vain for victims of war in other cities that have been bombed beyond recognition, to 'shells' and 'embers' (p. 171). The imagery utilised in 'The Dead Wingman', of 'guttering fires', of the 'darkness' of the carrier and such formidable aspects of terrain as the 'bleak walls of a crater' and 'black firs', emphasises the mood of grief. Interestingly, too, Jarrell's characteristic metaphors of childhood and sleep contribute to the portrayal of an exhausted and distraught unconsciousness: down below, the pilot observes 'a port of toys', and finally his dream ends in sleep.

The imprisonment of the airman by the new technology gives way to another sequence of poems such as 'Stalag Luft', 'Jews at Haifa', 'Prisoners', 'O My Name It is Sam Hall' and 'A Camp in the Prussian Forest', that are precisely concerned with the institutions and forms of imprisonment. 'Stalag Luft' works backwards as the 'I' of the poem, through a process of recall, interprets the experience of incarceration as analogous with keeping rabbits in 'wired-in hutches' or of playing childhood games of being captured. The past environment of rabbits, grass, dappled mustangs and leghorns is made to comment ironically upon present reality. The most significant line in the poem expresses how the child wakes into maturity: 'When I woke the rabbit was gnawing.' 'Jews at Haifa' historicises political captivity by apportioning a central importance to the displaced refugees shunted about 'on the edge/Of the graves of Europe' (p. 177). Such exiles, the poem infers, understand the reality of the modern world, because their experience holistically characterises the turmoil of the post-war West and also the Eastern bloc; the Jews rightly claim to have 'understood the world'. American troops in military prisons form the subject matter of 'Prisoners' and 'O My Name It Is Sam Hall', poems written in neutral tones whose meaning inheres in the conclusion of 'Prisoners':

The prisoners, the guard, the soldiers – they are all, in their
  way, being trained.
From these moments, repeated forever, our own new world
  will be made.   (p. 178)

Jarrell's inference here, of political pawns being shifted
through social relationship into ritualised captivity, is reinforced elsewhere in his war poetry, most prophetically in 'A
Camp in the Prussian Forest'.
  In 'A Camp in the Prussian Forest', a poem set in the
aftermath of a concentration camp, the poetic voice is
plangent, restrained, reverent, appropriate to a poetry of
mourning. An incident is related which dramatises the
immeasurably barbaric nature of the war: a load of dead Jews
is being collected by the Allies from a concentration camp just
after the war has ended, and is being transported for a decent,
orderly funeral. Ironically an American prisoner witnesses
with the narrator the fate of former Jewish inmates:

> Their corpses, stacked like sodden wood,
> Lie barred or galled with blood . . . .   (p. 180)

'A Camp in the Prussian Forest' draws upon imagery of bodies
being consumed by fire, and makes reference to traditional
Jewish symbolism, such as the Star of David, in order to
embody the reality of mass destruction. Jarrell's objective is to
mourn the dead Jews, and to indicate the scope and magnitude of the tragedy in as calm a way as possible. This he
attempts by presenting it in relation to the wooded
background against which the scene takes place. The tone is
consistently elegiac, allowing the horrific details and
obscenities, together with the narrator's own reaction, hysterical laughter, to be framed by a 'profitable' and 'living'
landscape that objectifies them, and makes the scale of the
horror more accessible

> I walk beside the prisoners to the road.
> Load on puffed load,
> Their corpses, stacked like sodden wood,
> Lie barred or galled with blood

By the charred warehouse. No one comes today
In the old way
To knock the fillings from their teeth;
The dark, coned, common wreath

Is plaited for their grave – a kind of grief.
The living leaf
Clings to the planted profitable
Pine if it is able;

The boughs sigh, mile on green, calm, breathing mile,
From this dead file
The planners ruled for them. . . . One year
They sent a million here:

Here men were drunk like water, burnt like wood . . .

The needles of the wreath are chalked with ash,
A filmy trash
Letters the black woods with the death
Of men; and one last breath

Curls from the monstrous chimney. . . . I laugh aloud
Again and again;
The star laughs from its rotting shroud
Of flesh. O star of men!   (p. 181)

'A Camp in the Prussian Forest' is one of Jarrell's finest war
poems, and one of the most effective American poems written
about the atrocities of the Second World War. It is rivalled
only by Louis Simpson's 'The Bird' and 'A Story about
Chicken Soup' and John Ciardi's two poems 'The Gift' and
'Captain Nicholas Strong'.
   Jarrell's war poetry exhibits an intense interest in ideological issues and principles, and in poems such as 'The Wide
Prospect', 'The Soldier' and 'The Sick Nought' the trade
values that the poet believes underpin the Second World War
are polemically treated. Generally Jarrell's statistical imagery
of commodities, exports, integers, units and arithmetical
ciphers functions in a rather nakedly doctrinaire fashion and
does not poetically carry the political thrust that it is intended
to have. Far more effective are poems demonstrating the
victims of war in their abandonment; such poems operate

dramatically to demystify jingoist rhetoric. 'A Ward in the States', 'A Field Hospital', and 'Terms', for example, show the casualties of war in horrific close-up in a manner reminiscent of Sassoon and Owen in the First World War. Most powerfully realised of all Jarrell's war victims, though, is the child: his poetry draws regularly upon the imagery of childhood as shown above, but certain poems – for instance, 'The Truth', 'Protocols', 'Come to the Stone...' or 'The State' – particularise the fate of the bereaved infant deprived of his family or of the symbols of his infant security such as his pets or toys. 'The Truth' most effectively represents this genre of poem; it is a dramatic monologue spoken by a child whose father and sister have died in a bombing raid upon London. Simplicity of language and authenticity of recall derive in 'The Truth' from the child's attempt to recreate an earlier experience, to mediate and interpret as accurately as possible. The reader links this Blake-like poem with earlier imagery of the goggled aviator, helpless above the clouds, or the prisoner of war likewise trapped. Such metaphors form the nucleus of Jarrell's war poetry. The reader has journeyed imaginatively from the airfield camp and transient barracks to the prisoner-of-war stockade, and finally, by way of the concentration camp, to the asylum which houses the disturbed child. All of these situations manifest a pervading psychological imprisonment similar to that suffered in reality by Louis Simpson, whose images often derive from neurasthenic origins.

Louis Simpson, who was born in Jamaica in 1923, served in the 101st Airborne Division of the US Forces. He suffered a breakdown after the war when his memory of battle was completely blacked out, and writing poetry helped him to recapture this. Like Howard Nemerov and John Ciardi, he has continued to write on the subject of war, and *Good News of Death* (1955), *A Dream of Governors* (1959) and *Selected Poems* (1966) incorporate occasional war poems. In *The Poetry of War, 1939–45* (1965), an anthology edited by Ian Hamilton, Simpson describes the therapeutic value of writing war out of his system:

Through poems I could release the irrational, grotesque images I had accumulated during the war: and imposing order on these images enabled me to recover my identity. In 1948, when I was living in Paris, one night I dreamed that I was lying on the bank of a canal, under machine gun and mortar fire. The next morning I wrote it out, in the poem 'Carentan O Carentan', and as I wrote I realised that it wasn't a dream but the memory of my first time under fire. So I began piecing the war together, and wrote other poems. 'Memories of a Lost War' describes the early days of the fighting in Normandy; 'The Battle', the fighting at Bastogne.

In the same passage he details his objectives in writing war poems:

What, in these poems, was I trying to do that had not already been done? I did not wish to protest against war. Any true description of modern warfare is a protest, but many have written against war with satire or indignation, and it still goes on. My object was to remember. I wished to show the war exactly, as though I were painting a landscape or a face. I wanted people to find in my poems the truth of what it had been like to be an American infantry soldier. Now I see that I was writing a memorial of those years, for the men I had known, who were silent. I was trying to write poems that I would not be ashamed to have them read; poems that would be, in their laconic and simple manner, tolerable to men who had seen a good deal of combat and had no illusions.[5]

Simpson's commentary states an intention to recall the war in 'laconic' and 'simple' literary fashion, an artistic mode appropriate to the consciousness of infantrymen 'who had seen a good deal of combat and had no illusions'. Such a theory provides an interesting framework within which to discuss the poet's war verse.

In *The Arrivistes: Poems 1940–49* several poems treat the experience of combat in the literary terms of ballad. Simpson's aesthetic selection renders a formal simplification of the war in which certain key emotions and situations are emphasised to the exclusion of others. The poet has stated above that he wished to order feelings within himself of pathogenic origin, and his war poetry, despite the frequent use of the 'I' voice (for instance, at the end of 'Carentan, O Carentan'), suggests an impersonal process of ordering. Simpson's early war poems, such as 'Arm in Arm' or 'The Men with Flame Throwers', present the war in a heightened, dramatic fashion which substitutes mythology for documentation. The realism of 'Arm in Arm' is the realism of folk ballad. Such an impulse towards objectivity or at least of focusing upon the autonomy of dream recollection is achieved through the poems' capacity to invent their own imaginative environment. A new mythology of war produces mythic figures, frequently as sinister as the warlocks of legend, who inhabit a terrain which initially appears to be Arcadian. The veneer of archaism and the rhythmic patterns of the poems (frequently written in traditional quatrains enlivened occasionally by trochaic variation) lull the reader into a false sense of security before he is confronted by some mysteriously ominous presence such as a man with a flame-thrower or, as in 'Carentan', a grotesque watcher in a leopard suit.

'Arm in Arm' employs Simpson's recurrent motifs. It ostensibly describes a 'Dutch dyke' where 'friend and foe' were piled, and warns the reader jauntily 'Step over as you go'. The Captain or some other member of the officer class is usually found in Simpson's work, and in this poem a dying captain is detachedly laid to rest by 'The little Dutch girl', who seems like a pretty porcelain figure:

> They laid the Captain on a bed
> Of gravel and green grass.
> The little Dutch girl held his head
> And motioned us to pass.
>
> Her busy hands seemed smooth as silk
> To a soldier in the sun
> When she gave him a jug of milk
> In which his blood did run.[6]

The imagery of masking and deception, also frequently found in the work of another poet who wrote of war, Richard Wilbur, is common in Simpson's discourse of myth; here it provides the basis of a lament that the Captain had been unable to protect the men under his command:

> O had the Captain been around
> When trenching was begun,
> His bright binoculars had found
> The enemy's masked gun.

The feelings of insecurity symbolised by this poem, which describes a scene of unmitigated horror, express themselves in hallucinatory language. Simpson's skilfully cultivated air of insouciance, partly carried by the fixity of metre, intensifies the terror of the situation, as, for example, the narrator describes the way the dead were buried, the new dead ranged alongside the old dead of the churchyard:

> Beside a Church we dug our holes,
> By tombstone and by cross.
> They were too shallow for our souls
> When the ground began to toss.
>
> Which were the new, which the old dead,
> It was a sight to ask.
> One private found a polished head
> And took the skull to task
>
> For spying on us . . . .

In Simpson's poetry enlisted men are often abandoned by officers and left to their fate. The conclusion of 'Arm in Arm' continues the distancing effect that the rhythm, imagery and metre have created. The rhyme and syntax of the adapted ballad form objectify the experience, emotion is severely held in check, and even the bombers, compared to shepherds, are rendered in harmless terms:

> Till along
> Driving the clouds like sheep,
> Our bombers came in a great throng
> And so we fell asleep.

A similar kind of visionary poetry, which is also powerfully and ambivalently direct, is the compressed, deceptively simple war poetry of Stephen Crane in *The Black Riders* and *War is Kind*: in both poets dream and reality are confused, and their basic narrative and aesthetic mode exploits pictorial imagery and presentational rather than explanatory symbolism. Like Crane also, Simpson's titles, as in 'Arm in Arm', or 'Carentan, O Carentan', frequently disguise his ironic intentions and serve, initially at least, to de-emphasise and leave unstated the real subject-matter of his verse. Often in these early war poems, Simpson works through structural inferences, and his poetic mode leans formally towards the narrative and fictive rather than the lyrical. Such a preoccupation with narrating a story characterises later war poems, too, such as 'The Bird' and 'A Story about Chicken Soup'.

Simpson's aesthetic and analogical transpositions as displayed in 'Arm in Arm' are similarly manifested in 'The Men with Flame Throwers' and the celebrated 'Carentan, O Carentan'. 'The Men with Flame Throwers' represents the voice of a terrified man, an authentic victim of war who feels himself to be threatened and hunted down by sinister figures, 'captains in cupolas', 'clipped commanders' who are out for blood. All the soldier or persecuted civilian can hope to do, the speaker implies, is to hide from this aloof military junta who remain 'stiff as starch' and who never 'touch blood'. Simpson's poem utilises historical references – for example, to Nagasaki and Flanders – to root the mythic dimension of the poem into reality. A similar historical reference provides the title of 'Carentan, O Carentan', which transmutes the poet's combat experience near this Normandy town with its deceptively romantic sounding name.

The poetic method of 'Carentan, O Carentan' is to employ a narrator to dramatise a situation of reversal. Through skilful deployment of regular quatrains and expressive syntactical repetitions, such as 'the sky was blue', the poem initially evokes a terrain seemingly the antithesis of war, a land peopled by lovers, where soldiers, although in 'combat-interval', meander themselves like sweethearts 'two by two'.[7] The symbolism at first suggests natural order, aesthetic grace and social harmony. Simpson, though, characteristically hints at war through the image of soldiers with rifles likened to farmers with pitchforks and through the reference to far-off artillery (the invasion battleships and destroyers, pounding the beach heads, still conducted their offensive, yet merely 'spoke' to invisible towns). Only in stanza 6 does the war intrude directly, when the narrative shifts dramatically to render an ambush where hostile onlookers, clad in 'leopard suits', seem to act out a preordained plan as they carefully take aim 'between the belt and the boot', intent apparently upon castration. The poem communicates the misery and chaos of battle through what appears to be psychotic recreation, and the soldier's voice implies the fundamental psychological change induced by war:

> I never strolled, nor ever shall,
> Down such a leafy lane.
> I never drank in a canal,
> Nor ever shall again.   (p. 4)

Short sentences here connote the sense of finality in the speaker's decision. Interestingly, Simpson reverses the earlier symbolism of natural proportion, when the flora in stanza 10 become distorted through the unnatural storm of steel, signifying war:

> There is a whistling in the leaves
> And it is not the wind,
> The twigs are falling from the knives
> That cut men to the ground.   (p. 4)

The narrator's address to the silent Master-Sergeant, the napping Captain and the 'sleeping beauty' Lieutenant rounds off the development of Simpson's poem, emphasising the solitary plight and helplessness of the infantryman. 'Carentan, O Carentan' shrouds war within the narrative of the unconscious mind; the speaker of the poem mythologises the events of war in colloquial recall in order to refocus their primal cruelty. 'Carentan, O Carentan', through its controlled anecdotal manner, underplays and ritualises the *danse macabre* of combat.

At its best, as in 'Carentan, O Carentan', Louis Simpson's war poetry suggests by its compression the 'Kubla Khan' genre of dream-inspired automatic writing. Simpson returns in *Good News of Death* (1975) and *A Dream of Governors* (1959) to the task of piecing together a war collage; incidents and memories are ranged alongside each other as the poetic mind selectively refocuses on long-forgotten details. In 'Memories of a Lost War', for example, the poet evokes from the recesses of his mind, as symbolism of human endurance, the tired eyes and thin hands of the soldier clutching the embers of a cigarette. 'I Dreamed that in a City Dark as Paris' from *A Dream of Governors* (we note the frequency of dream terminology of this period), like Simpson's earlier poems, presents another ghost-image of the war; this time the ghost is transubstantiated into the form of a French *poilu* abandoned in a desolate city near to the front. In this dream the 'I' narrating the poem experiences an incubus-like reincarnation into the brain of a *confrère*. Dream, the poem concludes, attains validity, since it offers a method of remythologising past wars:

> The violence of waking life disrupts
> The order of our death. Strange dreams occur,
> For dreams are licensed as they never were.
>
> (p. 39)

Simpson, like Randall Jarrell in his prose-poem '1914', treats the earlier war as if he had participated himself. In part IX of 'The Runner', for example, the parapets of the Great War are peopled by lost figures, forgotten by the living. Simpson's concern with the First World War represents the veteran's poetic reverence for former soldiers, an attitude commonly found among war poets.

Recall expresses itself in Simpson's poetry of the 1950s and 1960s through interesting formal patterning. In 'The Bird' one is reminded of the earlier trance-like ballad poems when the poetic instinct shapes itself narratively, moving fictively to tell a story. The objectivity of 'The Bird' intensifies its powerful investigative thrust, as the horrors of Dachau and Belsen are played down through the strongly stressed quatrain form written in jaunty tone. Historical truth supplies a dimension of actuality to 'The Bird', which, plangently at times, narrates the fates of two German boys, one of whom, Hans, acts as a concentration-camp guard shortly before the Russian occupation of the area. Hans's fate remains uncertain, although he is presumed dead, and his childhood friend, Heinrich, receives a letter returned to him marked 'deceased'. Technically 'The Bird' achieves its concentrated energy from a poetic technique of drastic simplification. Major historical events – for example, the mass execution of the Jews, the Russian liberation of Eastern Europe and the defeat of the German armed forces – frame a minor human tragedy, the loss of a humane German soldier and the separation of childhood friends. 'The Bird' approaches historical truth in a non-literal way; the autonomy of dream as a dynamic of poetic practice and creation produces in the poem the illusion that one is reading a folk interpretation of events and situations. The reader's sympathy is engaged by such features as the ballad form of presentation and the unifying symbolism of the bird itself. The poem's non-representational devices suggest the collective folk memory expressing itself; the truth of German involvement in the war (Nazi guilt and German innocence, symbolised through the concentration camp which is defended by the loyal soldier of the Reich) is inferred by the poem's aesthetics. 'The Bird' exploits dramatic symbolism to communicate a truth which is the very antithesis of trans-historical. The poet's adaptation of old forms, of ballad rhythms and metres, tightly controlled by end rhyme, enables him to articulate in his poetry not one death but many. The contrary tensions in 'The Bird' have their genesis in Simpson's own experience of war; the reader is moved along rapidly and impersonally by the normative and traditional fixity of the metre with its predictable rhyme scheme, and yet the poem also displays a seeming autonomy. The connotations of Simpson's language are public in their orientation: his bold syntax and traditionally textured vocabulary and structures, the regularity of his language, all combine to work ambiguously. The ultimate tensions of the poem, the arc of its feeling, produce unconscious meanings and curious resonances. For example, the story of the friends retains romantic pathos, and yet this is juxtaposed against the working of the gas chambers and also the suicide of the SS guards. Massive historical events seem to be transformed into fairy tale, and the German folk-song which opens and closes the poem suggests the possibility (reminiscent of ballad) of the hero's literal transformation into a bird. This device also enables the poem to offer two versions of events, one the human pogrom, and the other natural events shaped by the forestal environment:

> The banks were bright with flowers,
> The birds sang in the wood;
> There was a fence with towers
> On which armed sentries stood.   (p. 81)

'The Bird' succeeds in inferring, through its veneer of the picturesque, many interesting questions about patriotism, persecution and mass war death: it demonstrates a highly skilled attempt to unite historicism with popular poetic historiography.

'A Story about Chicken Soup', from *At the End of the Open Road* (1963), presents to Simpson's reader an evaluative and retrospective summary of his poetic position *vis-à-vis* the war viewed from over twenty years on. This recapitulation originates from a personal anecdote as the narrator (presumably Jewish) relates how 'there was always chicken soup', but the old-country family were wiped out by the Germans:

> I know it's in bad taste to say it,
> But it's true. The Germans killed them all.
>   (p. 101)

This clipped and truncated version of Nazi brutality becomes supplanted in the poem's second section when, with sharp recall, the 'I' speaker remembers an incident of war. 'In the ruins of Berchtesgaden' a golden-haired German child ran out: she resembled a cuckoo and appeared extremely undernourished; her flesh was 'not even enough to make chicken soup'. The poet and his comrades 'forgave' her, as they had killed her 'mechanical brothers'. Simpson's narrator, by this reference to Allied killing, presents the war in just perspective, as the earlier Nazi atrocities have now been measured against Allied killing. The imagery, of cuckoos and of the orphaned child as raw material for soup, enlivens the poem with a colloquial casualness which enhances its power. 'A Story about Chicken Soup' works through verbal directness; unlike 'The Bird' it exploits no 'literary' veneer. Its free verse form and subtle repetitions of syntax communicate an impact of authenticity: the historical situation, it seems to imply, is here stated in unambiguous and unemotional fashion. The poem's conclusion, separated off typographically from the two previous sections, conveys a note of regret that past events, of an unhappy nature, are believed to be determinants (in the eyes of the narrator's friends) of present conduct. The narrator, conversely, wishes to escape from the past's 'tragic world', which presumably includes the memory and dream of war. One may deduce from the poem the strong hold exerted by past events, including the war, upon the poetic imagination of Louis Simpson.

AESTHETICS AFTER WAR

The title of this section originates from Richard Eberhart's poem 'Aesthetics after War', which questions the notion of war as aesthetic paradigm, and includes the lines

> Was the Italian airman crazy
> When he saw aesthetic purity
> In bombs flowering like roses a mile below?
> He could not see nor feel the pain of man.
> Our own men testify to awe,
> If not to aesthetic charm,
> On seeing man's total malice over Hiroshima,
> That gigantic, surrealistic, picture-mushroom
> And objectification of megalomania.[8]

Eberhart's scholarly tone leaves open the proposition that war is inimical to aesthetic study, although it celebrates as aesthetic spectacle the harmonious beauty of precision instrumentation. The glowing and eerie radar screen, parked aircraft 'wings folded back ethereal as butterflies', and the arithmetical purity of the Mark 18 gunsight, such objects belie their own reality. In perceiving their formal perfection, the poet should also be aware of their illusory nature, for they contribute to a masking of machine-destruction. Such a poetic theme interested a large number of American Second World War poets.

Richard Wilbur, in *The Beautiful Changes, and Other Poems*

(1947) frequently contrasts the grace and elegance found in the setting of war against its true mechanised horror. In his short poem 'On the Eyes of an SS Officer', for example, his imagery attempts to crystallise the 'foul purities' of Nazism, when the officer's eyes remind the poet of 'violent virgin snows' or the 'acetylene eye' of an Indian saint.[9] The imagery of snow and coldness similarly characterises 'First Snow in Alsace' when the 'sparkling combs' and moth-like beauty of the snowfall mask the 'eyes of soldiers dead a little while'. In 'Mined Country' the scenic aspects of terrain are also illusory, since they hide explosive devices that can maim and kill. Wilbur, rather like Anthony Hecht in *A Summoning of Stones* (1954), subtly renders the war as a threat to humane codes of living. A measured and witty poetic attitude to the aesthetics of war is called for, expressed by Wilbur in 'Mined Country' as the writing of a new language to explore war's realities, one antithetical to the values of bullish militarism.

Anthony Hecht similarly expresses repugnance at increasing disorder consequent upon war: at least four of his muted war poems in *A Summoning of Stones* explore the theme of disproportion; they comprise 'Drinking Song', 'Christmas is Coming', 'A Deep Breath at Dawn' and 'Katharsis'.[10] Like the novelist William Eastlake, and his fellow poet Malcolm Cowley in 'Château de Soupir: 1917', discussed in an earlier chapter, Hecht's poetry registers despair at the ruination of the château, which symbolises the creative pinnacle of the European mind. Hecht, in 'Drinking Song', implies chagrin at the despoliation of such aesthetic perfection. In his poetry beauty of a lyrical kind abounds, but suffers quick strangulation: the aesthetic of war necessarily manifests itself as mimetic of the processes of death by instrumentation. In Hecht's 'Drinking Song' the magnificent interior of the château cannot mitigate the five dead Americans lying in the pasture outside. 'A Deep Breath at Dawn' and 'Christmas is Coming' similarly postulate a war-devastated landscape, its formal perfection violated.

Frequently aesthetics after war for those poets who had fought in the Pacific war zone consisted of a particularisation of tropical warfare. Robert Glenn Price, 1918–54, who served in the US army as a staff correspondent, was among the first American troops to occupy Japan. His little-known volume of war poems, *The Hidden Airdrome and Other Uncollected Poems*

(1956), accentuates the large number of civilian deaths
resulting from American aerial bombardment, and stresses
the d isparity between such pointless human suffering and the
idyllic surrounding of the tropics. 'Dead Girl: Saipan' utilises
scenic information to emphasise the corpse's lifelessness: the
native girl is 'sparkling dead', representative of fathers,
mothers and children who rushed into the sea in mass suicide.
Exotic landscape in 'The Fleet Leaves Saipan' is 'shorn', after
having been battered by the US navy. In 'Equinox' Price
employs an extended metaphor to dramatise allegorically the
act of destruction which forms the basis of warfare. The
tortoise's fragile beauty symbolises the reverence for beauty
that is obliterated by warships and aeroplanes, and the poem
compares the responses of two car drivers to the living
creature blocking the road:

> The year's passion – a glaze over a glaze –
> Is the bright occasion of equal day and equal night,
> When the orange husk of the bittersweet
> Opens upon its star-orange berry
> And the tortoise moving in its great suspended dome
> Due east and west across the road
> Is a different thing to two men
> Each driving his own automobile
>
> One swerves to keep from destroying
> The inimitable stroller
> Only to watch in the rear-view mirror
> The other car run down the turtle architecture.
> The thunder of the shell collapsing
> Makes a storm through which the drivers pass.[11]

Price's imagery depends upon the idea of dome-like and
structured harmony perforated by the mindless machine, a
trope central to the poetic understanding of the Second
World War. The image recalls Hecht's despoiled château and
Allen Tate's castigation, in his magnificent 'Ode to our Young
Pro-Consuls of the Air', of the 'gentle youth' who divebombs
ancient cultures and exterminates the Lama, the 'dying swan'
of 'old pain'.[12]

John Ciardi, whose early war poems are included in *Other*

Skies (1947), continues to display interest in the aesthetics of war in *As If, Poems New and Selected* (1955) and in *39 Poems* (1959). The life-style of the airman offers aesthetic possibilities, his propensity to be his own 'dramatist' as in 'Port of Aerial Embarkation' and to cultivate narcissistically gesture and role like an artist. Ciardi, as here, seems fascinated by the façade of war, its exterior beauty. Just as in the wry 'Valentine for a Soldier's Girl' he plays off images of cupids and angels against the reality of aerial combat, so in many of his poems he transforms the gestures and aestheticising self-instincts of men at war into a satire of war itself. His imagination seizes upon the decoratively inappropriate: how, for example, in 'Two Songs for a Gunner', tracer bullets are reminiscent of 'a wild fountain' of light or appear like a 'jewelled cobra', or, in 'On a Photo of Sergeant Ciardi a Year Later', he himself adopted a ludicrously 'fine bravura look of calm' that was utterly deceptive.

Like Robert Glenn Price, Ciardi draws upon the iridescent and the exotic elements of Pacific warfare, and similarly exploits sea and jungle terrain for its illusory beauty. In 'Poem for my Twenty-Ninth Birthday', for example, the papaya grove and tropical pine work poetically to signify the simple, outward 'darkness' of the native, which contrasts with the inner spiritual darkness of the American airman. As much as Eberhart or Jarrell, Ciardi finds shocking beauty in the airborn manoeuvres of the plane as it banks and turns. The geometric perfection of the plane's progress, dependent upon mathematical calculations and wind-computation, invests it with an incarnate god-like beauty: God has become the machine. In 'Massive Retaliation' from *39 Poems* the poem's language invents its own euphemisms to match up to the hiatus between appearance and reality epitomised in the plane's blazing beauty, as it deals its own heavenly law of destruction:

> It was a thousand of ourselves we saw.
> A thousand theorems spiraled from the sun
> to some proof statelier than the thing done.
> A sky-wide silver coming of the Law.[13]

Ciardi's periphrastic poetic diction, in which planes 'pinwheel' and bombs fan out like 'silver sharks', reaches a crescendo in the poem's concluding stanzas where the aerial apotheosis is articulated through apocalyptic symbolism, and the planes, 'like a marriage race of gods', transcend time and human capacities for reason.

Ciardi rejects the camera eye in treating the aesthetics of war; the prismatic charm of air, cloud and waves or the trajectory of the symmetrical, arrow-like plane squadron represent, like the tracer-bullet, diseased 'luminous sperm', the antithesis of life-giving human energy. Ciardi's analysis of war continues, in *39 Poems*, to express the poet's interest in the illusory nature of war situations. Perhaps the outstanding example of this poetic concern with deception occurs in 'The Gift', which portrays the post-war career of Josef Stein, a poet who survived the concentration camp and who continued, after the war, to live and behave as if normal. Stein so disguises his past torment that 'strangers could not tell he had died once'. A similar experience informs Ciardi's narrative poem 'Captain Nicholas Strong', when the Captain, who has entered the concentration camp as American liberator and discovered its horrors, 'dressed again' to face the post-war world. Despite the order of his civilian life, Strong cannot eradicate his loathing and self-disgust at murdering the German guards of the camp and, paradoxically, detesting the Jewish victims whom he rescued. The opening of 'Captain Nicholas Strong', an ornate descriptive passage which conjures forth a prettified dawn reminiscent of Thomas Gray or William Collins, may stand as emblematic of Ciardi's war poetry; for the pearl and blue soon change to horrifying scenes of human skeletons cramming food in their mouths, revolting living corpses which induce shame in the psyche of the beholder.

One of the most interesting formal attempts to poeticise war as an aesthetic paradigm is Richard Eberhart's cunningly structured 'Dam Neck Virginia'. The sane voice of Eberhart's poem, its coolly philosophical tone, balances up the paradoxical aspects of weaponry in motion. The configurations of gunfire, its hyperbolic visual glory, heightens Eberhart's intuition of its nature as illusory radiance. Eberhart's poem, through its restrained imagery of gentle celestial beauty and freedom (the movements of anti-aircraft fire are likened to the controlled motion of falling stars), evokes the ironic grace

of gunfire seen from a distance. The intricate tracery effects
so created seem to outshine natural phenomena in their
splendour of drifting balls of light and sailing parabolas.
Eberhart's principal intention, though, is to point up the
domination of man by the processes of machine war. The
artificial efflorence of gunfire manifests false transcendence,
because the operators of such systems cannot be fully aware of
the destructive potential of their technology. They have
become transformed into the victims of their own scientific
expertise, themselves mechanised spiritually, 'each specialist
himself precision's instrument'. The machine often provides
an emblem in Eberhart's war verse, as in 'The Preacher
Sought to Find Acceptable Words', of the human creature's
propensity, almost akin to a biological version of original sin,
to exterminate its own species. The beauty of gunfire or of the
astral aeroplane, frequently articulated through imagery of
ships and the sea, merely serves to complicate matters,
communicating in one of the poet's most penetrating phrases,
'the beautiful disrelation of the spiritual' (p. 90).

Eberhart frequently draws upon the language and concepts
of Christian philosophy in order to analyse poetically the
energies and situations of war; two of his most admired war
poems, 'The Fury of Aerial Bombardment' and 'At the End of
War', suggest the parameters of his position. 'The Fury of
Aerial Bombardment', written in a language of resigned
melancholy, questions the conceptualisation of a loving deity.
If a loving deity presides over human activities, then how may
pointless wartime killing be interpreted in Christian terms?
Eberhart's poetry frequently employs puns and double
meanings of ironic asides, and in 'The Fury of Aerial
Bombardment' the profound rhetorical questions directed to
interrogate the nature of Godhead cunningly switch, in the
concluding stanza, to comradely concern; such an enterprise
ironically fails because the young military assassins-cum-
schoolboys have been forgotten by the narrator; their deaths
are subsumed in technological devastation, and their names
have become as impersonal as the terminology used in a
training manual:

> Of Van Wettering I speak, and Averill,
> Names on a list, whose faces I do not recall

But they are gone to early death, who late in school
Distinguished the belt feed lever from the belt holding pawl.

The laconic verbal mode incriminates the operations of the
machine in their anonymous deaths: Van Wettering and
Averill, like the young men mourned only by relatives in
Eberhart's 'A Ceremony by the Sea', have been dehumanised
by industrial processes and reduced to statistics. Such an
underpinning characterises a sequence of Second World War
poems, perhaps the most famous being Howard Nemerov's
'The Place of Value' from his volume *The Image and the Law*
(1947). Nemerov's poem includes a terse reflection similar to
the observation made in the conclusion of 'The Fury of Aerial
Bombardment' quoted above. Nemerov's poetic inference is
that, in a civilisation without clearly defined moral values, the
random act of dying in warfare signifies nothing, but society
deviously manufactures social credentials to justify such
military slaughter. The intellectual position adopted by the
poem has a long cultural lineage, but Nemerov's articulation
exhibits a sharpness of focus, similar to Eberhart's, in theorising on the role of circuitry; Nemerov writes,

> I have known people to die
> By the failure of a cotter pin
> Who believed they were fighting for truth.[14]

Such a terse statement suggests the centrality of Nemerov's
war poetry; many of his poems suggest an imagination
seeking to revalue the events of battle, as in 'A Fable of the
War' from *A Guide to the Ruins*, whose ironic tenor and
visionary intensity recall Louis Simpson's 'I Dreamed that
in a City Dark as Paris'. American Second World War poets
frequently seem to write thus in dialectical relationship.
Nemerov, for example, in his study of a doomed culture and a
ruined civilisation, and in his treatment of associated themes
of post-war alienation and the disparity between public
attitudes to war death and the response of the veteran,
explores similar themes in his work to those managed by Karl
Shapiro, an analysis of whose work concludes this chapter.
    Many of the poets discussed in this chapter have concen-
trated in their work upon the soldier as a passive victim of

capitalist military systems operating beyond his control: in such a projection the weapon-machine usurps the functions and role of God in dispensing death and creating spectacle to outrival natural phenomena. This, of course, comprises only one way of regarding man at war, in which the soldier is observed as social being acted upon; in such a poetic analysis the stress is upon exploitation rather than upon sin and damnation. Simpson and Jarrell and Ciardi, for example, display in their war poetry little overt interest in endorsing an alternative counter-pattern of Christian conduct. Other poets, though, and one thinks particularly of Eberhart, Nemerov, Lowell and Shapiro, made poems out of the parabolic imagery traditionally used to dramatise Christian doctrines of evolution. They represent the war to be a setting for spiritual conflicts waged in soulless America, and adopt a scale of non-temporal values to envision the soldier as the lost type of a doomed species. Robert Lowell, a convert to Roman Catholicism, treats the war pedagogically as a morality play; its institutions and processes, the social organisation that approves the bomber, for example, is abjured as the demonic functioning of a ghastly and perverted eucharist. War to the early Lowell exemplifies blasphemy and ungodliness.[15] Howard Nemerov likewise blamed man and not the weapon in showing the war as a further collapse of Christian–Judaic values and assumptions. Nemerov's war verse offers a guide to the ruins of a fallen world, a state brought about through the irreligious conduct of man in creating war.[16] In order to focus more clearly upon the strain of religious war poetry noted in the work of men such as Lowell and Nemerov, one poet, Karl Shapiro, will be briefly considered to close our discussion of Second World War poetry. His work advances our argument in that his poetry dramatises the divine energy of the deity and reduces the machine, as in his poem, 'The Gun', to a mere cipher incapable of destruction without man's guidance. In Shapiro's war verse man not the gun is the villain (and the hero) of the drama.

Shapiro's war poetry presents the traditions and moral evaluations of Judaic religion as a strong counterpoise to war. Shapiro's soldier (and he frequently writes autobiographical poems) unselfconsciously reflects upon the agency of Christ; he reads the Bible, as in 'Christmas Eve: Australia', as naturally as he chews gum; he behaves and thinks at all times aware of the Scriptures, their law and their personalities, Solomon, Elijah, Paul and Jonah, supplying models of conduct by which to reaffirm or to measure present behaviour.[17] The consequence of drawing upon such a carefully nurtured cultural inheritance is that Shapiro's hero has a defence against the nihilistic energies of militarism. Like the figures in John Hersey's *The Wall*, the Bible reader or Christian dissenter can shelter behind 'a wall' (one notes the symbolic importance of such a concept in Jewish tradition).

In 'The Conscientious Objector' the religious values of the committed Christian soldier are approved by the poet. Shapiro's poem celebrates the rebellion of the pacifist which is soundly based upon principles of just dissent. The objector has earned his appellation as one of 'the heroes of our cause' because his choice has been taken out of conscience. After the Armistice such courageous action, the poem argues, will remain to provide moral sustenance, as it proves the power of conscience. Religious symbolism supplies the poetic means of affirmation. For example, the cells where the conscientious objectors are like martyrs incarcerated, take on the visionary properties of a Mayflower or a Noah's ark: the immobility of the prison cell is transformed into a spiritual pilgrimage of true heroism through the language of journeying and sailing into uncharted seas:

> A Mayflower brim with pilgrims headed out
> To establish new theocracies to west,
> A Noah's ark coasting the topmost seas ....   (p. 27)

Unlike the quirky objector in Cummings's poem 'i sing of Olaf', examined earlier in the book, Shapiro's objector is treated straightforwardly as a religious hero, one of 'the men of Bibles' who opposed military uniformity out of a passionate conviction to 'plain decencies'.

Whereas in the previous part of our discussion of Second World War poetry the machine has been observed as an instrument of man's destruction, acting upon him almost with a mind of its own, in Shapiro's verse no such transference takes place. Shapiro reveals little interest in the weapon as creator of illusory aesthetic spectacle either. In 'The Gun' his principal intuitions are crystallised. The poem's confessional tone apportions moral blame not to the weapon but to the soldier who operates it. It is the mortal sin of the specialist that ultimately matters, his choice to kill. Ironically, in 'The Gun' Shapiro calls for absolution for the weapon itself; the blame belongs wholly to himself:

> . . . I absolve from your name
> The exaction of murder, my gun. It is I who have killed.
> It is I whose enjoyment of horror is fine and fulfilled.
> You are only the toy of my terror, my emblem of blame.
>
> (p. 69)

The didactic tone of 'The Gun' infers the imperatives and theological referents of Shapiro's poems written explicitly of war, such as 'Homecoming'.

'Homecoming' portrays the war as a collective act of shame: the soldier needs to attain divine forgiveness to expiate his guilt. The returning ship signalises his guilt in gathering to itself the 'sickly-sweet stench of humiliation', and, unlike the imagery of Noah's ark freely in motion, or of the Mayflower pilgrims, the voyage from war manifests a paradigm of madness, sterility, and death:

> . . . even the majority, untouched by steel
> Or psychoneurosis, stare with eyes in rut,
> Their hands rabble to snatch the riches
> Of glittering shops and girls.   (p. 74)

Far from depicting the soldiers as returning heroes, the poem names the vessel a 'ghoul ship' which transports sick lunatics and 'imprisoned souls' returning to the USA bent only on plunder. The voice of 'Homecoming' as commonly noted in Shapiro's poetry alternates between the expression of firm social judgement and the slightly aloof impatience at observing a graceless, erring sinner. Ultimately Shapiro's finest war poetry, displayed in 'Troop Train' and 'Elegy for a Dead Soldier', displays preoccupation with time and eternity. The soldier, like all men, endures a temporal fate ('armies all repose in clay') and his military conduct is only to be expected, since he manifests through his actions his genealogy as one of the seed of Cain. Shapiro's best war poetry catches the intonations of psalm, the nuances of biblical language and its solemnity; this power characterises 'Elegy for a Dead Soldier', one of the greatest of all war poems written by an American, and also concomitantly one of the finest war poems of the English language.

Shapiro's formal choice of the elegy allows him to set the soldier's death within a traditional framework of mourning, and to employ dignified and elevated language to heighten its significance; for the young man whom the poet has witnessed dying attains in his casual-seeming death a tragic elevation, becoming a representative figure. 'Elegy for a Dead Soldier', in its sacramentalised opening two stanzas and its hints of Christian optimism in the epitaph, enacts 'glory and rebirth beyond the void' through its ritualised language. For example, the funeral ceremony, in stanzas 1 and 9, which structure the poem, sustains inferences of transcendence; here, the poem seems to imply, lies a dead Christian, the full spiritual significance of whose death calls for redemption; the possibility of such affirmation, the poetic assertion of regenerative alternatives to war, is stated in stanza 10:

> Hollow or firm,
> No man can ever prophesy until
> Out of our death some undiscovered germ,
> Whole toleration or pure peace is born.   (p. 45)

Shapiro's poem, in its meditative and philosophical manner, reflects upon two principal meanings of the young man's death. The first is its psychological function as an analogy for the onlooker's own death; for the watchers and, of course, the poet's readers, have inevitably, in their imaginations, occupied the centrepiece of such a drama:

> Who has not wrapped himself in this same flag
> Heard the light fall of dirt, his wound still fresh,
> Felt his eyes closed, and heard the distant brag
> Of the last volley of humanity?   (p. 43)

Secondly, the poem passes judgement upon American culture, its social values and conventions. In many ways the latter commentary supplies the substantiality of the elegy; it analyses American society in order to tell us how to live; its ultimate trajectory, as the work of any religious poet's is bound to be, is didactic. This social critique holds together the various emotional resonances and themes of 'Elegy for a Dead Soldier'. From the outset the poem carefully measures our self-identification with the loss of youth manifested in the boy's pointless death; the death, which can only be apprehended in personal terms, an 'aggregate of one', signifies the unique death of individuality, our own death's ultimate meaning. What raises Shapiro's lamentation to greatness is its penetrating and lofty survey of the soldier's life, his standards of conduct and convention; the poem is a lamentation by the poet–reader of Paul for the loss of spiritual energy in contemporary America, the 'new Byzantium' of our time: Shapiro's unexceptional solider, prejudiced, an observer of custom, politically naive, basically unintellectual, is above all a materialist. His involvement in the journey of war, as 'neither a victim nor a volunteer', signifies to the soldier an interruption in the pursuit of materialism:

> The journey was a detour that would steer
> Into the Lincoln Highway of a land
> Remorselessly improved, excited, new,
> And that was what he wanted . . . .   (p. 44)

The tenor of Shapiro's poem is to absolve the soldier from blame at suffering a social condition towards hedonism and money-values, and yet, at the same time, to emphasise, through imagery and tone, the futility (in a Christian time-scale) of such activity. War for Shapiro is a paradigm of irreligion and the soldier should be mourned for his sin, prayed for and understood, using the traditionally sanctioned myths and concepts of the Bible. By adopting the symbolic pieties and parabolic textures of religious language and imagery poets such as Shapiro dramatised in their work a powerful opposition to machine warfare and to the despair and anxiety induced by American 'death-culture'.

9 Towards Vietnam: Portraying Modern War

SATIRIC FABRICATION OR EPIC BIOGRAPHY?

The historical experience of Korea and Vietnam has generated a complex and radically new consciousness of war for Americans. In the immediate years following the Second World War the development of sophisticated nuclear technology and the continuing economic expansion of the United States seemed to presage an unbroken era of military supremacy; in reality America's involvement in Asia proved otherwise. Both Korea and Vietnam turned out to be wars significantly different from earlier 'conventional' wars; Vietnam, in particular, demonstrated both the limits of American power and the moral ambivalence of advanced technology. In the Second World War, the fight against fascism provided a ready legitimation for the involvement of the United States, and the American nation through its supply of material resources and manpower could fairly claim to have played a major part in the defeat of Nazism. Vietnam was different in that the war produced a backlash of public opinion, and ultimately it was impossible to win either militarily or politically. In counter-cultural terms such a national dilemma was dramatised in metaphors suggestive of irreconcilable and inherent moral contradiction. Mary McCarthy offers an example of how this unpopular war was presented to the American public by the literary intelligentsia in her book *Vietnam* (1967), an informal account of her visit to the war zone: the essence of her impressions crystallised in the portrayal of naïve Americans waging war in order to 'save' the Vietnamese peasantry. Another dominant image in the semantics of the American youth sub-cultures of the 1960s and early 1970s was that of the patriotic and idealistic Viet

185

Cong (VC) warrior resisting attacks from US saturation bombing. *Diary of an Unknown Warrior*, edited by D. McCullin (1973), falls into this genre of oppositional writing.

During the last two decades literary production of American war books has continued to be prolific. In the realm of 'serious' literature (and the great commercial and popular success of modern war classics such as *Catch-22* and *Slaughterhouse-Five* teaches one to be undogmatic about classification) the American war writer has drawn upon a situation of productive crisis rather analogous to that experienced by earlier Anglo-American modernists in the 1920s. John Barth, reflecting upon the period, has coined the useful phrase 'literature of exhaustion' to describe the intense formal experimentation whereby genre has been mined to the point of 'ultimacy';[1] Wylie Sypher, seeking to theorise about the demise of wider intellectual traditions, postulates 'loss of the self' as an indicator to the decline of liberal faith in the power of individual affirmation.[2] The years from 1960 are sometimes termed the era of post-modernism in the United States, when, after a cultural by-pass, the legacy of modernism has been realised through the explosion and dismemberment of traditional notions of genre.

A look at the books written initially in response to Vietnam seems to corroborate such a prediction; there does seem to be a vast amount of literature which attempts technical innovation. Drama serves as an example of such a development. Megan Terry's 'folk war movie' *Viet Rock* (1967) and Joseph Heller's *We Bombed in New Haven* (1968) both employ transformations, happenings and direct audience participation to achieve their effects. A similar process characterised, in Europe, Peter Weiss's socialist play *Vietnam Discourse* (1968), which drew upon German *Agit-propstücke* of the 1930s. In American poetry, too, copious formal innovation seemed to mark an openness of genre, an accessible plurality of conventions and options; this is displayed interestingly in John Balaban's *Vietnam Poems* (1971), where Anglo-Saxon religious verse supplies a linguistic model for treating the Indo-China conflict and integrating it within wider Christian–pacifist myths.

An attempt to present a comprehensive survey of the literature of war written during the last twenty years or so lies beyond the scope of this chapter, which is predicated upon such a recognition. It is useful, though, to acknowledge the practical situation of the war writer and to attempt very briefly to reconstruct his literary context. The ambiguous and shifting nature of literary production and its relation with such material conditions as readership and methods of distribution imply complexly evolving cultural relationships and forces. An example of particular relevance to the writing of specifically 'war' books is the fluidity and interchange of conventions and styles made possible in a mass paperback market aimed at a mix of readers. An interesting example of such a process of cultural dynamism may be observed in the diffusion of the 'Catch-22' mode of war writing; a recent paperback picked up at random, Robert Littell's naval story set in the Vietnam war, *Sweet Reason* (1974), proclaims on the cover that the book blends 'Portnoy and Catch-22'. The rapid growth of paperback sales had meant not only a more profitable market for the gung-ho type of war novel, but also, more interestingly, communication to a wider audience of some of the techniques of experimental fiction. This may help to account for the commercial success of Vonnegut's *Slaugherhouse-Five* and Eastlake's *Castle Keep*, both highly formal and technically sophisticated works of fiction.

An analysis of war literature draws strength from taking account of a range of war books. In the case of Vietnam this means carrying out a concurrent examination of such intricate experimental works as William Eastlake's *The Bamboo Bed* (1969) or Norman Mailer's two novels *Why Are We in Vietnam?* (1967) and *The Armies of the Night* (1968), and widely read popular works such as Robin Moore's best-seller *The Green Berets* (1966). The point of such a concurrent reading is to try to identify interpenetrations of genre and also the evolution of literary traditions. My own understanding of the South-East Asia conflict has been intensified through acquaintance with a wide range of popular artefacts, among them such books as William Wilson's *The LBJ Brigade* (1967), Richard Hooker's *MASH* (1970),[3] G. McCarthy's poems *War Story* (1977), and such films as *Dog Soldiers* and *The Deer Hunter*. The literary quality of such books may not necessarily be high, and yet they are worthy of study to investigate the nuances and inflections of cultural life.

The production of literature involves a mediated process of negotiations and interactions, conditions which prompt fundamental questions concerning the status of war books in symbolising external reality. An interesting series of questions revolves, for example, around the representation of collective military experience within literary form. A recent study, *The Military and American Society* (1972), has considered the massive impact, both social and economic, of the military–industrial complex within the United States. It has been estimated, for example, that over half America's adult males in 1970 had undergone some form of military service, seemingly a fact of enormous cultural importance.[4] In the face of such history how may literature articulate a specific and national response? How has a people as unmilitaristic as the population of the United States absorbed the increasing resources allocated to military spending? Of course such problematic issues are not easily resolved imaginatively in war books, yet one would expect to find some shaping awareness of them at work. It will be argued later that the vision of Joseph Heller in *Catch-22* of a vast military bureaucracy communicates a metaphorical awareness of such a situation. Adopting a more formalist perspective one looks for evidence of orientations towards tradition in recent war writing, a subtle attunement on the part of the novelist or poet towards the works of earlier authors. Questions similar to these will be posed in the substantive part of this chapter which examines two contending methods or literary modes of portraying war. I have, for the sake of argument, been polemical in writing about them as presenting opposing representations of modern warfare. The discussion will open with analyses of Joseph Heller's *Catch-22* and Kurt Vonnegut's *Slaughterhouse-Five*, and will argue that both works exhibit a profoundly new satiric exploration of war which finds expression through innovatory formal patterning and the fabrication of new myths.

Catch-22 (1961) has probably contributed more than any other work to the literary apprehension of war during the last two decades.[5] The interpenetration between literary form and the movements of history is clearly shown in the commercial success of Heller's labyrinthine novel: the symbolisation of war as a labyrinth has now become firmly established in the way that earlier myths had been (the First World War metaphor of the soldier's farewell to arms was a previous example of equally potent symbolism); such images act as primary vehicles for our consciousness of men at arms. It is hardly an exaggeration to say that the idea of an all-pervasive catch has become the most widely accepted image of battle Pentagon-style, its structures and forms. Heller's invention of a catch which simultaneously determines, reflects and distorts the attitudes of various ranks of soldiers to the deadness of military institutionalism symbolises most effectively the nature of hegemonic relations. The intellectual genesis of the catch is difficult to identify, although one can take pleasure in drawing analogies with the processes of formal logic or such complex constructs as those inspired by generative grammar. The catch, of course, coerces, yet in a barely perceived manner which relies upon intellectual beauty and coherence:

> Yossarian saw it clearly in all its spinning reasonableness. There was an elliptical precision about its perfect pairs of parts that was graceful and shocking, like good modern art, and at times Yossarian wasn't quite sure that he saw it at all, just the way he was never quite sure about good modern art.   (pp. 54–5)

The catch obliquely implies the reification of military procedures in its formal autonomy; its uses, as the novel reveals, are exploitative. Through its mystique and *Gestalt*-like powers the catch may be drawn upon in a variety of ways to instil loyalty and obedience to the military creed. It may provide legitimation for raising the number of bombing missions or justify the arrest of persons thought to be oppposed to the bureaucratic hierarchy. The metaphor of a catch works structurally and imaginatively to symbolise in microcosm the seemingly willing mass subjection of soldiers to the interests of the industrial–military complex. Colonel Korn's educational sessions supply an example of the infallible theory in operation: only men who never ask questions are admitted, and then the sessions are discontinued on the grounds that it was neither possible nor necessary to educate people who never questioned anything.

Taken at this level *Catch-22* embodies a satire upon system

building, a hypostastisation directed at grammarians, logi-
cians and positivists in a neo-Swiftian mode. Tony Tanner has
drawn attention to the abiding concern of American writers
with conspiracy theories, their fear that the simple 'unpat-
terned' life, inward-directed (and analogous with the mythical
past of the virginal continent) becomes impossible to achieve
in a world where individual identity is increasingly obfuscated
(as the extended word-play upon the names of characters in
Heller's masterpiece suggests); spontaneous conduct grows
more and more difficult. Tanner emphasises the role of
behaviourism and the linguistic sciences in convincing Americans that freedom of action is more and more constricted:

> American writers dread ... all conditioning forces to the
> point of paranoia which is detectable not only in the subject
> matter of many novels but also in their narrative devices.
> Narrative lines are full of hidden persuaders, hidden
> dimensions, plots, secret organisation, evil systems, all kinds
> of conspiracies against spontaneity of consciousness, even
> cosmic take over. The possible nightmare of being totally
> controlled by unseen agencies and powers is never far away
> in contemporary American fiction. The unease revealed in
> such novels is related to a worried apprehension on the part
> of the author that his own consciousness may be predeter-
> mined and channelled by the language he has been born
> into.[6]

Given that the long tradition (from Ortega Y Gasset to
Marcuse) of predicting the growth of dehumanisation has
authentic roots, the artist is increasingly likely to create
literary modes which permit him to portray a social world of
an indeterminate and anxious character, and one inimical to
the individual's rational understanding. Heller's fictional
work displays these features, and his formal procedures such
as the devices of satiric distortion, allegory, parody and
burlesque contribute to the formation of a vision of breakdown. His novel exploits the departure from literal truth in
order to arrive at a representation of the monolithic power of
modern institutions, in this case conveyed through the
metaphor of the army's hierarchy. Such bewilderment experienced by the reader throughout the novel seems war-

ranted if *Catch-22* is read in this way as a new kind of satire, one whose elaborate fabrications communicate a profound national *Angst*. One example should make this clear, the way individual generals ai e as helpless as their men, which is shown in their over-sensitivity to the media; their wish to be presented in a favourable light indicates that they are as much victims of 'the system' as the combat airmen trying to escape from flying more bombing missions. The image communicated throughout the novel is of men lost in psychological corridors.

If one accepts such an interpretation of the novel, *Catch-22* exhibits certain characteristics of its period. The novel, for example, bases its narrative upon a fluctuating rhythm of crisis. One may observe a parallel development in the public's response to war as conveyed through the media and newspapers: many of the latter reserve a section of their foreign news pages for the coverage of wars abroad, and the most acclaimed newspaper men tend to be those frequently prominent in front-line action. Another obvious relation of Heller's narrative devices of concealment to external reality may be deduced from the curious public oxymoron of a 'balance of terror': such a euphemism does not conceal nuclear technology's proliferation of new horrors, the development of weapons like the neutron bomb recently created, for instance, which outrival avant-garde art in breaking with convention and rendering obsolete all that has come before. Whether one conceives of literature as a strictly determined ideological form or as a cultural product which retains a relative autonomy, its seems probably that such a history of war as continuing literary event informs Heller's novel. Heller's sustained satire against the dullness of maladministration, his post-absurdist lament for the disappearance of identity, suggests that the thrust of war writing in the sixties changed focus, from the heroic struggles of the battlefield to the absurdities of the communications process itself. The strains and confusions endured by American democracy, throughout Korea, the Cold War and McCarthyism, seem to have found subliminal articulation in the lunacy of Cathcart, Korn and Major and in the disordered narrative of the novel.

The chief thematic polarity in *Catch-22* is the struggle between the fetishistic, admired and worshipped for itself, and the soldier's counter attempt to hold fast to personal identity. An extended satire upon naming informs the novel at many levels. The case of Major Major Major Major, permanently trapped by his cumbersome names, illustrates such a predicament. Major Major, 'born too late and too mediocre', discovers that he is being utterly taken over by 'prolix bulletins', and so he 'grew despondent'. One day he signed Washington Irving's name to a document, an act of rebellion which functioned as catharsis: henceforth he exploits as a counter-strategy the names of other famous writers, notably John Milton, in order to fight back. Of course, Major Major's insubordination brings forth a plethora of activity from security men (whose bizarre activities seem to anticipate fictionally the historical reality of Watergate a decade or so later). The fetishistic status accorded to trivial memoranda in *Catch-22* signifies an entire military code, the collective voice of a self-perpetuating bureaucracy whose directives alter consciousness.

Modern war in *Catch-22* appears essentially to be an administrator's war, the focus having shifted from the exigencies of combat to the rampages of bureaucrats whose methods of communication imply a new species of epiphenomenalism; the end result is a situation where the liberal concept of identity is so far eroded that it eventually vanishes altogether. This finds outstanding comic expression in the novel when literal truth and the falsified bureaucratic version of reality clash head-on. Such disjunctures are strewn throughout *Catch-22*, in the strange figure of the soldier in white, a powerful image of anonymity, or the unknown soldier Mudd, who, blown to bits in the sky, generates a persuasive synecdoche for men at war. The two most celebrated paradigms are the cases of the dead man in Yossarian's tent, the soldier who died in a dogfight over Orvieto before he was officially reported missing and is, therefore, deemed never to have died; and the diametrically opposite fate of Doc Daneeka, who is deemed to be dead because he was supposed to be on flight duty in a plane that was destroyed. Doc Daneeka's living presence does nothing to contradict the authorised report of his death. With capacious irony Heller plots the repercussions of his figurative death – for example, the cumulative benefits bestowed upon his 'widow', who eventually refuses to accept his letters, preferring to disown him and accept the official version of his non-existence. The lieutenant who has been killed in action but never officially 'arrived' in the squadron was simply a 'replacement' pilot, whose belongings insist for Yossarian upon the recalcitrance of death, a reality closed to Major Major, who allows Sergeant Towser to report him as never having 'arrived' at all. Such depictions infer the nature of modern war where the substantive reality of combat death often becomes unknowable and its actuality concealed within the labyrinthine processes of modern technology – the circuitry of electronic media, for example – that produce new kinds of mystification.

The reader of *Catch-22* encounters one of the recurrent preoccuptions of American war writers, the domination of combat men by unvalorous administrators. Sergeant Whitcomb, for example, feels delighted that twelve more men have been killed in combat (and they are sent duplicated 'personalised' letters of condolence) because his chances are increased of getting an article in *Saturday Evening Post* in praise of his commanding officer. The war increasingly becomes a publicity man's war where good aerial photographs rather than military tactics dictate the strategy of tight bomb patterns. Language uses, too, assume an important role in the mixed devices of concealment and self-advertisement employed by high-ranking officers: the officers most likely to succeed are those, such as General P. P. Peckem, who are highly sophisticated users of language, or those, such as Scheisskopf, whose crude instrumentation theories and encyclopaedic knowledge of trivial regulations result in promotion to the rank of general. An instance of Scheisskopf's pedantic lunacy occurs in his admiration of parades, the most redundant part of military routine. Beneath Scheisskopf's comic presentation, though, hides a sinister reality; his fixation upon swingless marching hints at a crucifixion mentality. Men, in Scheisskopf's opinion, should ultimately become as precise as machines:

> Lieutenant Scheisskopf's first thought had been to have a friend of his in the sheet metal shop sink pegs of nickel alloy into each man's thighbones and link them to the wrists by strands of copper wire with exactly three inches of play, but

there wasn't time – and good copper wire was hard to come by in wartime. He remembered also that the men, so hampered, would be unable to fall properly during the impressive fainting ceremony preceding the marching and that an inability to faint properly might affect the unit's rating as a whole.   (p. 84)

The literary technique deployed here characterises much of Heller's novel; it sustains awareness, through inventive distortion and departure from strictly literal truth, of the connotations of mechanised slaughter, the transformation of men into machines. As a hospital administrator says to Yossarian on another occasion, when considering the expendability of soldiers, 'one dying boy is just as good as any other or just as bad'. Yossarian learns, too, that his leg 'belongs' to the government.

Heller reveals an aesthetic predilection towards gradual revelation and partial disclosure: for example, the sparse and selective use of conventional literary realism heightens the reader's intuition of aerial combat, acting as a sharper lens. Such naturalistic scenes are framed in the novel, and their locations provide formal interplay within the overall strategy of derangement: they seem almost like set-pieces. The limited usage of 'realistic' presentation is also appropriate in a wider formal sense too, because in the institutionalised world of the novel traditional concepts of worth and epic heroism (which seem to emerge from such realistic presentation) prove obsolete and invalid. The environment of *Catch-22* spawns officers who act not out of moral considerations but only to defend or advance their own interests (as in the ironic promotion of Yossarian for breaking orders). It is wholly consistent, then, that fictional structures and narrative plotting should display a commensurate problematic of evasiveness and disorientation; such a consideration is raised if one examines the relationship of the novel to earlier traditions of war writing. In *Catch-22* many of the familiar conventions of the war novel are transformed into preposterous jokes: even the arrangement of Heller's novel parodies an earlier type of war narrative and movie. The narrative, based on the adventures of a group of officers and men, is broken up into a series of discontinuous sections, each of which only tenuously conveys the experiences of a character, such as Hungry Joe or Nately's Whore. Heller observes few rules in burlesquing the method of earlier naturalistic writers, such as William March in *Company K*, or admired contemporaries, such as Norman Mailer in *The Naked and the Dead*. It is a technique that relies minimally upon plot, and thus allows great organisational flexibility.

Heller's characteristic method may be described as neo-satiric as he frequently shifts the position of attack through a sophisticated usage of fictional apparatus, the deployment of hallucinations, *déjà vu* visions, nightmares, flash-backs and mystical projections that cohere to cloak his characters and ironically imply their occultness in a world where everyday reality seems to imitate the supernatural. Several critics, including Joseph Stern and Brian Way, have written of the symbolic and traditional formulas in Heller's novel.[7] The Soldier in White, for example, parodies the wounded soldier–hero, such as Dalton Trumbo's bandaged protagonist in *Johnny Got His Gun*, and also recalls Shakespeare's ghosts in striking the conscience. This fusion of the neo-satiric, a genre of avant-gardism, with the traditional distinguishes Heller as a war novelist. When Yossarian casts off his uniform and stands naked to receive his undeserved medal he is at one with such earlier deserters and rebels as Frederick Henry or John Andrews, but when he is absorbed into the Chaplain's mistaken vision, a naked man in a symbolic Tree of Life, he assumes briefly the aura of an Everyman, becoming part of a highly wrought pattern of imagery, like Hungry Joe's cat, which sleeps on his face and finally suffocates him. The planned obsolescence, redundancies and side-tracking in Heller's novel function in a similar manner; the reader can no longer cling to modes and assumptions of a well-tried kind; he finds himself in a satiric environment of constant confusion, and yet one which hints at the apocalyptic only to re-emphasise the material and the mundane, the impossibility of spiritual escape.

Kurt Vonnegut's outrageous subtitle to *Slaughterhouse-Five* (1969) infers the novel's satiric intentions through its self-advertisement as a novel 'somewhat in the telegraphic schizophrenic manner of tales of the planet Tralfamadore, where the flying saucers come from'.[8] Vonnegut's picaresque plot pivots upon the two contrary experiences of the unheroic Billy Pilgrim, who is taken prisoner by the Germans, incarcerated in a slaughterhouse and sees the aftermath of the Allied firebombing of Dresden, which, Vonnegut reminds us, was 'the greatest massacre in European history'. Billy also undergoes a different and more surreptitious form of imprisonment when he is captured by the inhabitants of the planet Tralfamadore and becomes a specimen of *Homo sapiens* in an other-worldly zoo. Vonnegut's narrative blends the techniques of science fiction with those of modern satire. The novel's sophisticated formal debate is conducted internally within the first chapter when Vonnegut engages in one of his favourite occupations, the undermining of genre. Speaking in his own voice, he attacks by implication fiction which treats war as a glamorous activity. He mocks also the pedantry of the war writer by describing his own clumsy attempts to make fictional capital out of the war. Such a task, of creating an exciting war novel, proves impossible, since the memories of war remain virtually submerged, emergent only in random and unstructured recollections: they stay for the most part unrealised, stubbornly resistant to the writer's mechanistic efforts to order them systematically (as Vonnegut, in Chapter 1, tries to invent a plot by constructing a crude model with his daughter's coloured crayons).

Vonnegut takes great pleasure in disclosing in Chapter 1 virtually all of the narrative events of the novel in order to dispose right away with the fixities of sequential narration; henceforth, and from the opening pages of the novel, he is released from any obligations to comply with conventional notions of genre. The formal innovation implied by such an undertaking matches the reinvention of his life undertaken by Billy Pilgrim, the novel's mock hero, who turns to science fiction for help after witnessing the firebombing of Dresden. *Slaughterhouse-Five* reverses almost all of the generic traditions of the Hemingway–Mailer–James Jones combat-centred line of war fiction: the novel contains no scenes of fighting; its controlling image of war is not the epic sweep of battle but the devastation of a beautiful undefended city and the mass death of its innocent citizens. Whereas previous traditions, and one thinks primarily of its extremities in, say, the Edenic and belle-lettristic metaphors of Alan Seeger in the First World

War, often emphasised the litanies of battle as a ritual of initiation, Vonnegut has no time for such celebrations: his novel prefers to flay the enemies of the common soldier in as prosaic manner as possible. Vonnegut's manner of narration and his prose style exploit the dispassionate and the detached, and the tone of the book is pitched deliberately in a low key.

This finds expression, too, in the characterisation of *Slaughterhouse-Five*: in place of Hemingway's Frederick Henry or Cummings's noble Zoo-Loo, the reader encounters flat, oafish creations such as the churlish and cruel Roland Weary or the violent and backbiting Lazzaro. Such figures as these and the freakish anti-hero, Billy Pilgrim, a certifiable lunatic, whose actions often belie the noble and allegorical associations of his name, display no charisma: instead of rising to the mantle of hero the novel's most moving character, the middle-aged high school teacher, Edgar Derby, meets an ignominious death, executed by a firing squad for stealing a teapot while all around him the ruins of Dresden testify to one of mankind's greatest crimes. (Any grand ironic ending for the novel is pre-empted early on in the narrative, when Vonnegut defuses the impact of Derby's death.) Vonnegut's satire, then, operates chiefly through a comedy of gesture and language. One of the most helpful guides to the nature of the novel is provided by the sub-title mentioned earlier, which describes the book as having been written in a 'telegraphic, schizophrenic' mode; the adjectives are helpful in a number of ways, 'telegraphic' because the novel is short and often cryptic and apocryphal, incomplete and unrealised in the abbreviated manner of a telegram, and 'schizophrenic' in its counterpointing of the two veiled crises in Billy's life; the novel's artistic modes blend elements of realism, fantasy and documentary (extracts from historical studies and speeches are drawn upon together with such facts and events of real history as Robert Kennedy's death). The novel's form, therefore, deploys several disparate and yet conterminous conventions in order both to create the illusion of historical authenticity and simultaneously to break down such an impression (one of the most hilarious examples of this is the Sears Roebuck furniture used to adorn Billy's geodesic dome on the planet Tralfamadore).

The most interesting formal innovation in *Slaughterhouse-*

Five is the use of the fantastic as a satiric lens. This works in a number of ways: the inhabitants of Tralfamadore have one major advantage over the people of earth – they can close their eyes to unwelcome reality; this simple device is learned by Billy, and through such a possibility Vonnegut is able to transcend his deterministic vision and invest his novel with beatific potentialities, as when Billy learns that death is merely a violet light and that one does not cease to exist after it. The fantastic dimension of *Slaughterhouse-Five* is related to the traditions of science fiction, and has both utopian and dystopian connotations; the former are illustrated when the Tralfamadorians break through time and the narrow confines of vision, and their similarity to Earth people is shown when they admit to Billy that they wage horrific wars on each other. Eric S. Rabkin has defined the fantastic as that where the ground rules of fiction are suddenly departed from: 'the fantastic is a quality of astonishment that we feel when the ground rules of a narrative world are suddenly made to turn about 180°. We recognise this reversal in the reactions of characters, the statements of narrators, and the implications of structure, all playing on or against our whole experience as people.'[9] Vonnegut's particular use of the fantastic draws upon a satiric impulse in science fiction which is especially helpful in allowing him freedom from a restricted time scheme.

The structural implications of such freedom are highly significant in the novel's articulation of meaning. When Billy dreams things, 'some of them true, and the true things were time travel', the reader's notions of truth are questioned. *Slaughterhouse-Five* manipulates temporality in many interesting ways: there are previsions, memories of the future, time warps and time windows; Billy is enabled to move backwards, forwards, sideways through time, seeming to verify a condition of the fiction of our time which is discussed when Frank Kermode in *The Sense of an Ending* (1967) speaks of the withdrawal from fiction of the consolations of form. He refers to Robbe Grillet and the new novel: 'we have a novel in which the reader will find none of the gratification to be had from sham temporality, sham causality, falsely certain description, clear story . . . the reader is not offered easy satisfactions, but a challenge to creative co-operation'.[10] Two ideas seem initially to stem from Vonnegut's bewildering use of time-shifts: the novel is able to suggest the world of modern science and, secondly its fluidity implies the freedom and movement of modern media. Vonnegut's well known interest in science is communicated through the novel's inference of relativity and in the 'switch' patterns of the fiction: in a single day Billy can blink in 1965, travel in time to 1958 – to blink in 1958 and travel forward to 1961 (p. 36). The mosaic effect gained here is surely suggestive of TV's seamless flow of images and its imaginative creation of myths. Vonnegut utilises such freedoms in a number of ways, principally to dramatise the uninterrupted rhythms of war, given expression in the novel through the simultaneity of the Second World War and Vietnam. Vietnam is mentioned throughout the novel, by means of direct reference to facts and figures or war dead, through the bellicose general who speaks at Billy's Lions Club, and in a number of narrative incidents, as when Billy treats a boy whose father has been killed in the battle for Hill 875 near Dakto. Vonnegut's technical experiments, therefore, allow him to present both a comprehensive critique of war-mongering and to treat war in a mode that reduces its glamour and conveys its real nature, which is to make its participants 'sick' and 'listless' and become the 'playthings' of 'enormous forces'; the reader takes the novel's main warning that there is nothing 'intelligent' to say about a massacre.

The two books most likely to become classics that have emerged from the Vietnam War, Philip Caputo's *A Rumor of War* (1977) and Michael Herr's *Dispatches* (1977), are non-fiction prose accounts of warfare retrospectively ordered upon personal experience. Although differing widely in the phases of the war treated, in structure and setting, point of view and certain formal and linguistic conventions, both books reveal a fundamental similarity of attitude. Caputo and Herr communicate a common intuition that war has epic significance; both suggest how Vietnam has come to be widely accepted as a metonymy for modern warfare, and how its historical energy proved the dominant influence upon a generation of young men who came to maturity in the American decade, the 1960s. Both writers, too, envision the war in South East Asia as one whose residual aura of defeat is likely to signify a profound change in the imagery and understanding of war. The American exodus and the notorious battles, such as those of Ia Drang, Hamburger Hill, the Rockpile and Dak To, have contributed to this altered public consciousness. In place of Kennedy's legendary Camelot, certain events such as the atrocity at My Lai and the Khe Sanh siege have become metaphors to connote national shame or military vulnerability rather like the mythic French humiliation at Dien Bien Phu. *A Rumor of War* and *Dispatches* are works that also acknowledge the rare and often gentle brotherhood forged under fire as Caputo and Herr testify to the courage and heroism of the foot soldiers whose collective biography they write. Both authors, in the main tradition of American war writing, are deeply sympathetic towards the resistance culture of the combat troops; this sub-culture implies a co-operative enterprise in endurance, a community of soldiers whose 'voice' is articulated through style, defiant humour, argot and close comradeship. Caputo and Herr both celebrate the loyalty and unacknowledged virtues of enlisted men in line companies, particularly 'grunts' or marines, and both writers deplore the inhumanities of command when disguised in the 'pentagonese' language of military politicians. The term 'epic biography' is meant to infer the way Caputo and Herr move beyond pure autobiography or journal in transforming the raw material of their own experience. Both writers concentrate less upon ingenious formal patterning and prefer instead to treat the Vietnam situation through mediated reportage and relatively accessible biographical form. They are commonly interested in portraying collective endurance and suffering as an extension of their own experience.

Philip Caputo's *A Rumor of War* (1977) recounts its author's first encounter as a young infantry officer in Vietnam during 1965–6. Caputo's marine unit was part of the first American Expeditionary force to serve in Indo China, and his period of nearly a year's active service ended with an honourable discharge after a court martial decision in his favour. In an epilogue Caputo (who was awarded a Pulitzer prize for war reporting in the Middle East) describes the completion of his Vietnam education at the American evacuation of Saigon ten years later. The vitality of Caputo's account inheres in its *Bildungsroman* quality, especially through the book's retrospective viewpoint as the reader is made aware of the author's two selves; the experience of the idealistic volunteer, who is infatuated with President Kennedy's Arthurian visions, is narrated by the war-weary veteran reporter who has covered war in the Golan Heights and elsewhere. The evaluations, images and balances achieved through such a mediated presentation enable Caputo to dramatise the lost generation overtones of Vietnam. His infantrymen are represented as naive victims of America's own self-delusion who undergo their 'primary sacrament' of war to uphold a mistaken notion that the United States is playing 'cop to the Communist's robber'.[11]

A Rumor of War purports to be a soldier's account of the early stages of the war. Caputo concerns himself pre-eminently with military matters, and in so doing finds little substantive evidence to confirm either the frontier heritage theory or the hypothesis that American troops conducted themselves violently towards Asian peasants out of a deeply ingrained racialism nurtured at home against ethnic minorities. His study of the Vietnam conflict emphasises the unique military character and colonial origins of the war. His own situation as an infantry soldier provides him with first-hand experience of the logistics of combat; for instance, his military training proves inadequate as it is premised upon a different set of tactical circumstances, those developed by the British in the Malayan counter-insurgency; this left him inadequately prepared for the specific kind of all-out jungle warfare of attrition he faced in Vietnam: the result was that he fell prey to his own worst fears and anxieties. Another example of the same process is narrated by Caputo when he asks to be transferred from an officer's desk job where his task is to act as 'death's book-keeper', to identify dead bodies and register details of their mortal wounds. After some time spent in this gruesome occupation he realised that he was in danger of losing his sanity and so he volunteered for a line company. The point in both cases is that the war in Vietnam, because of its sporadic nature and savagely intermittent rhythms, placed its combat troops in situations where they were especially prone to give vent to what Caputo calls 'a few minutes of orgiastic violence'. *A Rumor of War* conveys, through both its ironic arrangement of detail and its technical rendering of the conditions of battle (for example the 'gunship' role of helicopters and the strategic importance of mines and booby traps), a vision of warfare which generated extreme moral disorientation in its combatants. Previous American myths of the frontier spirit and doughboys 'over there' held no relevance for marines involved in a civil war waged in an alien climate and culture. Caputo expertly creates a context for the war in portraying its jungle setting, the endless skirmishes with a seemingly phantom enemy, and the indoctrination of combat soldiers through their own commanders' jargon of kill ratios, high body counts and such maxims as 'if he's dead and Vietnamese he's V. C.'.

Unlike Michael Herr in *Dispatches*, who creates a witty and colloquial sub-language, Caputo's linguistic mode is relatively 'literary' in echoing the cadences of previous war writers, especially Hemingway and James Jones. Although he does not borrow directly from these writers, Caputo absorbs their rhythms, and his thematic dispositions often parallel theirs; for example, like Jones he celebrates the selfless communion between enlisted men (shown in his fine portraits of his fallen comrades, Sullivan and Levy). Other kinds of 'brotherhood' interest Caputo too, as in the following passage, where he engages in a favourite pursuit, epic portraiture :

The colonel looked, and was, every inch a field marine, a brusque, hulking man with a face that manged to be ugly and attractive at the same time. His nose, banged-up, and too big, the seamed flesh and hard, worn eyes told more about where he had been than the words in his service record book and the ribbons on his chest. It was an ugly face, but it had the dignity that is conferred upon those who have suffered the bodily and emotional aches of war. The colonel had paid his dues under fire, and so belonged to that ancient brotherhood to which no amount of money, social pedigrees, or political connections can gain a man admittance.   (p. 61)

The phrases 'dues under fire' and 'ancient brotherhood' recall the Hemingway of *Across the River*, where a similar lexical stress is placed upon the redemptive power and dignity conferred by combat duty.

The communication or communion theme, of central importance in Caputo's narration, is also cleverly exploited to symbolise the breakdown of disciplined troops into what he refers to as 'an incendiary mob'. Battle fatigue, or the military necessity of taking punitive action, cannot mitigate these sudden 'disintegrations' as when, behaving as stereotyped Apaches, whooping and torching buildings, they utterly destroy the village of Ha Na. Such an act of collective crime and wanton destruction is later outdone when the author, under extreme pressure and responding to the inducements of his superiors to kill more of the enemy, persuades a couple of men in his platoon to kill two innocent Vietnamese civilians. Here the previously dignified bond between soldiers degenerates into blood-lust; in reviewing what happened, Caputo writes, 'There was a silent communication between us, an unspoken understanding; blood was to be shed' (p. 317). The incident, for which Caputo was court martialled but had most of the charges against him dropped, remains a metaphor of chilling horror. Caputo's deceived younger self, the morally confused infantry officer, stands as another type of the 'assailant–victim' figure noted in American literature by Frank Ross, the soldier who is sickeningly brutalised by war.

The writer seeking to capitalise upon his war experience faces initially two basic problems, to redefine the war from his own fragmentary memories, and, secondly, to symbolise information of a factual nature. In the process of presenting a vision of Vietnam, for example, the writer needs to order and recreate his own memories, and then to communicate an aesthetic 'version' of the realities he faced. In analysing a recent compilation of the poetry of Vietnam, I noted eight subjects that comprised poetic themes: geographical conditions, economy and climate; the desecration of Vietnamese culture; forms of combat; death and wounding; atrocities on both sides; the daily living patterns of soldiers; enemies within one's own camp – for example, insensitive civilians or generals; overt political, religious or moral protest. The best American combatant poets, such as Michael Casey or Basil T. Paquet, offer to the reader precise renderings of small incidents in the war, personal anecdotes or insights calling upon technical knowledge which make the fighting accessible. As John Felstiner has convincingly argued, though, lyric poetry of a traditional kind has proved inappropriate to communicate the character of the Vietnam war, its remote-ness, its jargonised recapitulations, its seeming impervious-ness to aesthetics.[12] A look at *Winning Hearts and Minds*, a comprehensive anthology written by war veterans, seems to validate Felstiner's arguments:[13] the war is, in general, pre-sented in a rather repetitive, stereotyped, ahistorical and conventionally 'realistic' way; only in occasional poem such as Michael Casey's 'A Bummer' or 'The LZ Gator Body Collec-tor', Don Receveur's 'Cobra Pilot' Stan Platke's 'Gut Catcher' or Basil Paquet's 'Morning – A Death' does the war seem actualised, made urgent through its particularity. What clearly is lacking is an available artistic mode of a sustained kind, an extended formal utterance or discourse in which the war's distinctive technical nature as well as its moral nature can be realised. Even the outstanding poets (such as Casey and Paquet), who write in a hard, imagistic style and who fashion metaphors out of the technology, medical and military, around them, fail to achieve this sustained encoding of protest. They do not appear to possess language resources, myths and imagery powerful enough to counter the anti-language conventionalised by the media and the military command. Wilfred Owen, the English war poet, faced a similar problem in writing of the First World War, and his solution was to exploit as a working tradition the language of certain Romantic poets, such as Keats and Shelley, whom he admired, and occasionally living ones such as Sassoon, blended with a modern technical knowledge. Such a resonant literary language supplied Owen with locutions in which he could speak compassionately, bitterly and ironically in turns and write poetry counteractive to the dead rhetoric of slogan makers and politicians. I want to argue that Michael Herr's idioms, drawn from a variety of contemporary sources, supply him with a vigorouly esoteric analogical language in which to write of Vietnam. He writes epic biography in the slang rhythms of the street and the counter culture.

In form and language *Dispatches* embodies a critique of conventional war journalism (which, Herr writes, 'could no more reveal the war than conventional firepower could win it').[14] Whereas orthodox war-reporting is a 'communications pudding', anchored by set conventions and established language practices, Herr's journal is impressionistic, image-laden and open to new ways of receiving and codifying experience. *Dispatches* treats the Tet offensive, the battles of Dak To, Khe Sanh and those fought at the Citadel of Hue, and is written to memorialise the 'grunts' who adopted the author. The heroes of the account are marines such as the 'big bad spade' gone wrong, Day Tripper, and Mayhew, or his quirky fellow correspondents, such as the battered and 'wigged' Englishman, Tim Page, or the karmic Sean Flynn. Such charismatic individuals, who radiate generosity and style, comprise the resistance culture at work in Vietnam. On one occasion Herr refers to the more sophisticated elements of this group as an 'authentic subculture': 'There were more young apolitically radical, wigged-out crazies running around Vietnam than anyone ever realised; between all of the grunts turning on and tripping out on the war and the substantial number of correspondents who were doing the same thing, it was an authentic subculture' (p. 189). Essentially Herr seeks unhampered and wide artistic perception, as an aid to which he frequently takes drugs and writes of the 'Highs' and 'spaced out' visions induced by them; he perceives too that Vietnam offers a paradigm of American culture, its competing value systems and tensions. From the implications of such an insight the war, as well as being military spectacle and existential wilderness, takes on the ritualistic impulses of social theatre. Developing this latter aspect, Herr forever tries to 'make connections', to act as a semiologist of culture, reading the signs of war, observing its objects, tokens, mannerisms. His prose illuminates the dress, graffiti, tones and inflections of his fellow correspondents and marines, crazies, media freaks, sharp soldiers, black soul brothers, fellow eccentrics, sadistic bureaucrats, long-haired radicals of the counter-culture. Herr notes the words written on helmets and flak jackets (for example, Day Tripper's calendar of his overseas service), and, with probing wit, deciphers the semantics, the argot, the ensembles, relating such phenomena to the system of social relations that pins it all together. He loves those with taste and style, such as the erudite Page; the men of sensibility – those, for example, who protect each other, such as Mayhew and Day Tripper, or those who cherish the English language; and, as a corollary to this, he is merciless in attacking the myths and evasions of the insensitive. He is particularly devastating in his satire of the 'Command psyche' and its attendant 'jargon stream'. For example, he describes Pacification as 'a swollen computerised tit being forced upon an already violated population, a costly, valueless programme that worked only in press conferences (p. 173). Such a formulation implies Herr's intelligence and his priorities.

The 'jargon stream' of 'cheer crazed language' provides Michael Herr with a constant source of irritation in *Dispatches*, and he suggests how its incongruity can hide the reality of moral outrage, how a 'discreet burst' for instance could mean a grandfather and two children ripped to pieces. Herr's mockery often results in his own weird concoctions of clichés, as when he writes in parody, 'Well, in a war you've got to expect a little mud to get tracked over the carpet, we took a real black eyes but we sure gave Charlie a shitstorm, we consider this a real fine kill ratio . . .' (p. 179). Herr's own language uses comprise the most spectacular element of *Dispatches*; he writes in an idiom which creatively fuses hippie catchwords, black slang, pop lyrics, military jargon, technical press terms, and the vocabulary and colloquialisms of the American youth and drug cultures. The war is presented in a language that opposes it, a discourse rich with a generational consciousness of 'life', of belonging to a revolutionary ambience whose spokesmen were such cultists as Mick Jagger and the Stones, Jimi Hendrix, Frank Zappa, and the Mothers of Invention. The resistance of rock and roll, its borrowed energies and cadences, is instrumentalised as an alternative voice to war.

Herr's voice seems the most original and intelligent to speak of Vietnam, and the only one (apart from Caputo's) which persuades the reader, on the basis of its imagery and referents, that the suffering was contested *within* Vietnam, opposed by alternative energies; Herr's book pays tribute to the generosity and comradeship he encountered in Vietnam, yet it does not condone the suffering and consistently opposes the war's treacherous side. An extract from *Dispatches* will make the point that Herr's book moves beyond autobiography to wider historical awareness and that its metaphors resist the innoculation of the 'jargon stream':

The Mission and the motion: military arms and civilian

arms, more combatant between themselves than together against the Cong. Gun arms, knife arms, pencil arms, head-and-stomach arms, hearts-and-minds, flying arms, creeping-peeping arms, information arms as tricky as the arms of Plastic Man. At the bottom was the shitface grunt, at the top a Command trinity: a blue-eyed, hero-faced general, a geriatrics-emergency ambassador and a hale, heartless CIA performer. (Robert 'Blowtorch' Komer, chief of COORDS, spook anagram for Other War, pacification, another word for war. If William Blake had 'reported' to him that he'd seen angels in the trees, Komer would have tried to talk him out of it. Failing there, he'd have ordered defoliation.) All through the middle were the Vietnam War and the Vietnamese, not always exactly innocent bystanders, probably no accident that we'd found each other. If milk snakes could kill, you might compare the Mission and its arms to a big intertwined ball of baby milk snakes . . . .   (p. 42)

Such a passage infers the ethical confusion and misplaced energy that often characterised the American experience throughout the Vietnam War. The paragraph also demonstrates a mode of war writing which makes creative use of modern colloquial language; in such a way it offers one linguistic solution to the problem of verbalising modern warfare.

Notes

NOTES TO CHAPTER ONE: INTRODUCTION

1. J. Felstiner, 'American Poetry and the War in Vietnam', *Stand*, 19, no. 2 (1978) 4–11.
2. Michael Herr, *Dispatches* (London, 1978) p. 48. Textual references are to this edition. First published in 1977.
3. F. Ross, 'The Assailant–Victim in Three War Protest Novels', *Paunch*, XXXII (1968) 46–57.
4. Philip Caputo, *A Rumor of War* (London, 1978), Introduction, p. xviii. Textual references are to this edition. First published in 1977.

NOTES TO CHAPTER TWO: POETIC LANGUAGE

1. H. Kenner, *The Pound Era* (London, 1972) p. 202.
2. D. Davie, *Ezra Pound, Poet as Sculptor* (London, 1965) pp. 41–7.
3. Ezra Pound, *Collected Shorter Poems*, 2nd edn (London, 1952) p. 208.
4. S. Cooperman, *World War I and the American Novel* (Baltimore, 1966) pp. 3–45.
5. B. Bergonzi, *Heroes' Twilight: a Study of the Literature of the Great War* (London, 1965) pp. 24–31; and R. N. Stromberg, 'The Intellectuals and the Coming of War in 1914', *Journal of European Studies*, 3, no. 2 (June 1973) 109–22.
6. J. Felstiner, op. cit.
7. Edith Wharton, *The Marne* (New York, 1918) pp. 56–67 and section VII.
8. Harry Crosby, *War Letters* (Paris, 1932) pp. 218–19.
9. W. Archer (ed.), *Poems of Alan Seeger* (New York, 1916) p. xxxii.
10. Ibid., pp. xxxv–xxxvi.
11. Ibid., pp. 131–3. The full title of this poem is 'The Aisne (1914–15)'.
12. R. C. Holliday (ed.), *Joyce Kilmer: Memoir and Poems*, vol. I (New York, 1918) p. 108.
13. F. W. Dupee and George Stade (eds), *Selected Letters of E. E. Cummings* (London, 1972).
14. E. E. Cummings, *Complete Poems 1913–1935*, vol I (London, 1968) p. 230. Textual references are to this edition.
15. Norman Friedman, *E. E. Cummings, the Growth of a Writer* (Carbondale, Ill., 1969) p. 79 (Friedman is writing of *Vi Va*).
16. E. E. Cummings, *Complete Poems*, p. 271.
17. See B. E. Stevenson (ed.), *Poems of American History* (Boston, Mass., 1950) for examples of popular war verse.

18. Malcolm Cowley, *Blue Juniata* (New York, 1968) p. 32. (See 1929 edition.)
19. Archibald MacLeish, *Streets in the Moon* (New York, 1926).
20. Cowley, *Blue Juniata*, p. 58. Compare this version with earlier drafts.
21. Allen Tate (ed.), *The Collected Poems of John Peale Bishop* (New York, 1948) p. 219.
22. Ibid., pp. 13–14.
23. John Curtis Underwood, *War Flames* (New York, 1917).

NOTES TO CHAPTER THREE: TWO MODERNIST WAR NOVELS

1. F. J. Hoffman, *The Twenties* (New York, 1965) p. 87.
2. Friedman, *Cummings*, pp. 22–3.
3. E. E. Cummings, *The Enormous Room* (London, 1928) p. 309. Textual references are to this edition.
4. See K. Widmer, 'Timeless Prose', *Twentieth Century Literature,* 4 (Apr–July 1958) 3–8.
5. David Lodge, 'The Language of Modernist Fiction: Metaphor and Metonymy', in M. Bradbury and J. MacFarlane (eds), *Modernism* (Harmondsworth, 1976).
6. Natan Zach, 'Imagism and Vorticism', ibid., p. 239.
7. E. Hemingway, *A Farewell to Arms* (London, 1932) p. 13. First published 1929.

NOTES TO CHAPTER FOUR: RADICALISM

1. See Laurence Stallings, *Plumes* (New York, 1924) ch. 6. Textual references are to this edition.
2. Laurence Stallings, *The Doughboys: the Story of the AEF* (New York, 1962) p. 3.
3. Ibid.
4. Ernest Hemingway, *Men at War* (London, 1966) p. 10. The original edition, published in 1944, included a longer introduction, written in 1942.
5. David Sanders, 'Lies and the System: Enduring Themes in Dos Passos's Early Novels', *South Atlantic Quarterly,* LXV (1966) 215–28.
6. Henri Barbusse, *Le Feu* (Paris, 1916) p. 339.
7. John Dos Passos, *One Man's Initiation: 1917* (Ithaca, NY, 1969) p. 2. First published 1920.
8. Jonathan King, 'Henri Barbusse: *Le Feu* and the Crisis of Social Realism', in Holger Klein (ed.), *The First World War in Fiction* (London, 1976) p. 46.
9. Ibid., pp. 45–6.
10. John Dos Passos, *Three Soldiers* (Boston, 1949) pp. 211 and 343. Textual references are to this edition. First published 1921.
11. J. W. Aldridge, *After the Lost Generation: a Critical Study of the Writers of Two Wars* (London, 1959) p. 68. First published 1951.
12. S. Cooperman, *World War I and the American Novel.*
13. John Dos Passos, *One Man's Initiation*, pp. 60–1.

NOTES TO CHAPTER FIVE: LOST GENERATION AT WAR

1. William Eastlake, *The Bamboo Bed* (London, 1969) p. 115.
2. John Hersey, *The War Lover* (London, 1959) p. 217.
3. Karl Shapiro, *To Abolish Children and Other Essays* (Chicago, 1968) pp. 153–4.
4. William Styron, *The Long March* (New York, 1952) pp. 55–6.
5. Ernest Hemingway, *A Moveable Feast* (Harmondsworth, 1966) p. 27.
6. Arthur Mizener, 'The Lost Generation' in R. E. Spiller (ed.), *A Time of Harvest* (New York, 1962) pp. 81–2.
7. Malcolm Cowley, 'Après la guerre finie', *Horizon*, xi (Winter 1968) 112–19.
8. C. A. Fenton, 'American Ambulance Drivers in France and Italy, 1914–18', *American Quarterly*, iii (Winter 1951) 326–43.
9. Cowley, 'Après la guerre finie'.
10. Edith Wharton, *A Son at the Front* (New York, 1923) p. 365. Textual references are to this edition.
11. See Dorothy Canfield Fisher, *The Deepening Stream* (New York, 1930). Textual references are to this edition.
12. Wharton, *A Son at the Front*, pp. 187–8.
13. Peter Buitenhuis, 'Edith Wharton and the First World War', *American Quarterly*, xviii (1966) 493–505.
14. Willa Cather, *One of Ours* (New York, 1922; repr. 1953) p. 375. Textual references are to this edition.
15. See ibid., pp. 172–3, for a guide to Claude's idealistic motivation.
16. Scott Fitzgerald, *This Side of Paradise* (London, 1960), vol. iii of the Bodley Head Scott Fitzgerald, p. 166. Textual references are to this edition.
17. Scott Fitzgerald, *Tender is the Night* (London, 1961), vol. ii of the Bodley Head Scott Fitzgerald. Textual references are to this edition.
18. See also A. Turnbull, *Scott Fitzgerald: a Biography* (New York, 1962).
19. See Arthur Mizener (ed.), *Afternoon of an Author: a Selection of Uncollected Stories and Essays of Scott Fitzgerald* (London, 1958) for an interesting commentary on this short story.
20. Turnbull, *Scott Fitzgerald*, p. 88. He comments upon Fitzgerald's bravery in the incident on the Tallapoosa River.
21. H. H. Waggoner, *William Faulkner: from Jefferson to the World* (Lexington, Mass., 1959).
22. William Faulkner, *Soldier's Pay* (London, 1957) p. 146. Textual references are to this edition.
23. A. C. Bross, 'Soldier's Pay and the Art of Aubrey Beardsley', *American Quarterly*, 19 (Spring 1967) 3–23.
24. William Faulkner, *Sartoris* (London, 1964) pp. 12–14.
25. Waggoner, *William Faulkner*, p. 24.
26. Olga W. Vickery, *The Novels of William Faulkner: a Critical Interpretation* (Baton Rouge, La, 1964) p. 17.
27. William Faulkner, *Collected Stories of William Faulkner* (New York, 1951) p. 473. Textual references are to this edition.

Notes

Notes

211

28. W. R. Moses, 'Victory in Defeat: "Ad Astra" and *A Farewell to Arms*', *Mississippi Quarterly*, XIX (1966–7) 85–9.

NOTES TO CHAPTER SIX: HEMINGWAY AND BESSIE: EDUCATION IN SPAIN

1. Ernest Hemingway, *For Whom the Bell Tolls* (London, 1941) p. 50. Textual references are to this edition. First published 1940.
2. Ernest Hemingway, *The Fifth Column and Four Stories of the Spanish War* (New York, 1969).
3. W. Carlos Baker, *Ernest Hemingway: a Life Story* (London, 1969) pp. 424–5.
4. Alvah Bessie, *Men in Battle: a Story of Americans in Spain* (New York, 1939) pp. 135–6. Textual references are to this edition.
5. Alvah Bessie, *The Heart of Spain* (New York, 1952).

NOTES TO CHAPTER SEVEN: SECOND WORLD WAR FICTION

1. Norman Mailer, *The Naked and the Dead* (London, 1965). Textual references are to this edition. First published 1948.
2. Lee S. Halpin, 'American Liberalism, Literature and World War II', *Minnesota Review*, III (Winter, 1963) 179–92.
3. Cooperman, *World War I and the American Novel*, pp. 230–2.
4. J. P. Diggins, 'The American Writer, Fascism and the Liberation of Italy', *American Quarterly*, XVIII (1966) 599–614.
5. Aldridge, *After the Lost Generation*, pp. 145–6.
6. John Horne Burns, *The Gallery* (London, 1957). Textual references are to this edition. First published 1947.
7. Frank Ross, 'The Assailant–Victim in Three War Protest Novels', *Paunch*, XXXII (1968) 46–57.
8. Ernest Hemingway, *Across the River and into the Trees* (New York, 1950). Textual references are to this edition.
9. Philip Young, *Ernest Hemingway: a Reconsideration* (London, 1966) p. 160.
10. Peter Lisca, 'The Structure of Hemingway's *Across the River and into the Trees*', *Modern Fiction Studies*, XII (1966) 236–50.
11. James Gould Cozzens, *Guard of Honour* (London, 1958) p. 373. Textual references are to this edition. First published 1948.
12. F. J. Hoffman, *The Modern Novel in America* (Chicago, 1963), 'The Last Ten Years'.
13. Maxwell Geismar, *American Moderns: from Rebellion to Conformity* (London, 1958) pp. 225–38.
14. James Jones, *From Here to Eternity* (London, 1965) p. 165. Textual references are to this edition. First published 1951.
15. Jones refers to the 'solar system' of the army.
16. Geismar, *American Moderns*, p. 180.
17. John Hersey, *The Wall* (New York, 1967) p. 382. Textual references are to this edition. First published 1950.

NOTES TO CHAPTER EIGHT: SECOND WORLD WAR POETRY

1. Shapiro, *To Abolish Children and Other Essays* pp. 152–3.
2. W. R. Brown, 'American Soldier Poets of the Second World War' (University of Michigan dissertation, 1965).
3. Karl Shapiro, *Poems 1940–1953* (New York, 1953) p. 119. Textual references are to this edition.
4. Randall Jarrell, *Selected Poems* (London, 1956). Textual references are to this edition. First published in 1955. (In addition to the sections listed here, there is also included a classification entitled 'The Trader'.)
5. Louis Simpson, *The Poetry of War, 1939–45*, ed. Ian Hamilton (London, 1965) p. 172.
6. Louis Simpson, *The Arrivistes: Poems 1940–48* (Middletown, Conn., 1949). Textual references are to this edition.
7. Louis Simpson, *Selected Poems* (London, 1966) p. 3. Textual references are to this edition.
8. Richard Eberhart, *Collected Poems, 1930–1976* (New York, 1976) pp. 123–4. Textual references are to this edition.
9. Richard Wilbur, *The Beautiful Changes, and Other Poems* (New York, 1947), p. 11.
10. Anthony Hecht, *A Summoning of Stones* (New York, 1954) pp. 89–90.
11. Robert Glenn Prince, *The Hidden Airdrome and Other Uncollected Poems* (Rowe, Mass., 1956).
12. Allen Tate, *Poems* (New York, 1960) pp. 16–17.
13. John Ciardi, *39 Poems* (New Brunswick, NJ, 1959).
14. Howard Nemerov, *The Image and the Law* (New York, 1947).
15. Robert Lowell, *Land of Unlikeness* (Cummington, Mass., 1944) and *Lord Weary's Castle* (New York, 1946).
16. Howard Nemerov, *Guide to the Ruins* (New York, 1950).
17. Karl Shapiro, *Poems 1940–1953*.

NOTES TO CHAPTER NINE: TOWARDS VIETNAM

1. John Barth, 'The Literature of Exhaustion', originally published in *Atlantic Monthly*, Aug 1967.
2. See Wylie Sypher, *Loss of the Self in Modern Literature and Art* (New York).
3. *MASH*, written of the Korean war, comments effectively upon Vietnam in the new mode of satiric fabrication.
4. S. E. Ambrose and J. A. Barber Jr (eds), *The Military and American Society* (New York, 1972) p. 151.
5. Joseph Heller, *Catch-22* (London, 1978). Textual references are to this edition. First published 1961.
6. Tony Tanner, *City of Words* (London, 1971) p.16.
7. Joseph Stern, 'War and the Comic Muse: the Good Soldier Schweik and Catch-22', *Comparative Literature*, xx, no. 3 (1968) 193–216; and Brian Way, 'Formal Experiment and Social Discontent, Joseph Heller's Catch-22', *American Studies*, ii, no. 2(1971) 253–70.

8. Kurt Vonnegut Jr, *Slaughterhouse-Five* (London, 1978). Textual references are to this edition. First published 1969.
9. Eric S. Rabkin, *The Fantastic in Literature* (Princeton, N J, 1977) p. 41.
10. Frank Kermode, *The Sense of an Ending* (London, 1967) pp. 18–20.
11. Caputo, *A Rumor of War* p. xii.
12. Felstiner, 'American Poetry and the War in Vietnam'.
13. L. Rottmann, J. Barry and B. T. Paquet (eds), *Winning Hearts and Minds*. The anthology (1972) is subtitled 'War Poems by Vietnam Veterans', and contains poems written over ten years by thirty-three poets. It was published by First Casualty Press, Brooklyn, New York.
14. Herr, *Dispatches*, p. 175.

Index

Numbers in bold indicate major discussion of works; numbers in parenthesis indicate entries referred to but not actually named.